IMAGES
of America

SALUDA

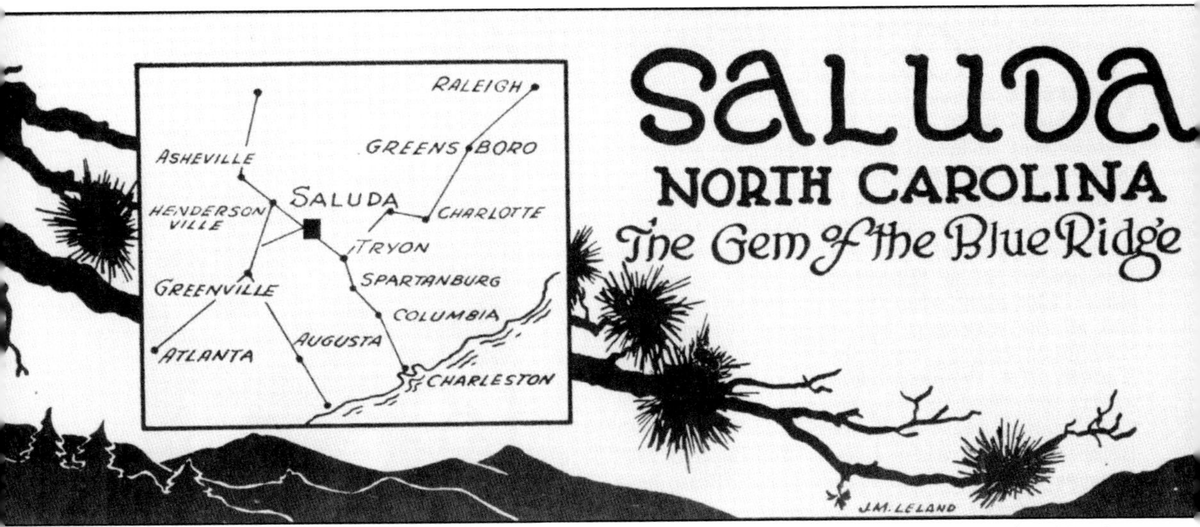

This map, signed by J.M. Leland, can originally be found in the *Saluda Magazine*, Vol. I, No. I, from 1936. The accompanying article begins, "Saluda, a restful, pleasing name left on mountain and stream by the Indians who wandered over this section, was chosen as most fitting for the little village which, like a gem, nestles amid its peaks on the very top of Saluda Mountain." (Courtesy of Cindy Stephenson Tuttle.)

On the Cover: William "Billy" Morris, known as the Keeper of the Century-Old Fire, lived in a log cabin on Holbert Cove Road and became famous for helping to keep a fire burning for 164 years. The fire was started by his grandparents in 1780. Billy loved to play the fiddle, and his companion was a dog named Booker T. After Billy passed away in 1944 at the age of 84, the fire went out. (Courtesy of *Carnegie Survey of the Architecture of the South*, Library of Congress.)

IMAGES
of America

SALUDA

Historic Saluda Committee

ARCADIA
PUBLISHING

ISBN 978-1-4671-2169-9

Published by Arcadia Publishing
Charleston, South Carolina

Printed in the United States of America

Library of Congress Control Number: 2013952610

For all general information, please contact Arcadia Publishing:
Telephone 843-853-2070
Fax 843-853-0044
E-mail sales@arcadiapublishing.com
For customer service and orders:
Toll-Free 1-888-313-2665

Visit us on the Internet at www.arcadiapublishing.com

This book stands on the strong shoulders of two women who captured Saluda's heart and soul with their writings. They knew Saluda as a very special place and left an irreplaceable legacy for us to build on in our book. Our heartfelt thanks go to Anne Riggs Osborne and Charlene Pace.

Contents

Acknowledgments

Without the countless members of our community who have loaned us their photographs, given time for interviews, and demonstrated unwavering enthusiasm for this project, this book would not have been possible. We are greatly indebted to everyone who opened their doors to us and shared family history, and we hope that this book is a testament to their willingness to share.

We are indebted to the Saluda city officials who in 2010 saw the value in forming a committee that wished to "preserve Saluda's past for its future." The board of commissioners at that time included George Sweet, John Morgan, Leon Morgan, and Johnnie Kinard, and the mayor was and remains Fred Baisden. We would also like to recognize the current city commissioners: Lynn Cass, Carolyn Ashburn, Leon Morgan, and Mark Oxtoby, who continue to support our work.

With the formation of the Historic Saluda Committee, the oral history project began. The stories shared by longtime Saluda residents and summer folk, names too numerous to list here, were the inspiration and foundation for this book. Many of the photographs they shared have rarely been seen outside of their own homes, and many are included in this book.

Also to be acknowledged for their major role in bringing this project to fruition are several others, including Charlene Pace, who has been an invaluable resource with her knowledge of history and extensive collection of Saluda photographs. Serendipitously, during the writing of this book, Jim Boyle was able to acquire a rare assortment of early Saluda photographs, including 16 originals by O.B. Garren, a local photographer who documented the early days of the town. He graciously shared these with the Historic Saluda Committee for the purposes of this book. Others have generously given of their time, talent, and knowledge, including Anna Pack Conner and the Polk County Historical Association, the Saluda Public Library, Dr. George Jones with the Henderson County Genealogical and Historical Society, James Metcalf, R. Clark Thompson, Ruth Anderson, Judy Ward, Leon Morgan, Bob and Linda Whitaker, Martha Ashley, Chuck Hearon, Janet Clayton, the family of Dr. D. Lesesne Smith, and many more. Lastly, we would be remiss without thanking our family and friends who tolerated our tunnel vision as we strove to bring this book to life.

Introduction

Long before the railroad cut through the steep gorge along the Pacolet River to what is now Saluda, North Carolina, there was Pace's Gap or Pace's Ridge. Located on Saluda Mountain, Pace's Gap was a crossroads for traders who carried goods and drove livestock along the path where the old Howard Gap wagon road to the Blockhouse Fort met the Winding Stairs Road down to the Lowcountry of South Carolina and Georgia. Pace's Gap was home to a drover's inn run by the Pace family, which provided accommodations for weary travelers and pens and fenced areas to secure their livestock for the night.

The very first settlers in Henderson County set up homesteading in the Mountain Page community. In 1777, by treaty, the Cherokee Indians moved from the extreme southeastern portion of Henderson County, known as the Mountain Page area, leaving this land vacant for settlement. This was prior to the 1785 treaty, which cleared the way for land settlement in the remaining portions of Henderson County. In 1805, Burrell Pope Pace received a land grant of 300 acres, which included the Old Mountain Meeting House in the Mountain Page community, later known as Pace's Gap.

The Pace family came to Jamestown in 1607 on the ship the *Marmaduke* and received a large land grant in Virginia from King James. Some descendants moved across Virginia and down through the mountain passes into what is now Spartanburg, South Carolina. Burrell Pope Pace married Lydia Woodruff in the village named for her family in South Carolina. He is buried in the old Mountain Page Cemetery, in the oldest known grave, with 1816 as his date of death. His son Moses Pace owned and operated the Pace House once located on the old drover's trail on Howard's Gap, which was later run by his son Ransom Woodruff Pace.

Records indicate the Thompsons were in the area by the early 1800s. John Thompson, one of the seven brothers who came from Ireland to settle in Pennsylvania, Virginia, Georgia, and later in the Carolinas, moved to Lynn, North Carolina, in the early 1800s. One of his sons, Frank Thompson, built a house at the foot of Warrior Mountain, and another son, Ashbury "Berry" Thompson, constructed a home in the fork of the road where Holbert Cove Road splits from Howard Gap Road. This house was used as a stagecoach stop between Spartanburg and Asheville, North Carolina, and also served as a trading post, election center, and the Tryon Post Office from 1839 until the railroad came up through Pace's Gap in 1878.

Though the old saying goes, "If you pass a Pace on one side of the street in Saluda, you are bound to pass a Thompson on the other side," early records indicate that families with the surnames of Hipp, Williams, Forrest, Morgan, Middleton, Metcalf, Holbert, Laughter, Johnson, Staton, Guice, Gordon, and Morris were early settlers in the area, too. In addition to Burwell Pope Pace, some of the earliest residents of Saluda included Benjamin Staton, William Metcalf, and Samuel Gordon. The latter three are buried in the Metcalf graveyard in the Fork Creek community. Some historians believe Benjamin Staton to be the first white man to live in present-day Henderson County. Many of the original families were Scotch Irish who left Pennsylvania around the time of the Whiskey Rebellion in the early 1790s.

When the first passenger train of the Spartanburg & Asheville Railroad chugged up the Saluda Grade on July 4, 1878, Pace's Gap was forever changed. By February 1881, the growth and prosperity of Pace's Gap had escalated to the point that it was chartered as the town of Saluda, named for Saluda Mountain, which is actually not a mountain but a group of mountains with the Saluda River at its feet It is said that the Saluda River was named for an Indian chief whose name means "corn river" in Cherokee, which sounded to white men like "Saluda."

Spread over seven hills, Saluda has an elevation between 2,096 and 2,200 feet. Considered an enchanted destination, it is rich with history, arts and entertainment, fine dining, and plenty to see and do. Saluda, located in two counties, primarily Polk and partially Henderson, celebrated its 130th anniversary in 2011 and has a population of just over 700 people.

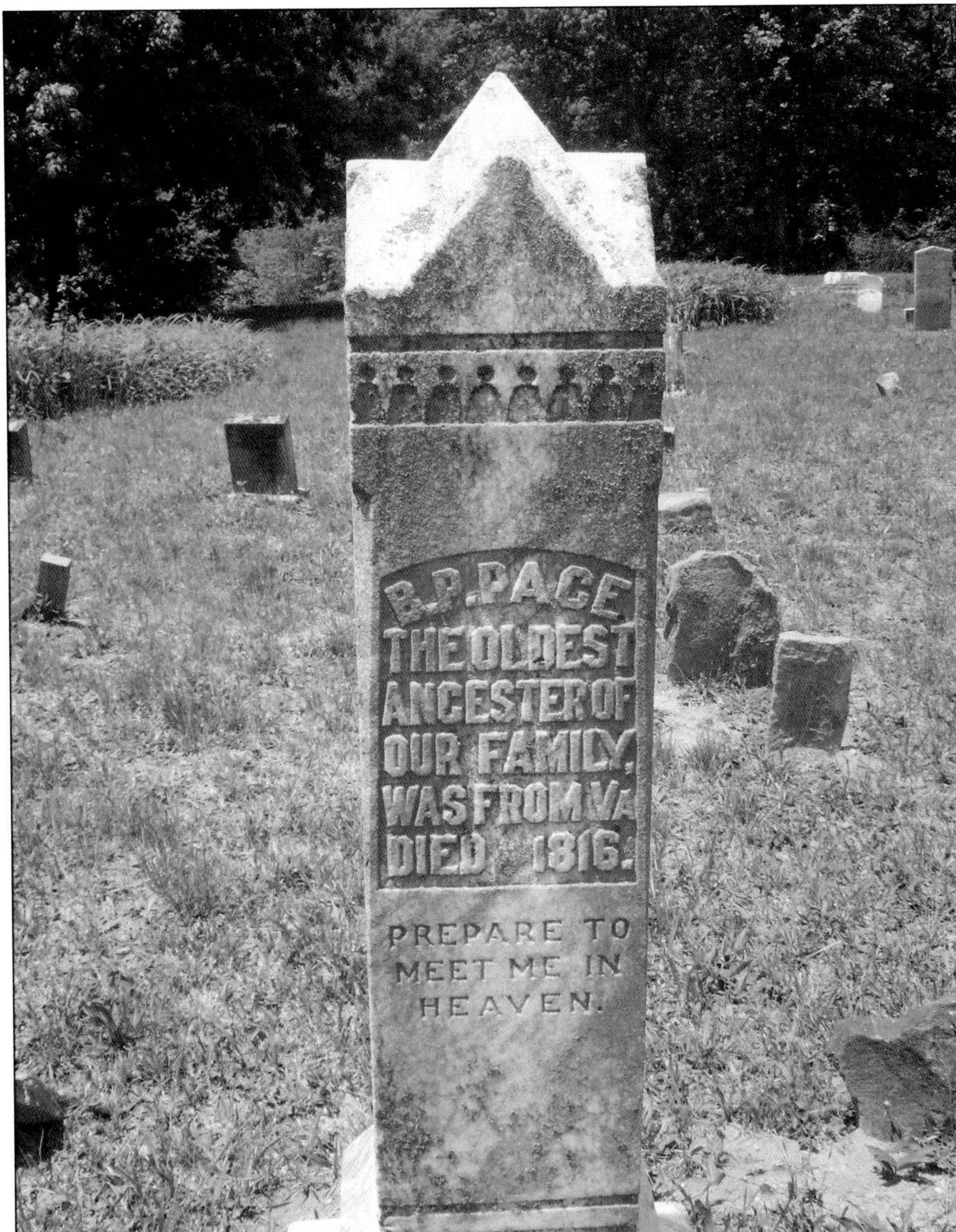

Burrell Pope Pace's gravestone is the oldest known grave in the old Mountain Page Cemetery, with 1816 as his date of death. Pace was a Revolutionary War veteran, enlisting in the Patriot Army in 1776 and attaining the rank of sergeant in Col. John Henton's regiment. (Courtesy of Cindy Stephenson Tuttle.)

One

The Railroad Meets the Grade

The Saluda Grade opened to rail traffic on July 4, 1878. At the top of the grade the tracks cut through the land of Cornelius Pace. However, the idea for tracks across the mountain came about as early as 1832, when the demand became great to move goods, livestock, and humans up the mountain away from the stifling heat of South Carolina and Georgia. When surveying began, it became apparent that the best route was the one taken by the early settlers to travel to the new lands—Howard Gap Trail.

It was not until 1877 that Capt. Charles Pearson, a former Confederate army officer, was assigned chief engineer. Pearson's ultimate challenge was to bring the line of the Spartanburg & Asheville Railroad (reorganized in 1881 as the Asheville & Spartanburg Railroad) across the Blue Ridge from Tryon to Asheville. This created quite a challenge since the early surveys revealed no route was available to ascend the mountains at a reasonable grade. Rejecting the route along Howard's Gap due to the instability of the ground, Pearson selected a route that followed the Pacolet River up the steep gorge, an almost vertical wall. This route begins at the bottom of Melrose Mountain at 1,081 feet and climbs to the town of Saluda, cresting at an elevation of 2,097 feet and creating a grade upwards of five percent, which is more than double a more reasonable grade of two percent. Without the help of convicts, mostly black, the line to Saluda would not have been completed. But the price paid by all workers, free or otherwise, was high due to sickness and accidents resulting in a high death rate. Despite this adversity, the tracks reached the top of the grade three months after the convicts began work on the project, resulting in the completion of the steepest main line standard-gauge railroad in the United States.

Once completed, the Saluda Grade proved to be treacherous due to runaway trains. Twenty-nine railroad men lost their lives before an injured railroad worker came up with the idea for safety tracks redirecting trains into a 60-foot pile of dirt.

The last passenger train crested the Saluda Mountain on December 5, 1968, thus ending the era for passenger service in Saluda. Norfolk Southern suspended freight traffic between East Flat Rock, North Carolina, and Landrum, South Carolina, in 2001, thus ceasing operations on the Saluda Grade.

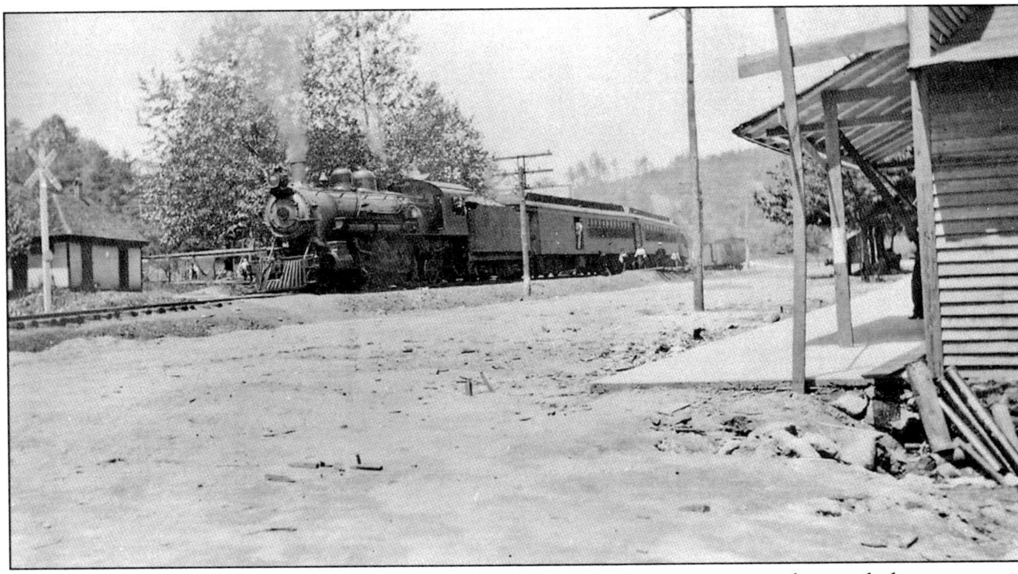

This photograph of early Saluda shows a passenger train preparing to descend the mountain toward Melrose, probably checking its brakes before tackling the grade. The early trains were not universally accepted in the beginning, as they were loud and monstrous beasts, often scaring children and horses. The spewing smoke and shrill whistles of the trains soon became an accepted part of life in Saluda and are greatly missed today. (Courtesy of the City of Saluda.)

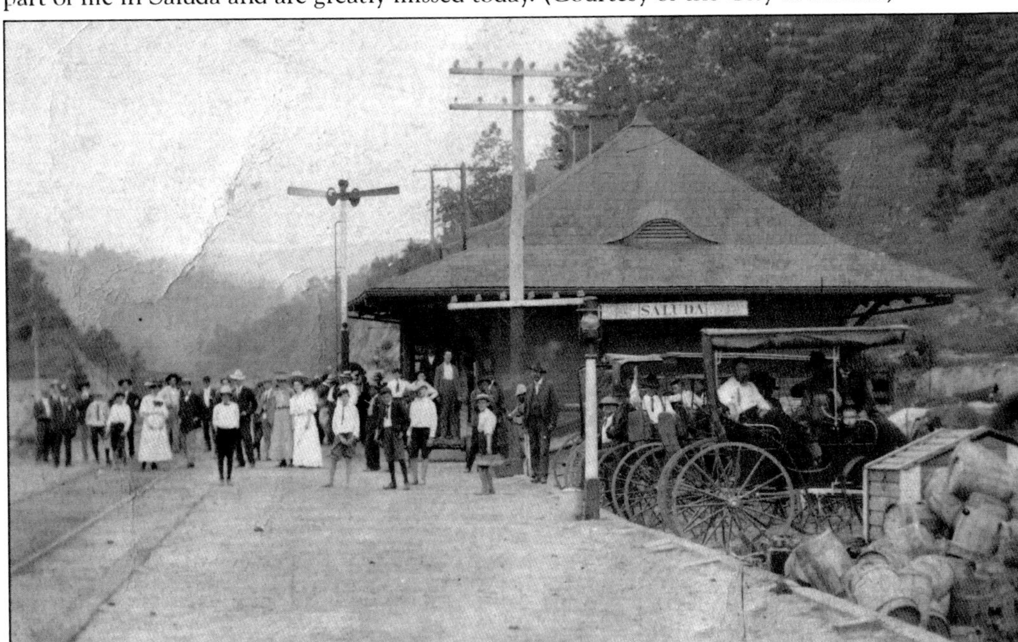

This photograph taken around 1910 depicts the depot that was located a quarter of a mile from town. The luxury Pullman and coach train the *Carolina Special* brought passengers from the Lowcountry for many years. Passengers, often dressed in fashionable attire, were greeted by horse-drawn carriages with drivers willing to transport heavy steamer trunks and luggage to one of the many inns and boardinghouses. (Photograph by O.B. Garren; courtesy of Martha Coates Ashley.)

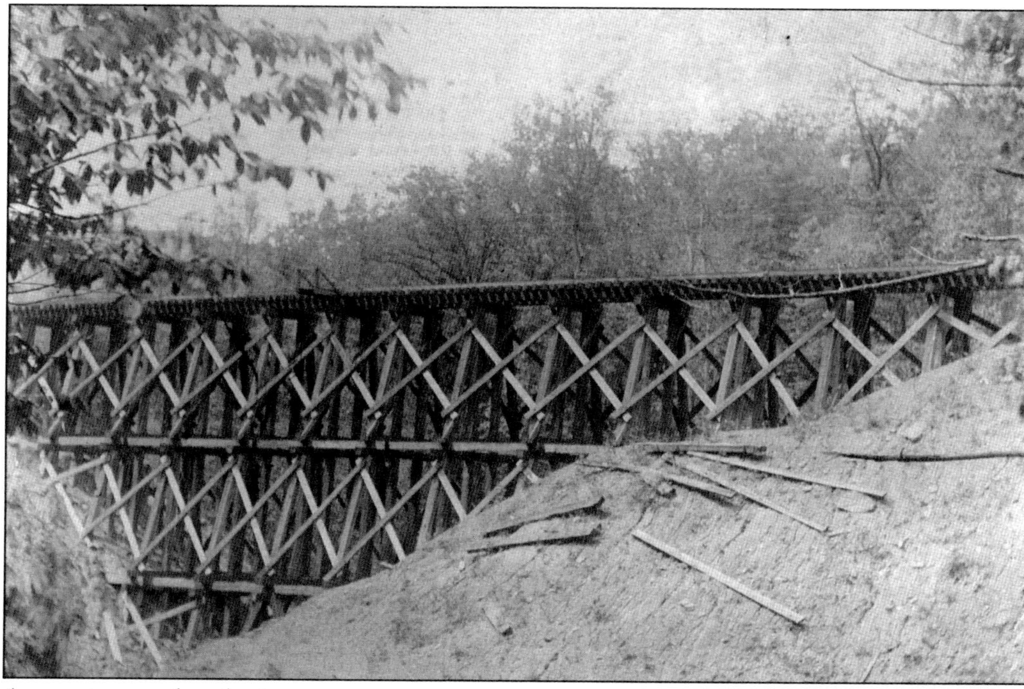

A notation was handwritten on the mat around this photograph, "Death Holler Bridge near Saluda, N.C., just after coming out of Big Cut." Accidents on Saluda Mountain claimed 29 lives, but none of them were passengers. (Photograph by O.B. Garren; courtesy of Jim Boyle.)

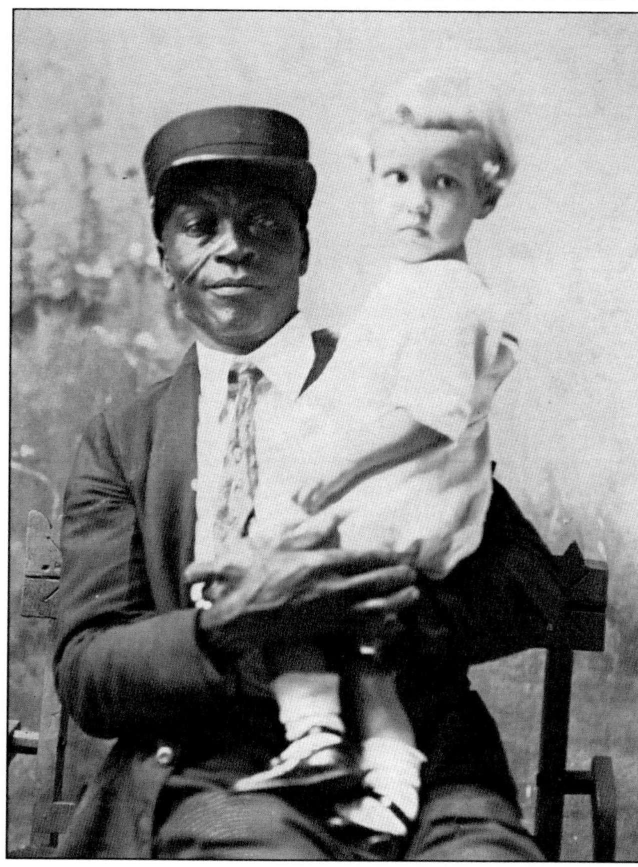

Many African Americans came from the Piedmont of South Carolina to find work during the railroad boom or visited in the summer with their employers as cooks and housekeepers. The railroad provided ample work for many, and others found work with the prosperous inns and boardinghouses that had sprung up to accommodate the railroad. (Courtesy of Charlene Pace.)

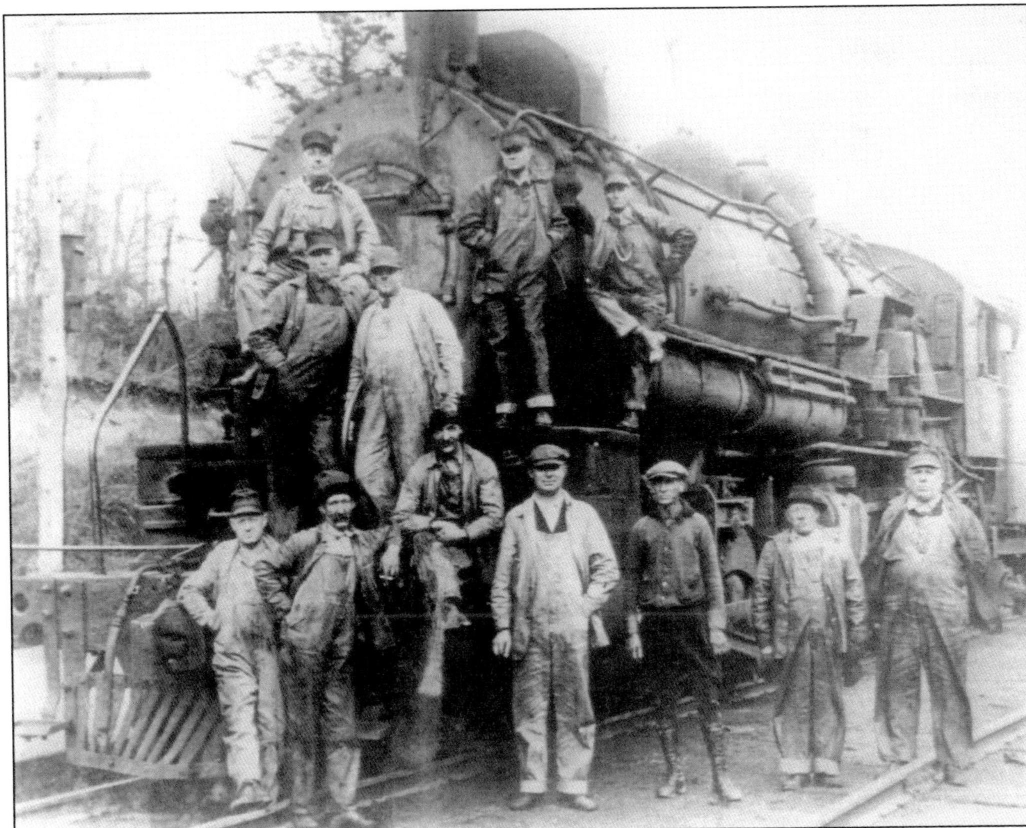

Pictured here are two images of the helper engine and its crew. The Saluda Grade drops 600 feet to the mile and is a 4.7-percent grade, according to the Association of American Railroads. This necessitated the helper train, which was built for traction rather than speed and had 10 smaller driving wheels, instead of the usual eight. Down the mountain in Melrose, the helper was connected to the rear of the train, and it pushed while the regular engine pulled up the grade. Sometimes it took multiple attempts to make it up the mountain. In the photograph below, the building in the background was a commissary for railroad men. It was located across the tracks from Saluda City Hall and built by Andrew Tanner. (Both, courtesy of Charlene Pace.)

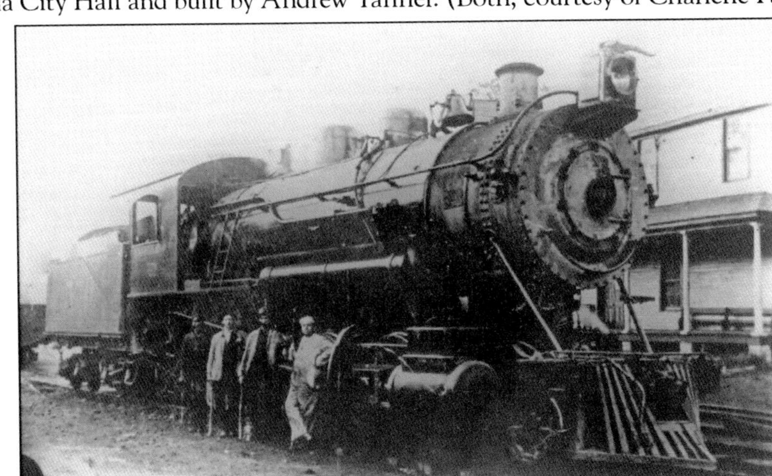

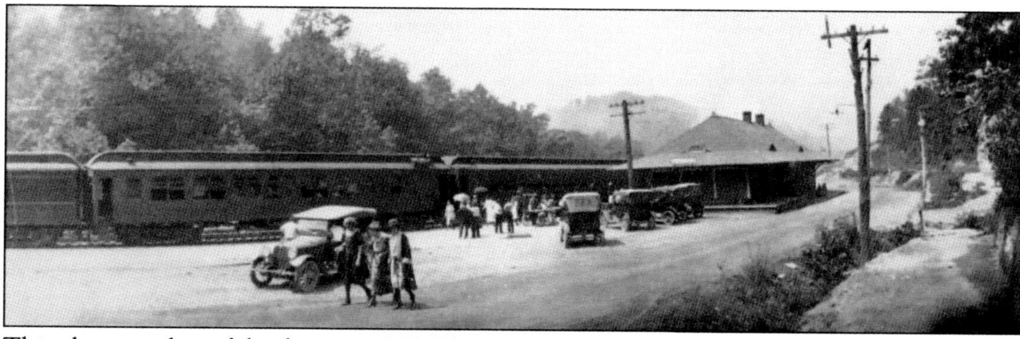

This photograph is of the depot in 1925. The automobile replaced the horse-drawn carriages that met the early trains. Many passengers traveled through Saluda, especially during the summer months, as evidenced by the number of passenger cars connected to this train. (Courtesy of the City of Saluda.)

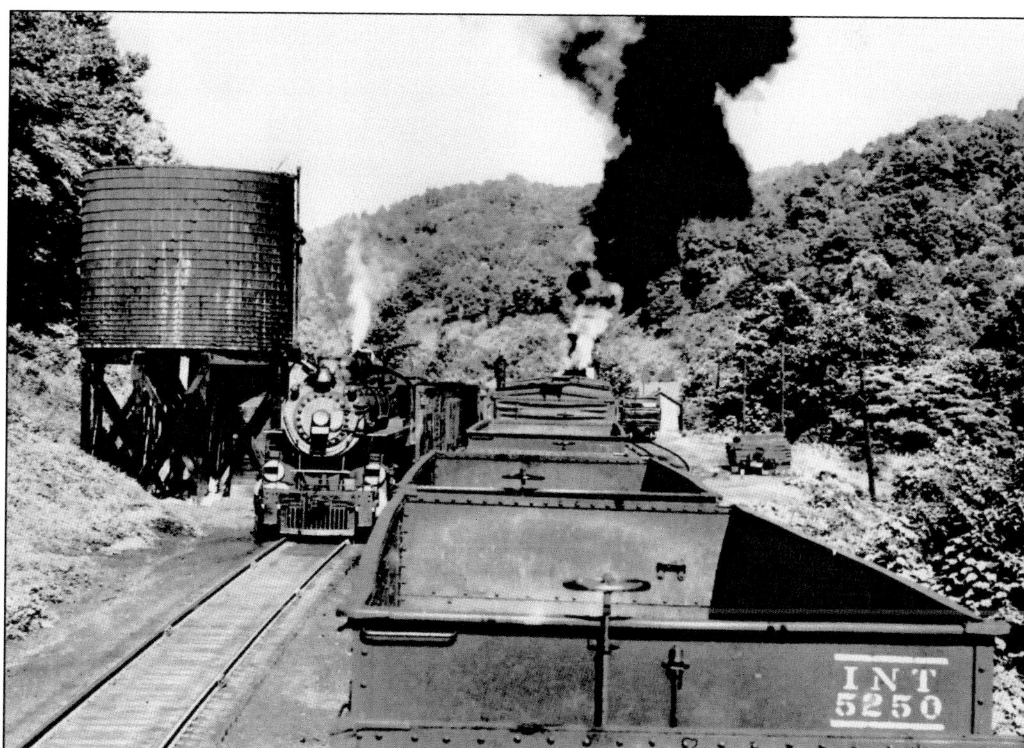

This train was en route from Asheville to Hayne, South Carolina, and stopped in Melrose while the fireman refills the water supply. This water tank was kept full by piping in spring water from high up on a mountain more than a mile away. In the wintertime, there was always the danger of the water freezing so railroad workers had to continually monitor it. (Photograph by Frank Clodfelter; courtesy of Charlene Pace.)

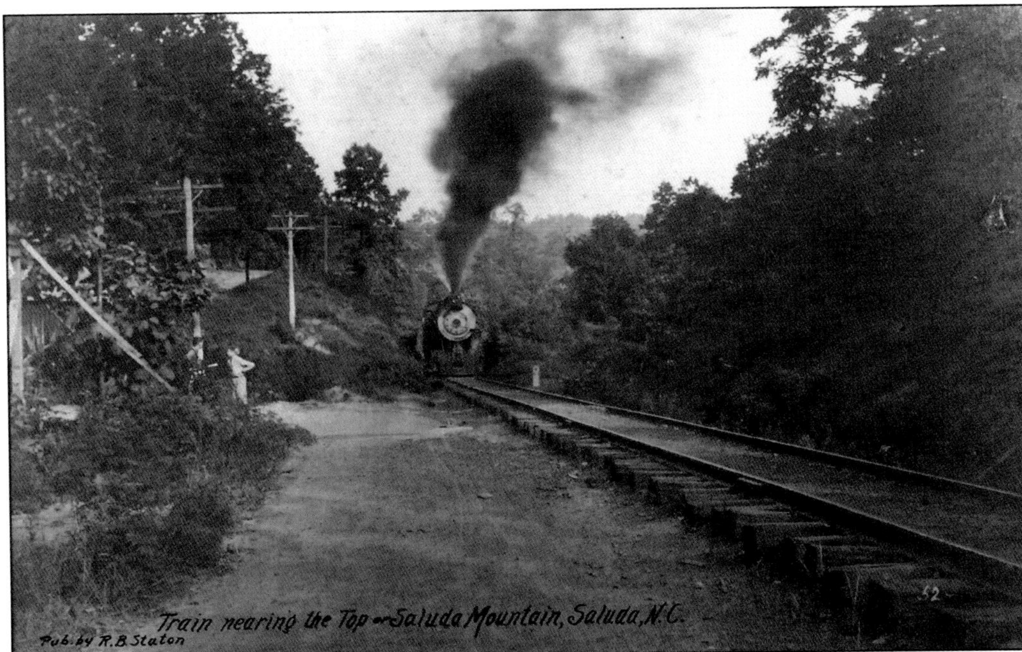

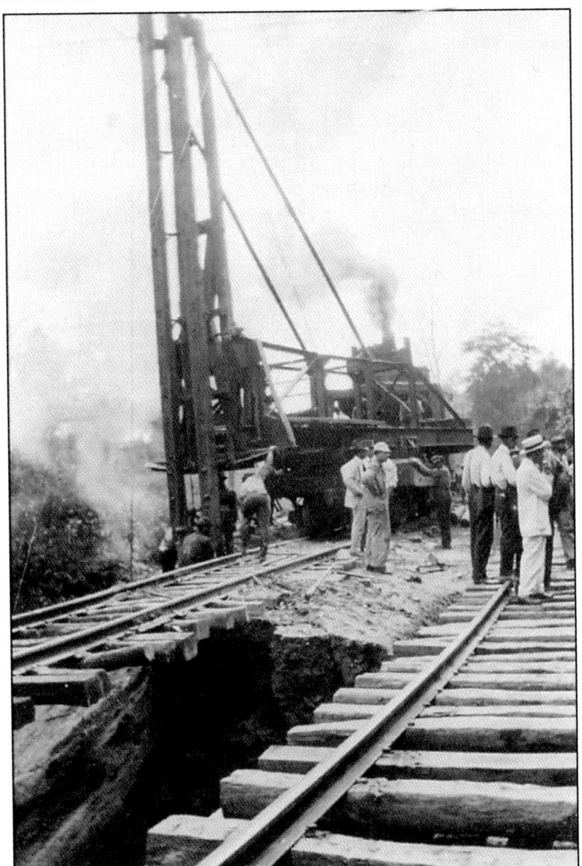

This postcard by R.B. Staton depicts the train topping Saluda Mountain. When the first train topped the mountain in 1878, it was an excursion run from Spartanburg. It was met by folks from miles around who came by foot, horseback, carts, buggies, and wagons. A big picnic was held to celebrate the occasion. (Courtesy of the City of Saluda.)

This photograph was taken in 1916 at the site of frequent washouts and is identified as "pile driver at Rockclif and waiting for the train." The reference to Rockclif may be referring to the rock quarry where they carved out the rock for the railroad. Men employed by the quarry lived in a shantytown nearby, resulting in the formation of a town near Melrose called Rockliff, which had its own post office between 1906 and 1919. (Courtesy of Catherine Nicholson.)

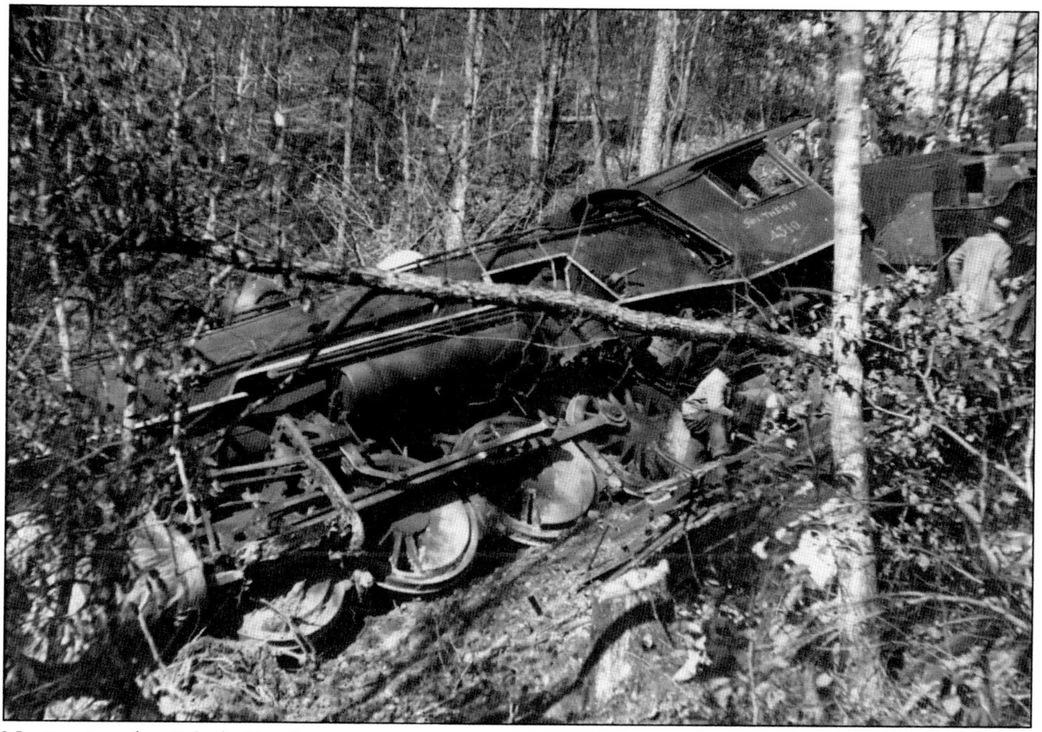

Navigating the Saluda Grade was anything but easy for railroad workers. Between 1880 and 1894, there were four bad wrecks in which men were crippled and killed. In 1880, a total of 14 men were killed, and 10 years later, three were killed. In 1893, three men were killed and one lost his leg while a carload of cattle was killed when No. 559 careened down the Saluda Grade and ended up in a tangle of twisted metal. Thus, Slaughterhouse Curve became a household name. In 1903, after his engine and a load of coal plunged over the embankment at Big Fill, Pitt Bellew, though crippled from his jump to safety, came up with a solution. Safety tracks were put in use to assist in slowing the trains down rather than plunging down the mountain, in the event of a runaway. The photograph at right was identified as "Big Cut near Saluda N.C. where three terrible wrecks occurred since 1892." (Above, courtesy of Martha Coates Ashley; right, photograph by O.B. Garren, courtesy of Jim Boyle.)

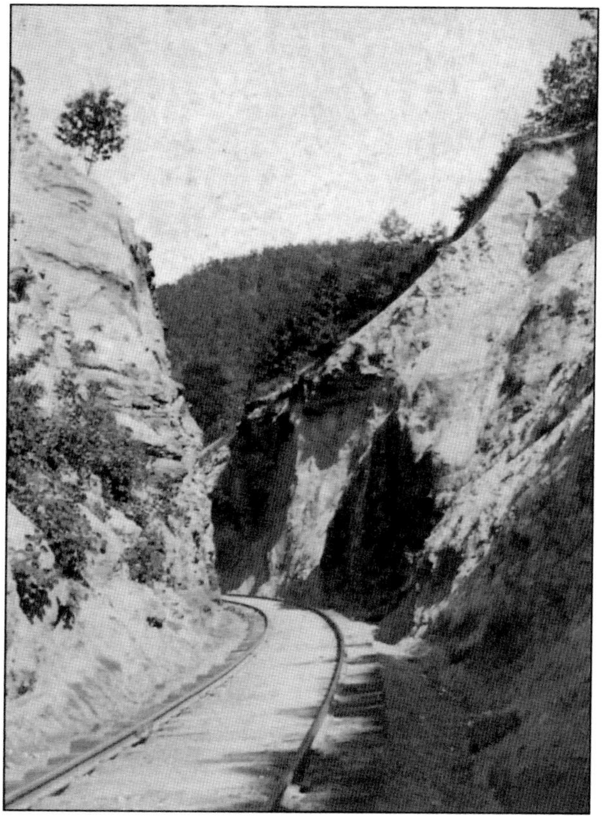

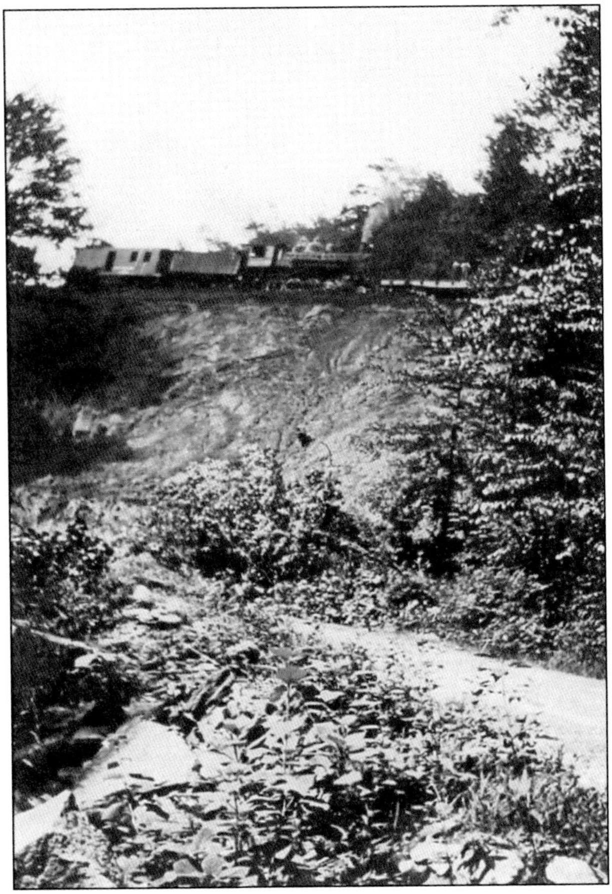

This photograph is of the primary safety track located in the curve at what was called the Big Fill. For many years, the safety tracks were left open at all times unless a train signaled to the switchman on 24-hour duty that the switch could be closed to send the train down the main track. During the 1950s, Weston Pace was a switchman, as was Clarence Pace. (Courtesy of Catherine Nicholson.)

This postcard from 1920 shows the railroad tunnel located on what is now Pearson Falls Road. The train would cross above, while horse and buggies and later automobiles passed through the tunnel, which cut through the mountain and crossed Joel's Creek before it flows into the Pacolet River. Today, the tunnel is still in operation for automobiles, and the unpaved Pearson Falls Road is a veritable wonderland of wildflowers and nature. (Courtesy of Charlene of Pace.)

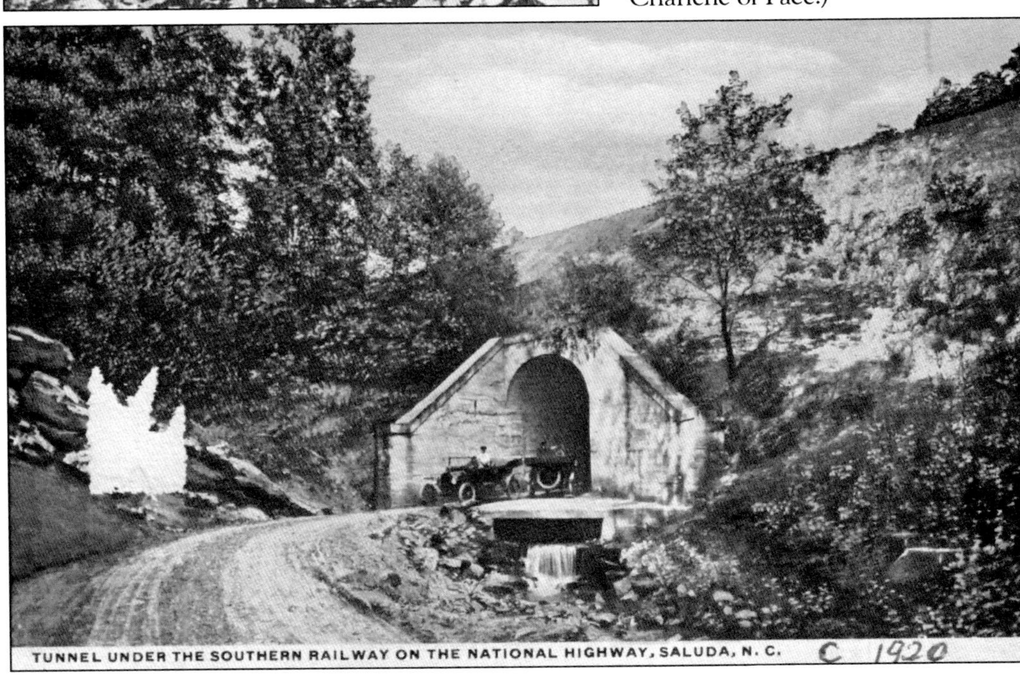

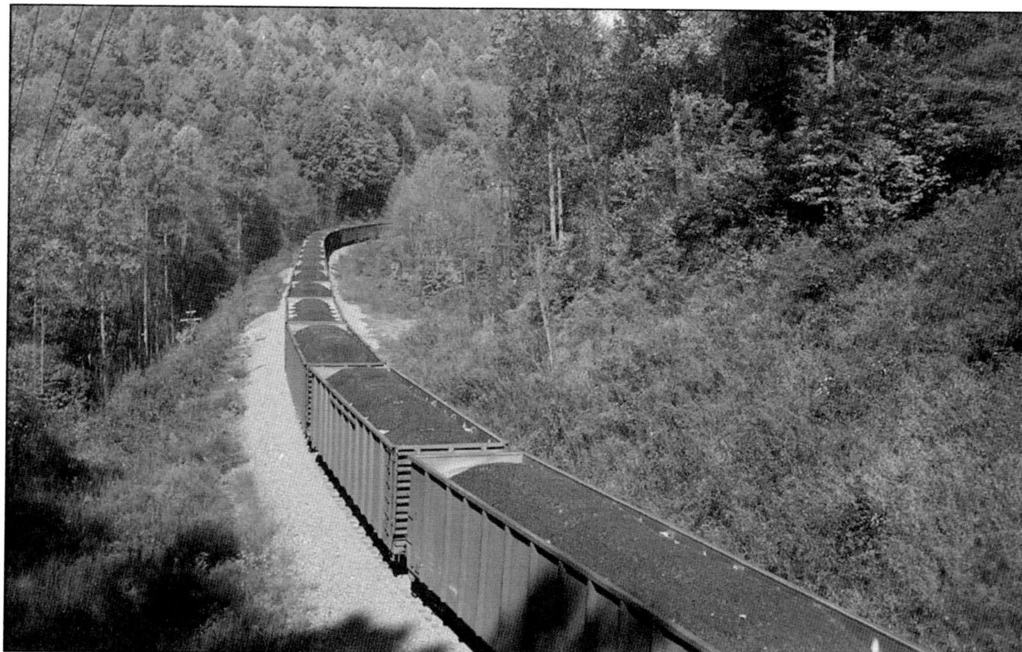

In 1980, this train is en route from Asheville to Hayne, South Carolina, with loaded coal cars passing Saluda Station on the Carolina Division of the Southern Railway System. The train is approaching the crest of the hill to go down Saluda Mountain to Melrose at the foot of the hill. (Photograph by Frank Clodfelter; courtesy of University of North Carolina at Asheville.)

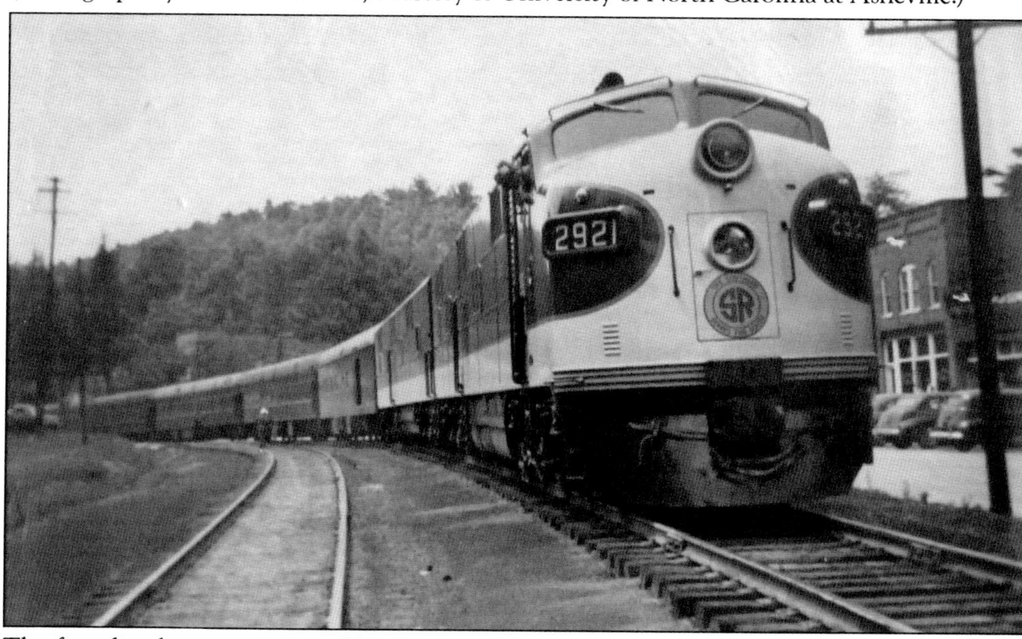

The first diesel engine, pictured here, cruised up the grade in 1949. In 1955, Southern Railway removed the first safety track due to its confidence in the new engines and safety procedures. However, runaway trains occurred in 1964 and 1971. Damage may have been minimal had the first safety track been left available. Instead they were brought to an abrupt stop two miles down the tracks at Melrose traveling down a five-percent grade. (Courtesy of Bill Holbert.)

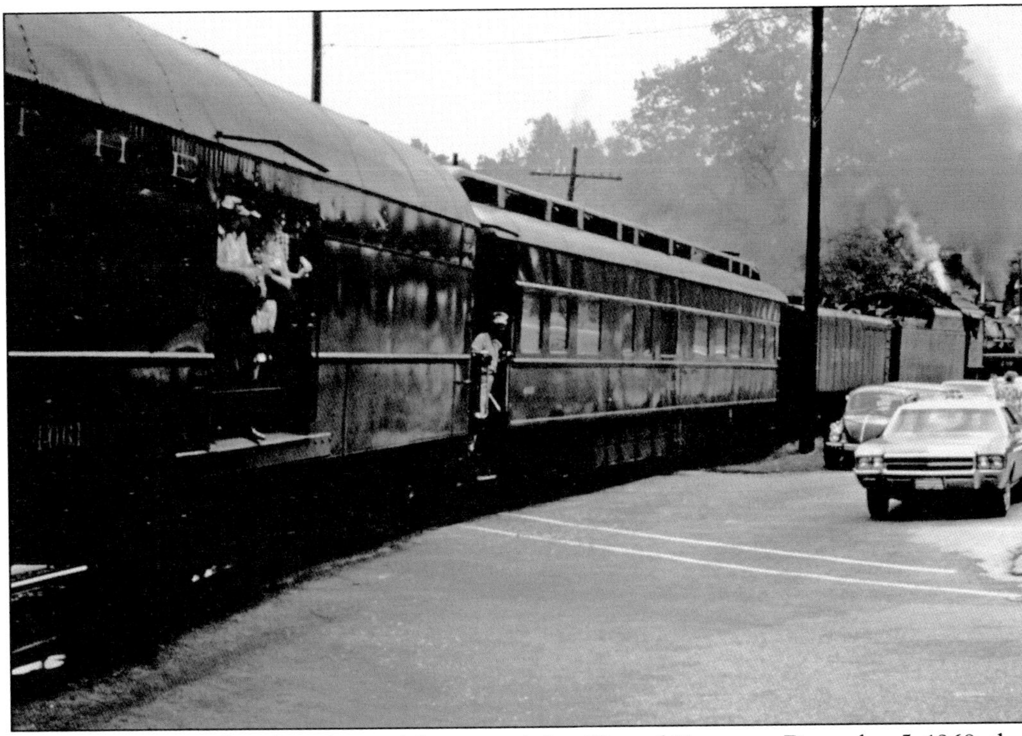

The *Carolina Special* made its last trek between Asheville and Hayne on December 5, 1968, thus ending the era for passenger service in Saluda. According to Frank Clodfelter in an article in *Trains Magazine*, November 1984: "During its prime years it consisted of mail and baggage cars, coaches, a diner, and Pullmans—an observation car proudly marked *Carolina Special*." (Courtesy of the Polk County Historical Association.)

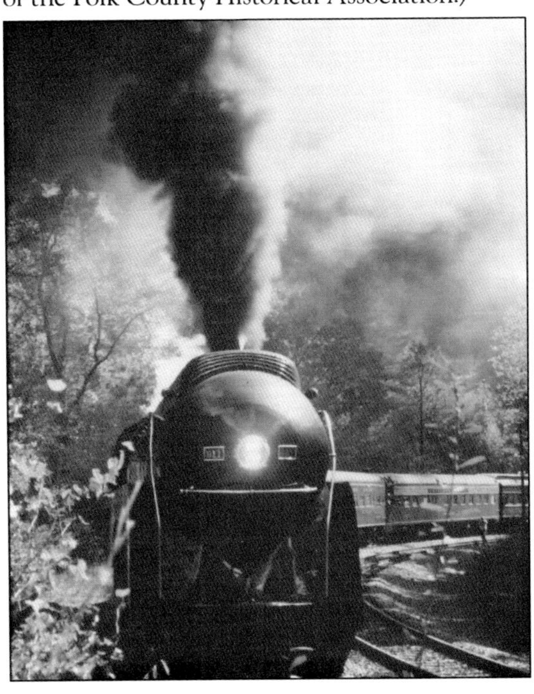

In October 1992, the Norfolk Southern 611 passenger steam engine took a spin through western North Carolina, including a daring trip up the Saluda Grade. Proving this stretch of railroad had not lost its might, the 611 stalled near the top of the mountain, with four heavy weight cars in tow, due to wheel grease on the tracks. Previously, the additional cars had been hauled up the grade by diesel-powered engines. (Courtesy of R. Clark Thompson.)

Two

Pace's Gap and Early Saluda

In the early days, the new settlement of Saluda had to accommodate the needs of the railroad workers who were in need of food, lodging, and supplies. Since the line to Hendersonville was not completed until 1879, Saluda was at the end of the line on the Spartanburg & Asheville Railroad for a year. Travelers going west to other resort towns such as Flat Rock and Hendersonville had to stop in Saluda to transfer to other modes of transportation, such as the stagecoach. These people and the rail workers had similar needs, increasing the demand for commerce in Saluda.

For many, Saluda remained the end of the journey once they discovered the natural beauty, pleasing weather, and the ozone-rich, healthy climate. Thus began the legacy of the grand inns, hotels, and boardinghouses providing fine accommodations for railroad workers and passengers alike.

For the first four or five decades, Saluda was one of the most exclusive resort towns in western North Carolina, primarily due to the influx of wealthy families from the Lowcountry, midlands, and even from the north. Many built grand Victorian summer homes that survived the Great Depression, and even today many are still in the possession of the original families. During this time, work was plentiful, and many came to Saluda to find employment.

The Great Depression had a huge impact on the inns and boardinghouses. Many mysteriously burned, rumored to be for insurance money. However, several were rebuilt and remained opened until World War II put a stop to extended road and train travel. With the end of the passenger trains in 1968 and the modernization of the highway system, Saluda has seen its ups and downs since then. Despite difficult years, Saluda has always managed to reinvent itself, making it an attractive and pleasing place to live year-round or seasonally. In 1996, the downtown district was placed in the National Register of Historic Places. In Saluda, whether exploring the past or present, it is hard not to feel connected to those glorious days of yesteryear.

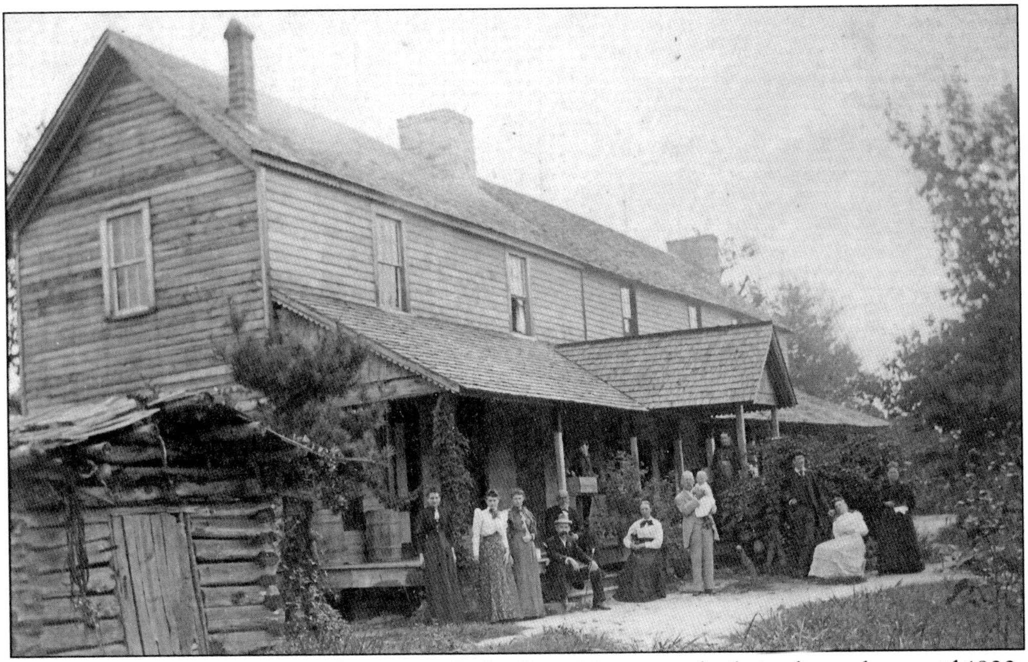

Located on the Howard Gap drover's trail, the Pace House was built in the early to mid-1800s by Moses Pace, son of Burwell Pope Pace, and was later run by his son, Ransom Woodruff Pace. According to family oral history, the house originally sat on at least 500 acres of land. It was operated as a drovers inn, boardinghouse, and even provided accommodations for boys attending the Saluda Seminary. (Photograph by O.B. Garren; courtesy of Jim Boyle.)

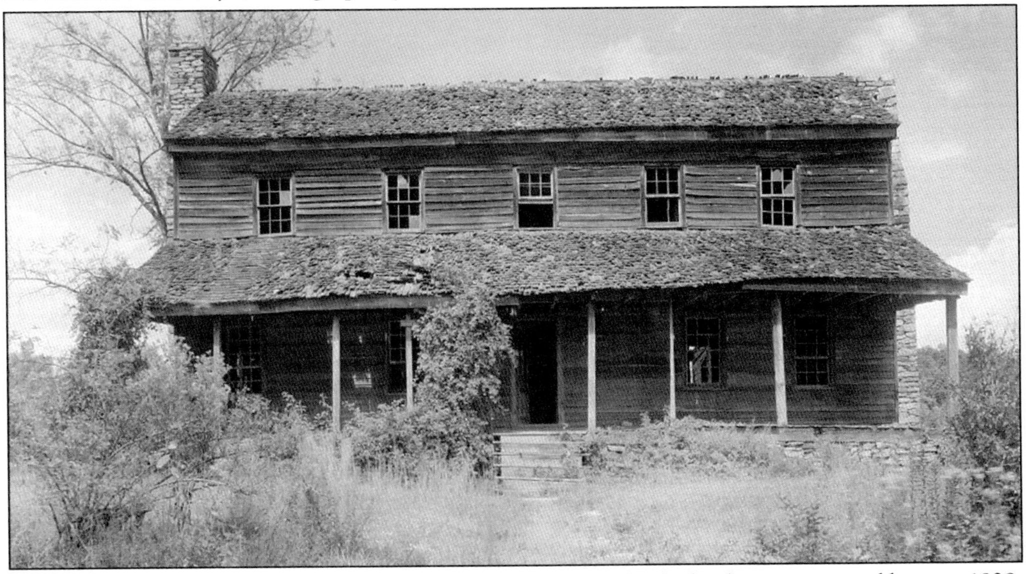

Around 1820, Frances Asbury "Berry" and Jane Thompson built this home, pictured here in 1938, in the fork of the road where Holbert Cove Road splits from Howard Gap Road, becoming a stop for the stagecoaches between Spartanburg and Asheville. In 1839, it became the first Tryon Post Office. Asbury Thompson served in the Civil War and was elected to the North Carolina Legislature, in which he served two terms. (Photograph by Frances Benjamin Johnson; courtesy of the *Carnegie Survey of the Architecture of the South* (CSAS), Library of Congress.)

The Guice family came from Scotland in the 1780s and settled near the Howard Gap Trail, at the top of a downward slope to the Green River crossing. The family built a drovers' inn, gristmill, blacksmith shop, and stock pens to accommodate travelers. A son, Peter, built a wooden bridge to replace the ford where the Howard Gap Trail crosses the Green River. Today, the Interstate 26 bridge crosses the Green River at almost the identical spot and bears his name. (Courtesy of Cindy Stephenson Tuttle.)

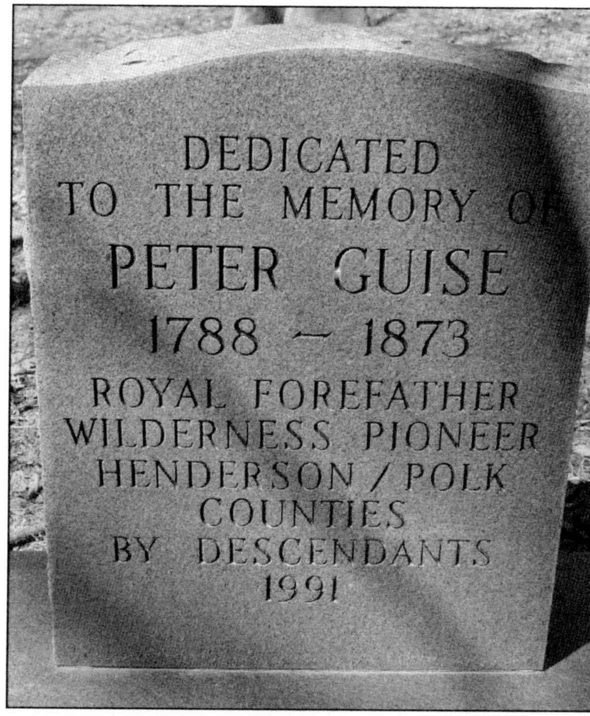

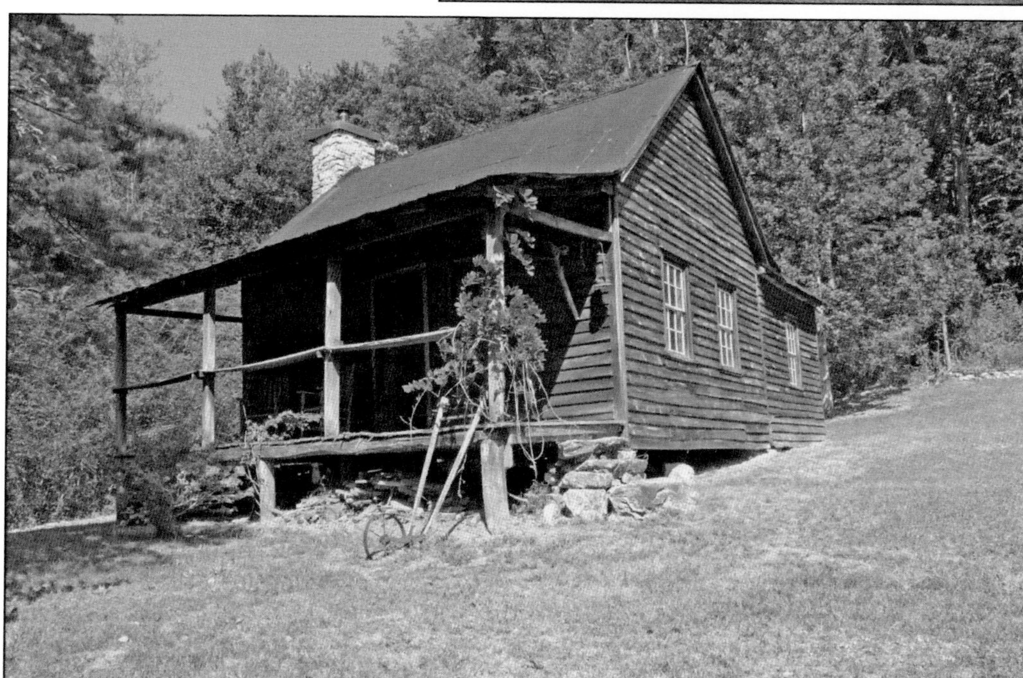

The John Hiram Johnson House, listed in the National Register of Historic Places, is the oldest intact and unaltered home in Polk County. Built in 1887, after John married Sarah Ellen "Sallie" Bradley, the Johnsons lived there until 1910. Located on the Holbert Cove Road outside of Saluda, the property was acquired in 1979 by Susan Dart and John McCutcheon, who have stabilized it and preserved its character and integrity. (Courtesy of Carolyn Ashburn.)

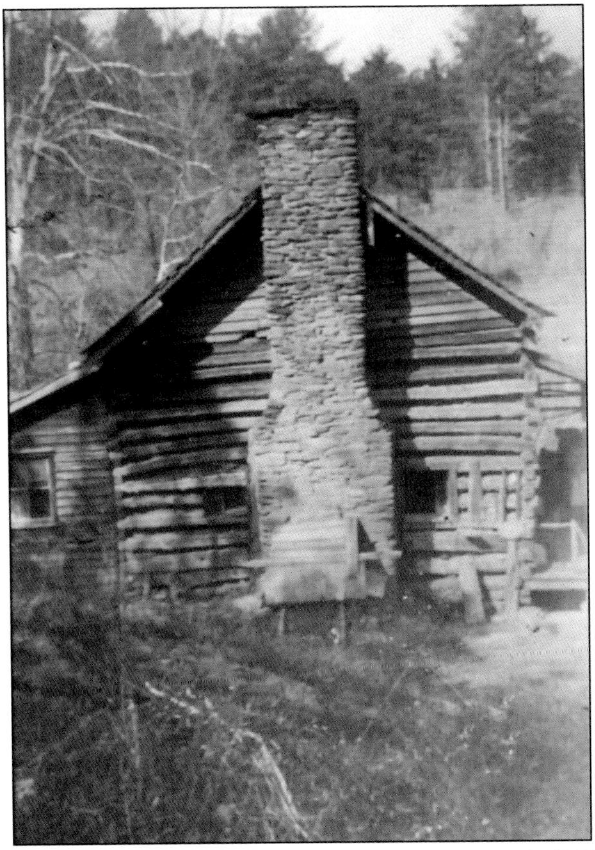

The Baxter Johnson House is located in what is referred to as the Shand Hill part of town. Though very old, it has been well preserved by its present-day owners. According to an oral history interview with Baxter Johnson's grandson Roy L. Johnson Jr., Baxter's wife died when Roy's father was very young. He raised his three children alone through years of hardship, at times surviving on only molasses and corn bread. (Courtesy of Roy L. Johnson Jr.)

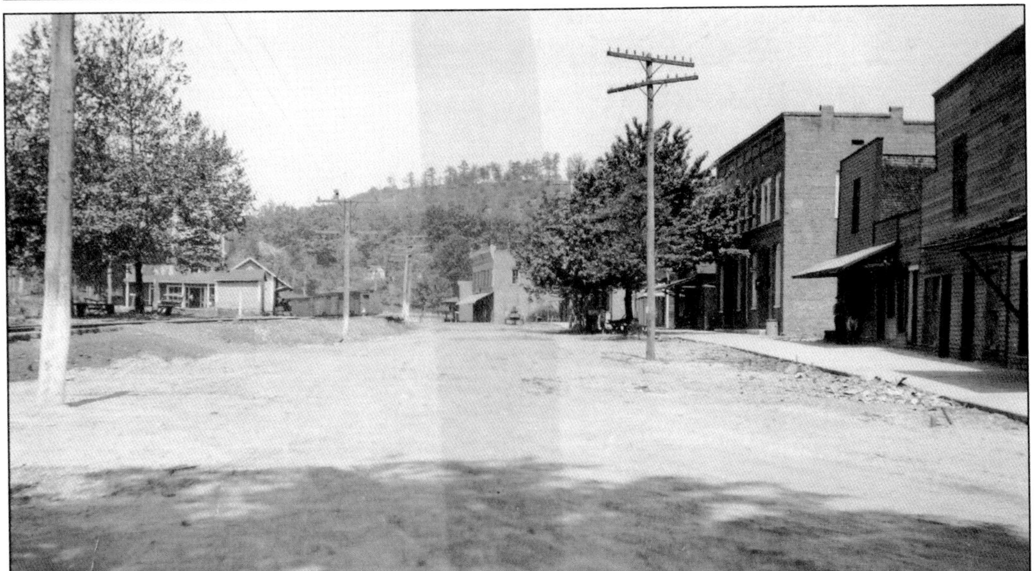

This early street scene shows a dirt Main Street with wood-framed buildings. The two brick buildings in view are the M.A. Pace Store and Saluda City Hall. Between these two buildings, but hidden from view, is Thompson's Store, and in the far distance, one can see what is now the Saluda Public Library. On the left is the original train depot. (Courtesy of Cindy Stephenson Tuttle.)

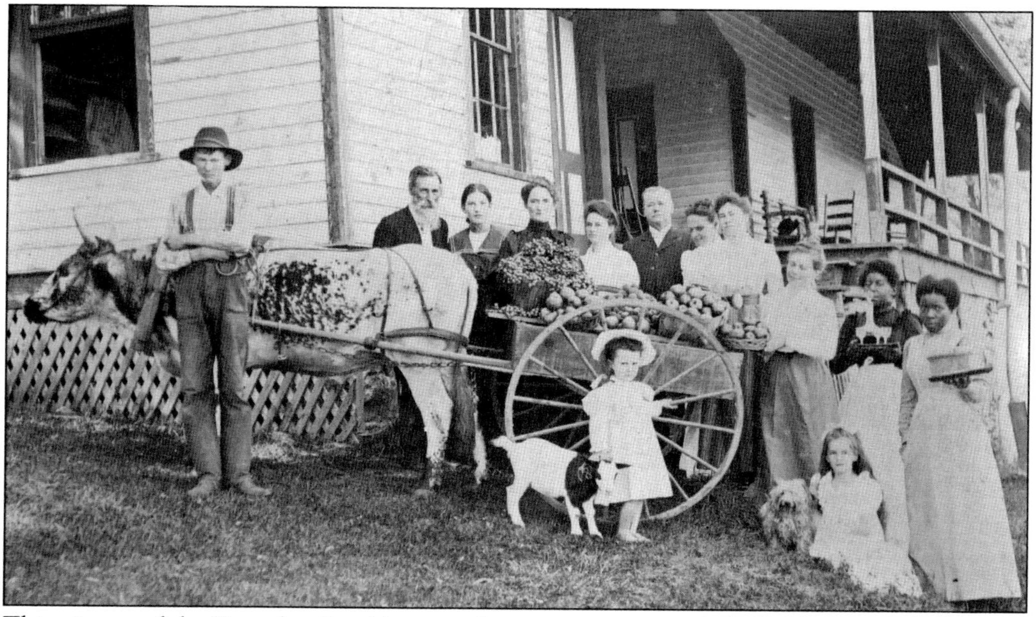

This picture of the Frost family with guests has an inscription on the back that reads, "Saluda, NC, 1900, Miss Stone and Wilma, Mr. Pearson and Sophy, Servants, Minnie and Belle." Below that the name "Mary P. Frost" is written. Two of the guests identified are Capt. Charles Pearson, chief engineer for the Spartanburg & Asheville Railroad, and his daughter Sophie D'Auge Pearson. Frost Road, originally named Frost Path, was named for the Frost family, who began spending summers in Saluda in 1885. (Courtesy of Nancy Leland Barnett.)

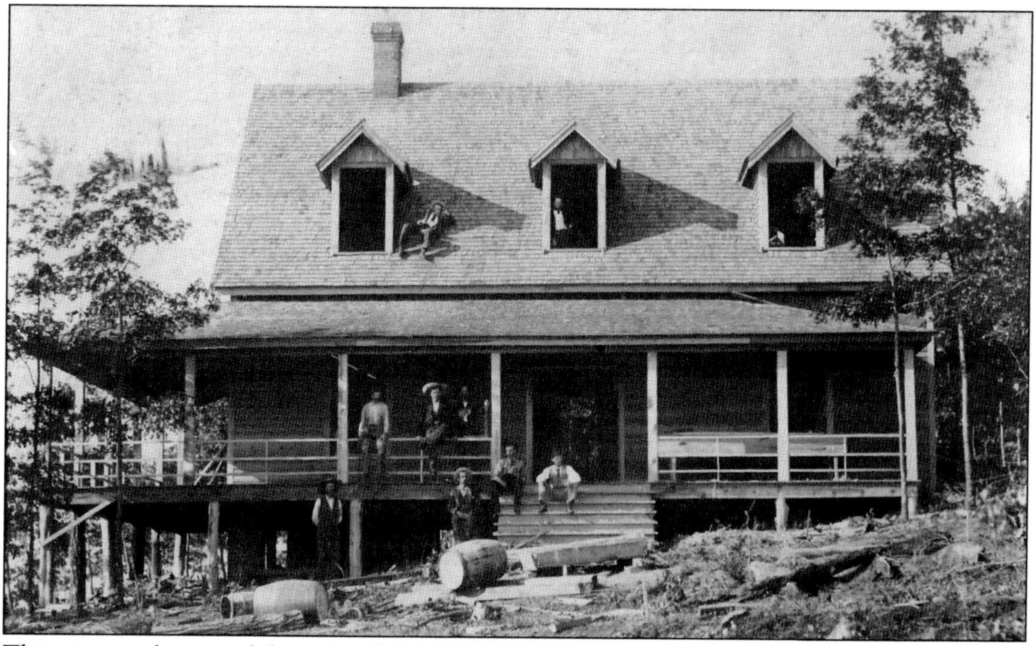

This vintage photograph has a handwritten notation that identifies it as a private summer cottage. During the boom of the early years, year-round residences and summer homes were in much demand. This photograph was taken by O.B. Garren, an early photographer and a contractor who built many of the original homes in Saluda. (Courtesy of Jim Boyle.)

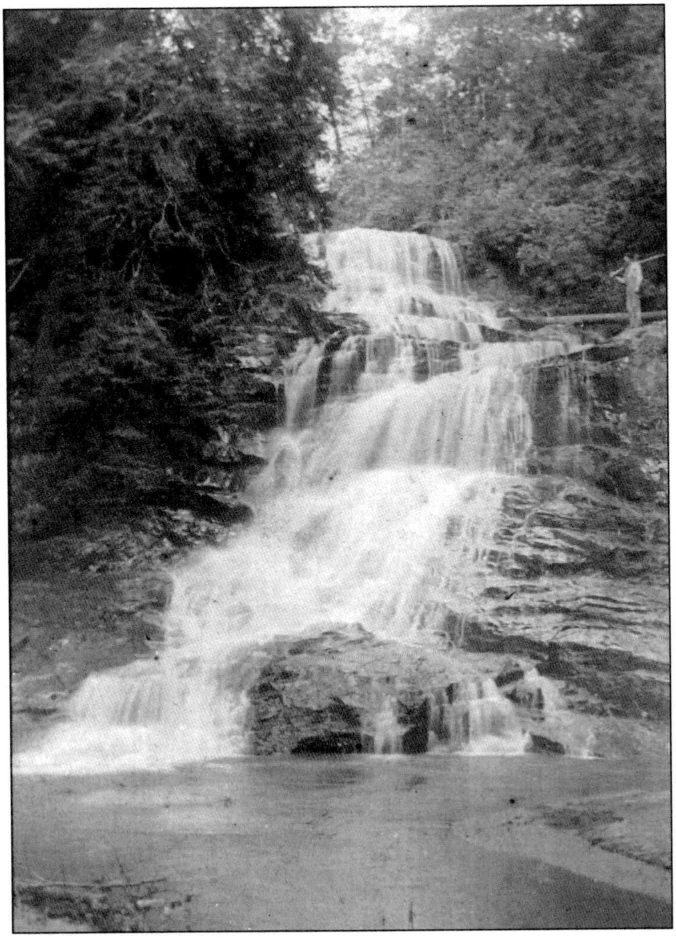

The natural beauty of this mountainous region attracted early settlers. This vintage photograph of Pacolet Falls has a handwritten notation that indicates it has a 92-foot drop. The falls are located about three miles from Saluda, and the Pacolet River runs parallel to the Saluda Grade. (Photograph by O.B. Garren; courtesy of Jim Boyle.)

The apple industry was one of early Saluda's most valuable economic resources. This photograph is of the Overbrook Orchard House, located in an apple grove originally planted by Dr. John C. Bushnell. It was the first commercial orchard planted in Polk County and contained Stark's Delicious and Stayman Winesap trees. It was sold to Henry P. Corwith in 1912 and later owned by the Staton family. (Courtesy of Martha Coates Ashley.)

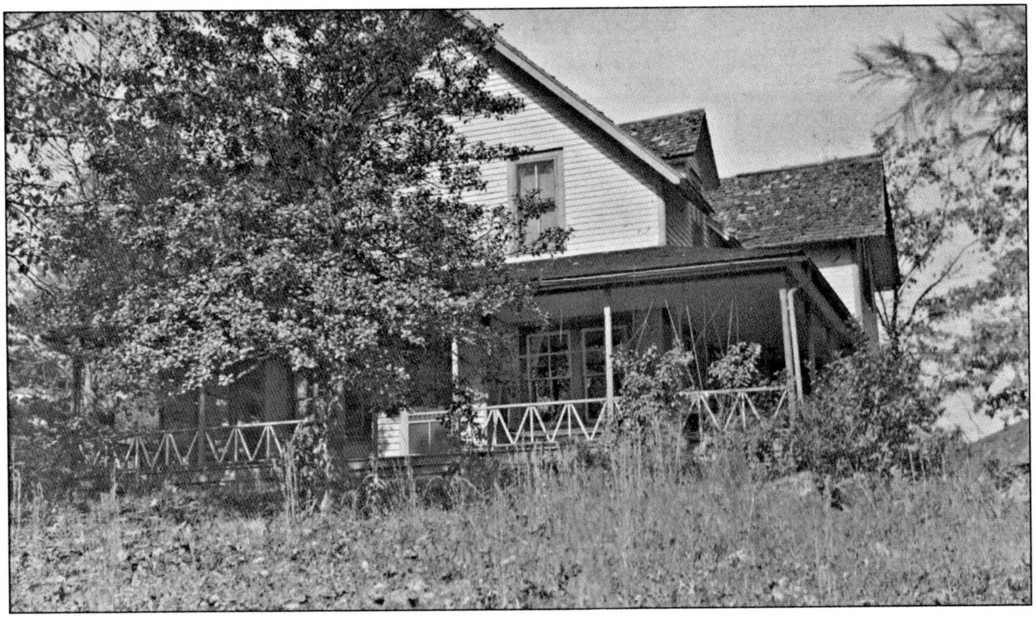

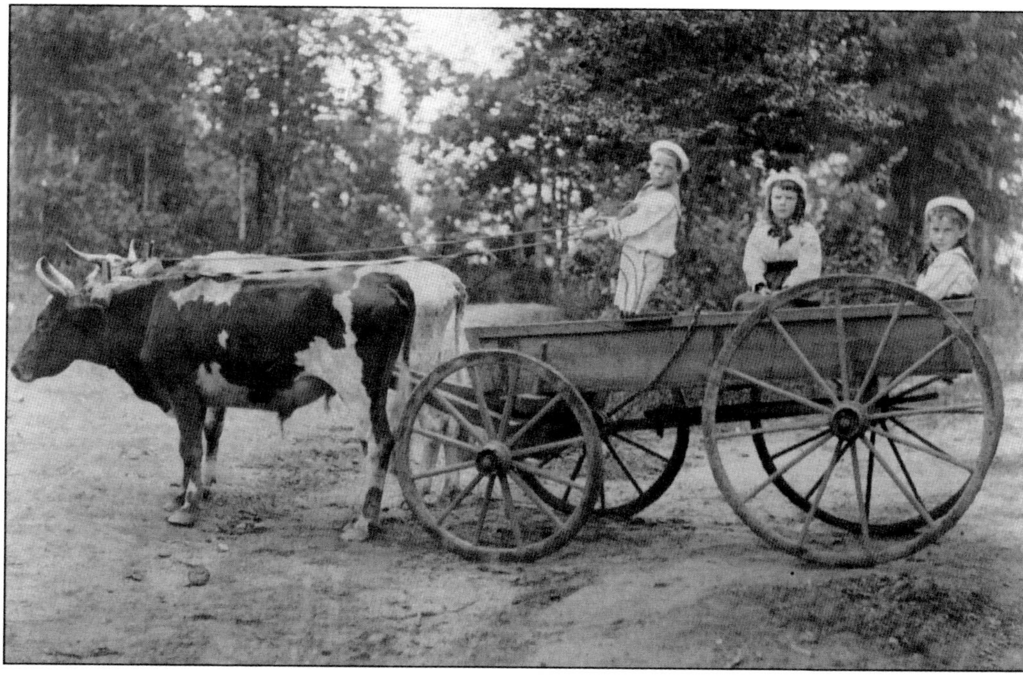

These two early photographs taken by O.B. Garren reflect the affluence of the day. Families dressed in their finest clothing were professionally photographed in their buggies and carriages. The photograph shown at the top has a handwritten notation that says "A Quiet Drive, Saluda N.C.," and the one below reads, "Riding Out in Saluda, N.C." (Both, courtesy of Jim Boyle.)

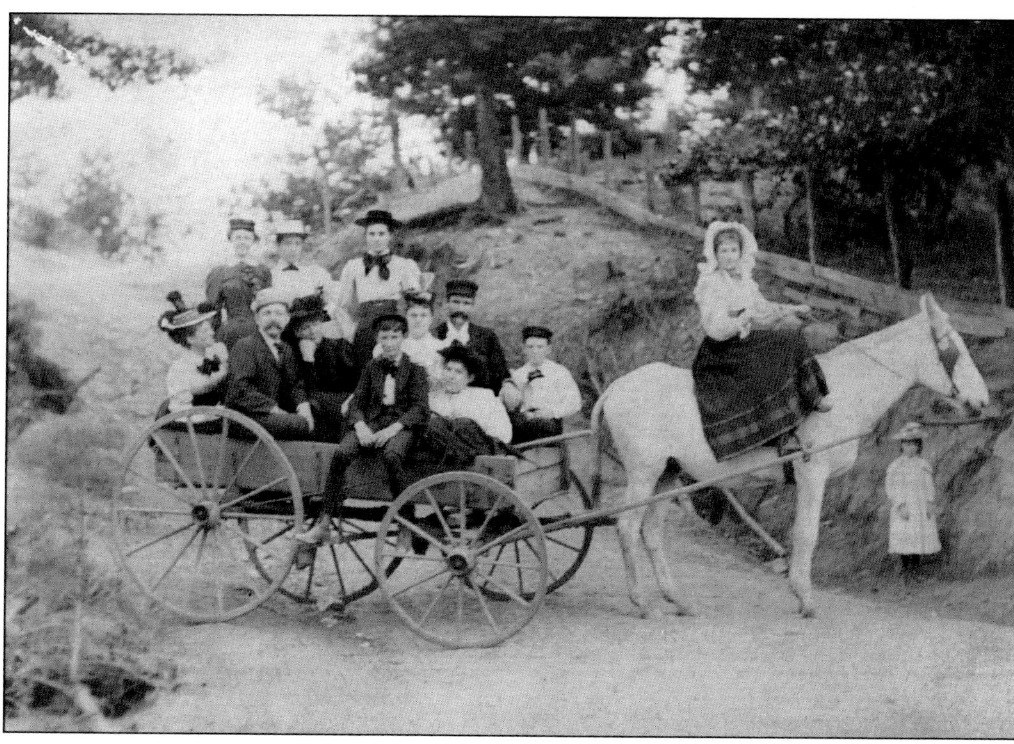

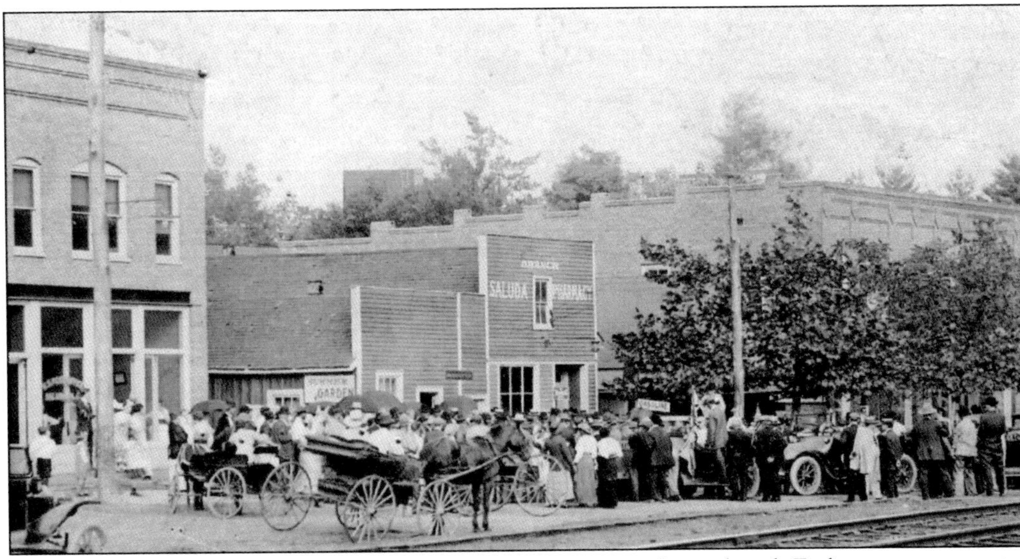

By 1887, Saluda was considered the best-paying station on the railroad. Eight passenger trains passed through the town daily, and during 1887, around 3,000 visitors came to Saluda. Mail was delivered to Saluda four or five times daily by train, resulting in a crowd of people flocking to town to retrieve their mail or just to see who was out and about. (Courtesy of Charlene Pace.)

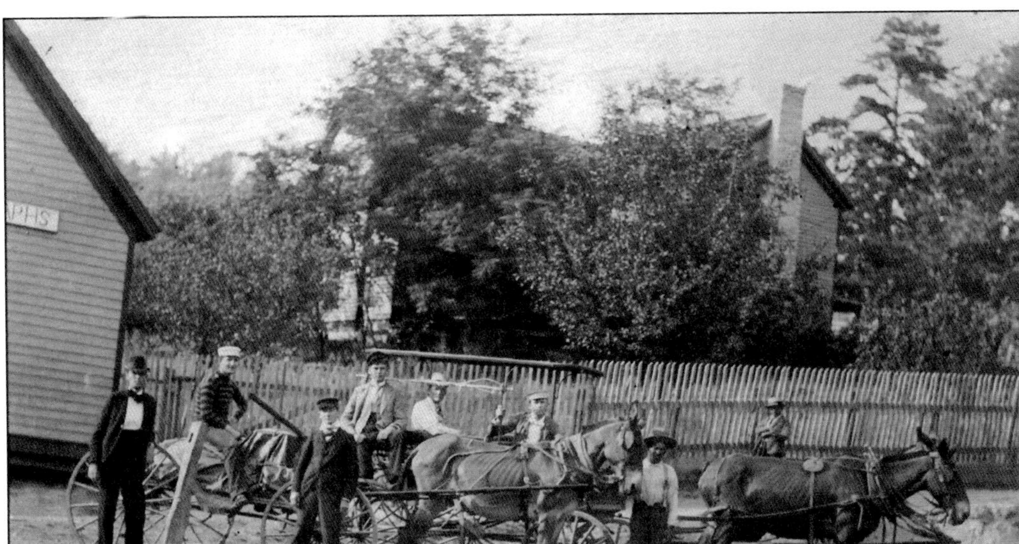

This early photograph taken by O.B. Garren beside his photography studio has a handwritten notation that reads, "Spike Team from the Great Smoky Mtn. N.C." Though no other information is given, it is assumed the men were brought in to work on the railroad. (Courtesy of Jim Boyle.)

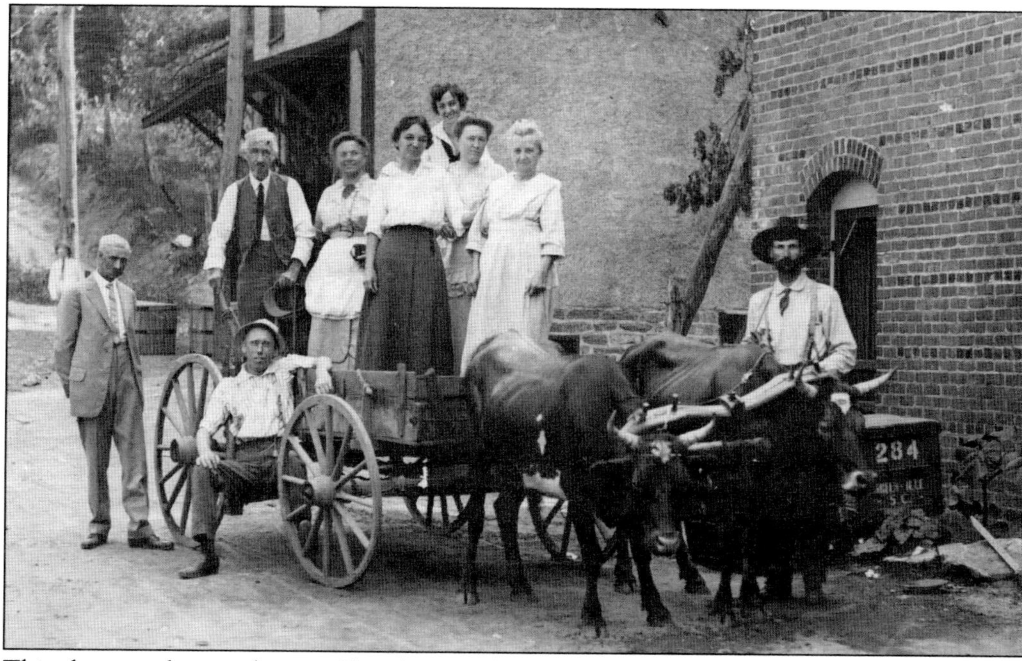

This photograph was taken on Church Street beside the current city hall building. The identities of the people are unknown with the exception of Marion Gordon, also known as the fiddle maker, who is on the right, wearing a hat. The pebble-dash building in the background features a method of exterior finishing popular in the first part of the 20th century in which pebbles are mixed with mortar for a textured surface. (Courtesy of Pauline Gordon Corn.)

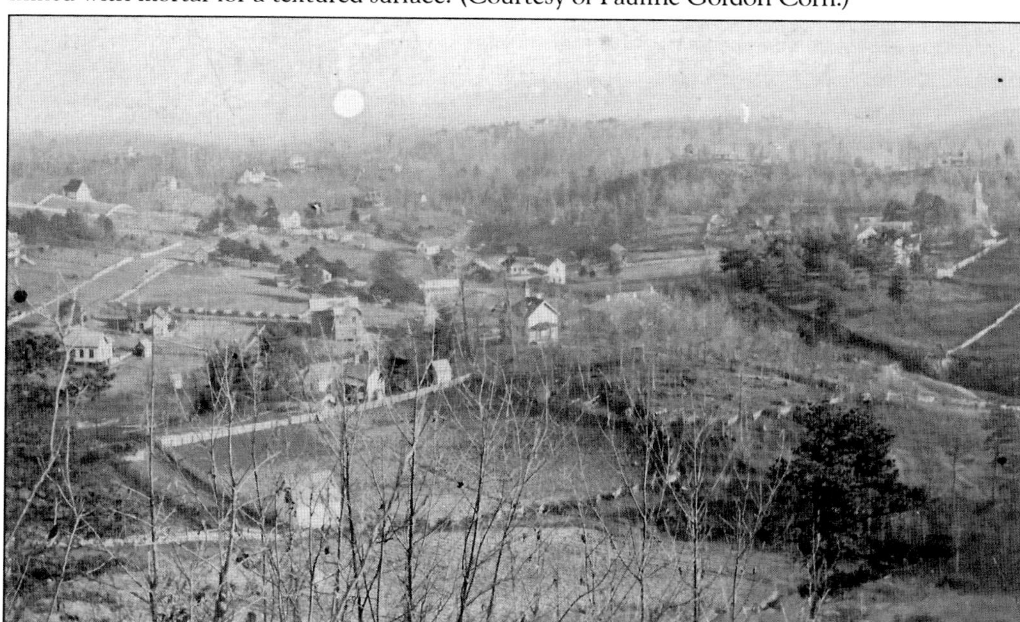

Taken from Piney Mountain, this early photograph by O.B. Garren shows an almost aerial view of Saluda. Piney Mountain is now privately owned by the Ogden family and located within the city limits. In the late 1930s, Bill Ogden put an access road in and built a little cabin, which is still used by the family today. (Courtesy of Jim Boyle.)

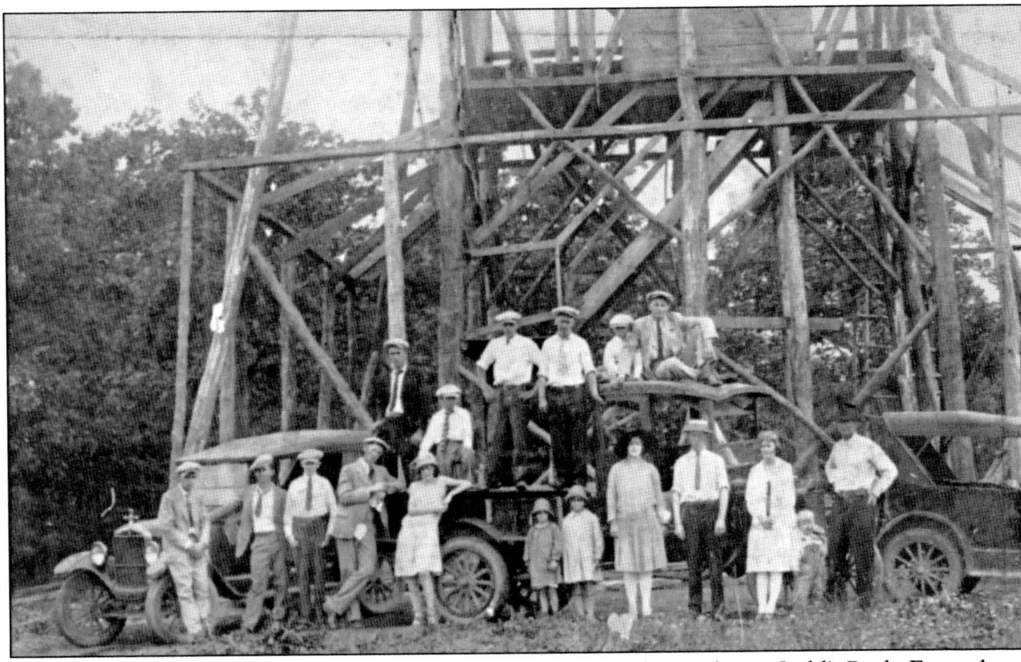

A favorite pastime was to climb the observation tower once located atop Judd's Peak. From there, one could get a good view of Saluda, Tryon Mountain, Mount Pisgah, and Mount Mitchell, all at the same time. Judd's Peak is located less than two miles from downtown Saluda. Though the tower is no longer there, the views are still breathtaking. (Courtesy of Charlene Pace.)

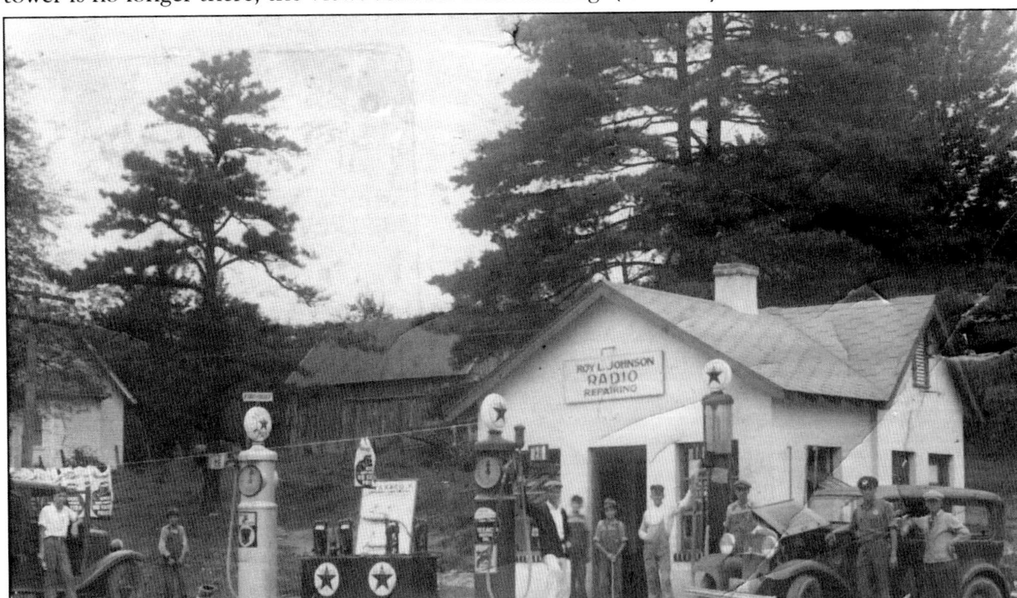

Roy Lee Johnson Sr. (second from the right) operated this service station and radio repair shop. He built the first radio in Saluda from parts he ordered. Visitors would come to his shop to listen to this new invention, and skeptics were known to peak behind it to see if anyone was hiding. The white building pictured to the left is located at the rear of the Saluda Presbyterian Church. (Courtesy of Roy Lee Johnson Jr.)

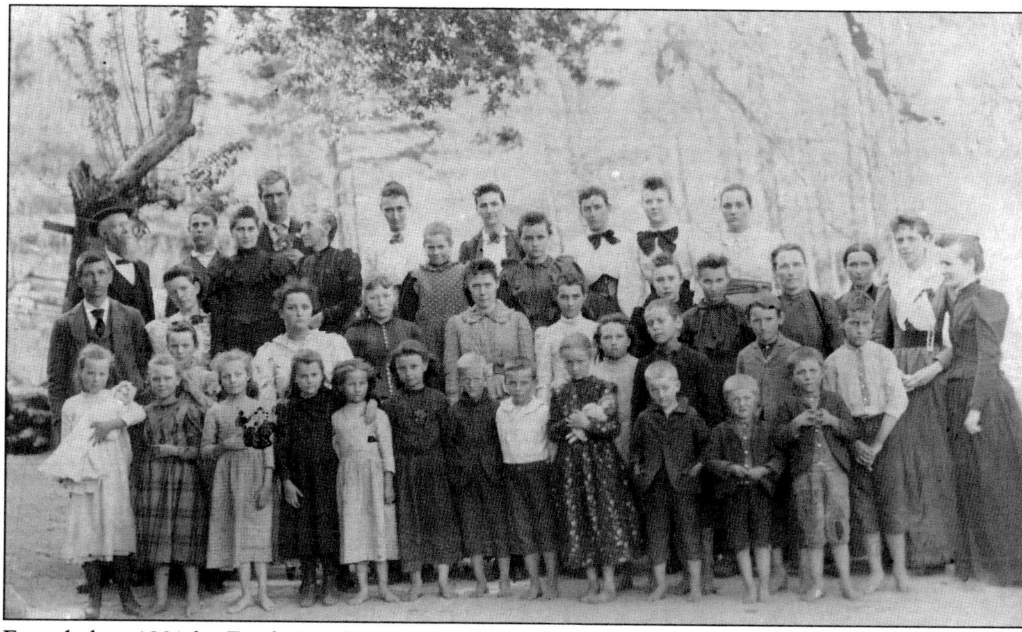

Founded in 1891 by Emily Prudden, the Saluda Seminary offered an excellent education that many otherwise would not have had. Her mission was to educate disadvantaged children in the region, and according to a 1906 brochure, the seminary offered instruction in writing, arithmetic, geography, health, physiology, history, composition, rhetoric, and music. A written notation on this photograph says, "A part of Saluda Female Seminary, Girls and Primary Class, Photographed during vacation 1893." (Photograph by O.B. Garren; courtesy of Jim Boyle.)

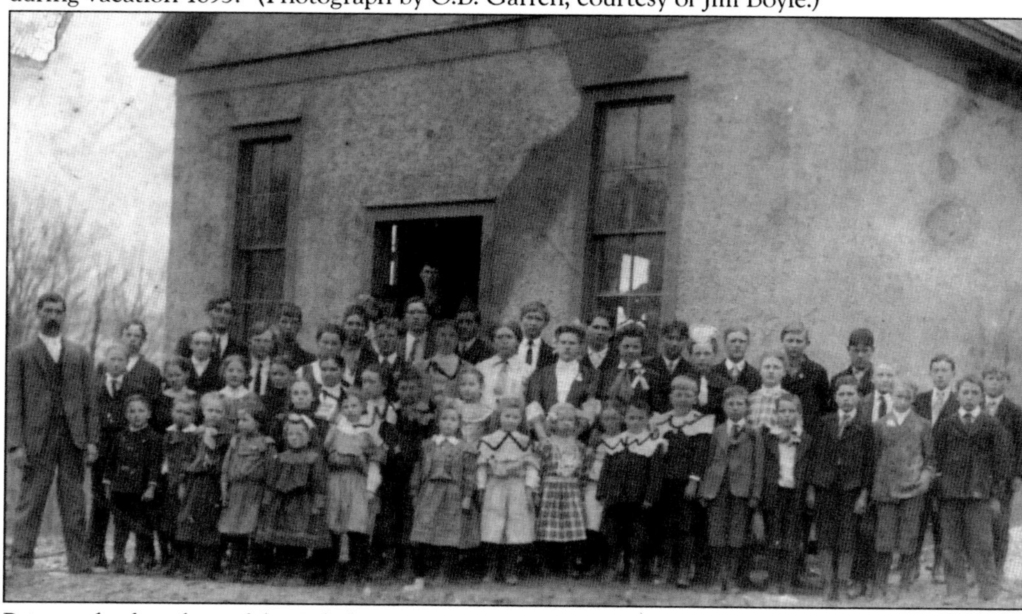

Prior to the founding of the Saluda Seminary in 1891, only a few other subscription schools existed in the region. These small, scattered schools were located at Friendship Church, Macedonia, and Mountain Page. This photograph, discovered in the personal belongings of Donivee Russell Hipp, now deceased, is of Mountain Page School, which closed around 1934. The school was located next to the present-day Mountain Page Church. (Courtesy of James Metcalf.)

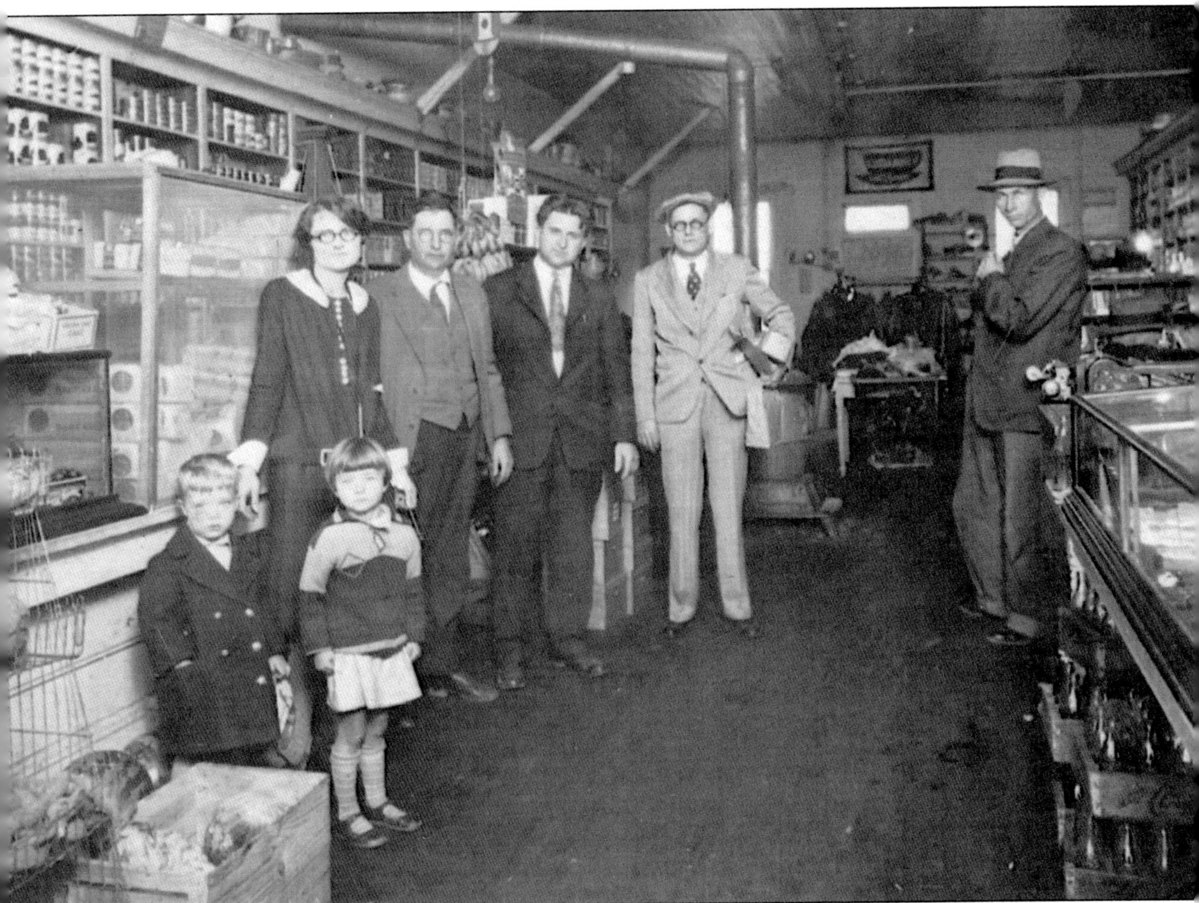

Two iconic businesses that remain in operation today in the historic district of downtown Saluda are the M.A. Pace Store and Thompson's Store. Records for the M.A. Pace Store indicate it was opened in 1899 by M.A. Pace. The Thompson family's early records show that George Lafatte Thompson first became involved in the mercantile business as early as 1890. Lola Thompson Ward grew up working in her father's business in the early 1900s. Reflected in this photograph, the two stores were once in operation together and coexisting in the current M.A. Pace building. Leon Morgan, current owner of the M.A. Pace Store, still has a letter from M.A. Pace to D.M. Ferry Feed Company dated February 24, 1927, notifying the company that Thompson and Pace had dissolved. Pictured here are, from left to right, Tommy Thompson, Betty Jo Thompson, Lola Thompson Ward, George Lafatte Thompson, unidentified, M.A. Pace, and unidentified. The M.A. Pace Store remains in operation at the same location, and Thompson's Store is located a short distance up the street. (From the album of Lola Ward, courtesy of Judy Ward.)

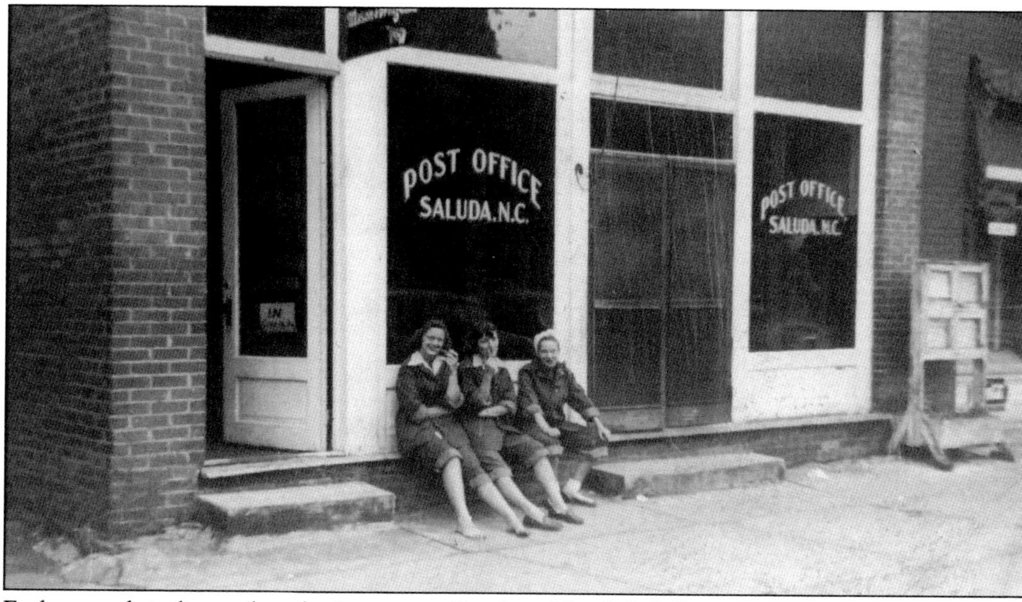

Early records indicate that the first post office listed for Saluda began on May 7, 1878, with John R. Tanner listed as the first postmaster. Since Saluda was not chartered until 1881, it is assumed the post office began under another name. This photograph shows the post office in the 1940s; it remained in this location until 1966. The post office has always been a great place to catch up with friends and neighbors. (From the album of Lola Ward, courtesy of Judy Ward.)

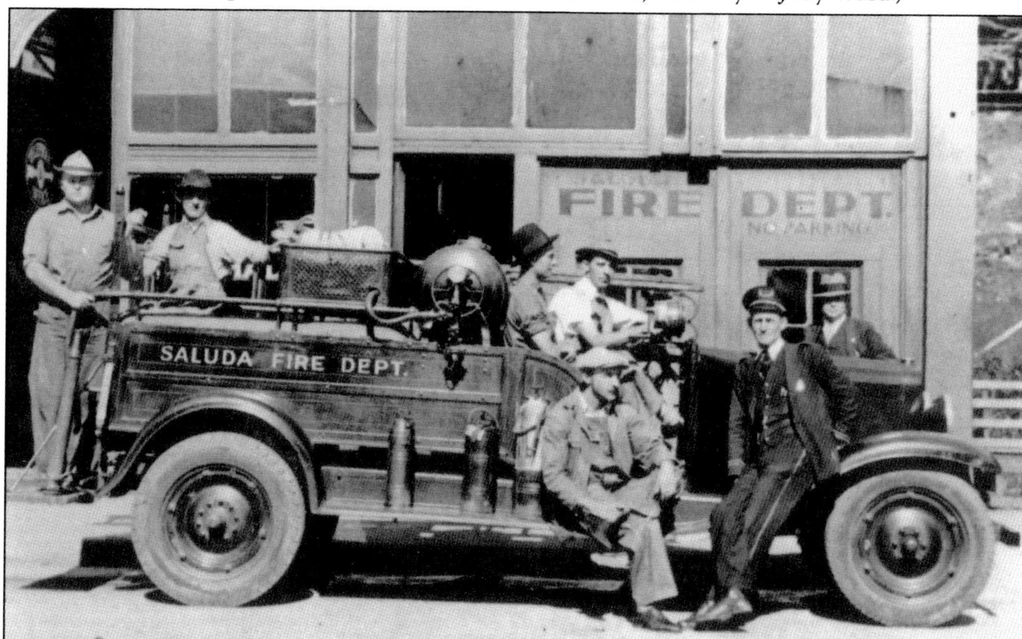

Pictured here in 1936 is the Saluda Fire Department volunteer fire squad and their dog Queen, who was raised at the fire department and described as the night watchman. The squad claimed it always "gets its fire." Pictured here are, from left to right, Laulley Fisher, Ed Johnson, Queen, Art Hipp, Roy Ward, Ernest Thompson, Chief H.G. Laughter, and Baty Hall. (Courtesy of R. Clark Thompson.)

Before you dial a number, take time to listen for the dial tone.

\- - - - -

To reach the long distance operator, dial Zero She will handle all out-of-town calls and give all information pertaining to them.

\- - - - -

For local information, dial 2117. If there is no answer, dial 2601.

\- - - - -

If you are on a party line and want to call a number on your line, dial "9", followed by the last digit of your number, and the last digit of the number you want to call. Now while the receiver is at your ear, press down the switch-hook button with your other hand and wait for your phone to ring. The other person's phone will be ringing at the same time. When your phone stops ringing, it indicates that the other party has answered. Now remove your finger from the button and talk.

If your phone does not stop ringing, it indicates that the party is not going to answer his phone. Remove your finger from the button and hang up the hand-set.

In 1936, Ed Leland paid the Appalachian State Telephone Company $800 and renamed the business the Saluda Mountain Telephone Company, starting out with one magneto switchboard and 16 telephones, the hand-cranked wall variety. Ever the pioneer, in 1945, Leland converted to the dial system at the same time Asheville did, but he did it all by himself. Leland ran the company for 32 years until his son E. Cater Leland Jr. joined him in 1968. By 1970, the company had 462 subscribers. Ed Leland was known for his hard work and lack of debt, along with keeping the rates low and the customer service superb, thus landing him in the *Wall Street Journal* and on *CBS Sunday Morning*. The Saluda Mountain Telephone Company was sold to Telephone and Data Systems, Inc., now referred to as TDS, in 1990. This image from a 1951 telephone directory provides instruction on the use of the party-line system. (Courtesy of E. Cater Leland Jr.)

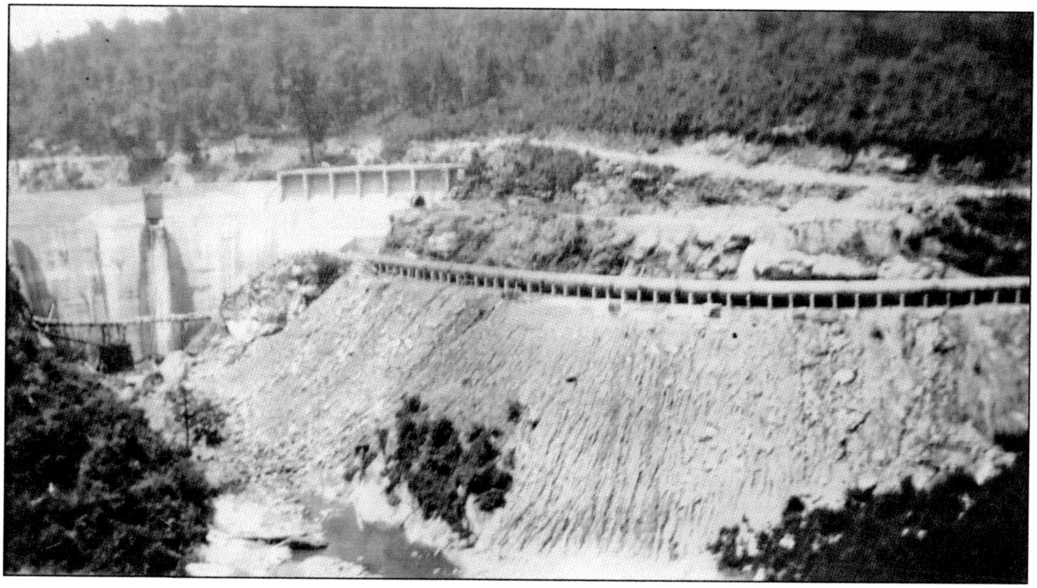

The founders of the Blue Ridge Power Company wanted to supply cheap electricity for their textile plants in Spartanburg, South Carolina, so they planned to build three dams on the Green River. Lake Summit and the dam, near Tuxedo, were built around 1916 or 1917. The flume was made of wood, as metal could not be obtained due to World War I. It was at this time that Blue Ridge Power Company built lines from Tuxedo (Lake Summit) to Spartanburg and substations in Landrum, Tryon, and Saluda. The Tuxedo plant was opened in 1918. Duke Energy still operates a hydroelectric facility on the lake's eastern end. The above photograph shows the Lake Summit hydroelectric dam under construction along with the wood flume. The image below, taken around 1948, shows Alex Salley walking atop the Lake Summit Dam. (Courtesy of Alex Salley.)

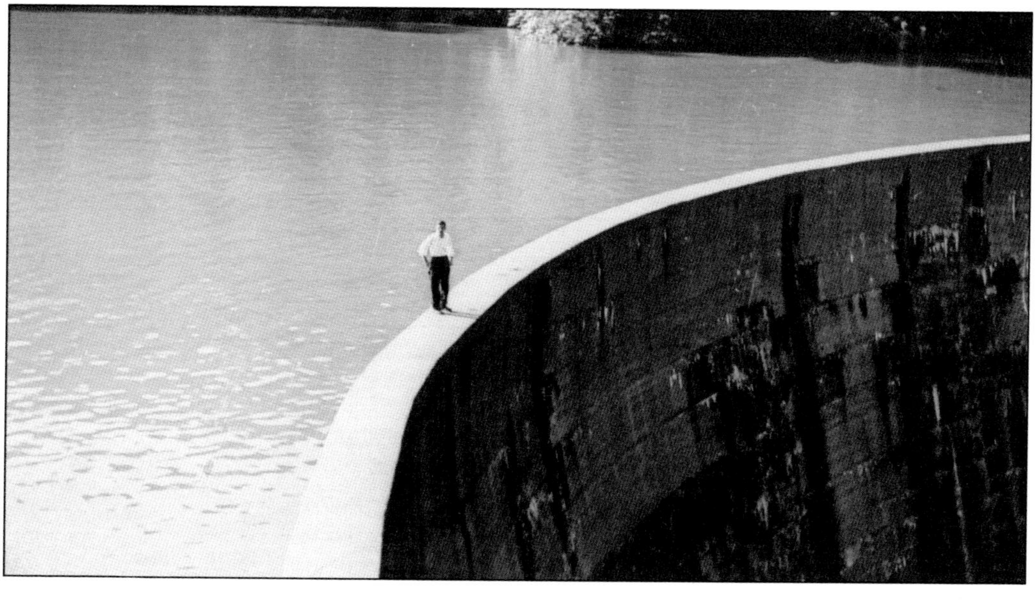

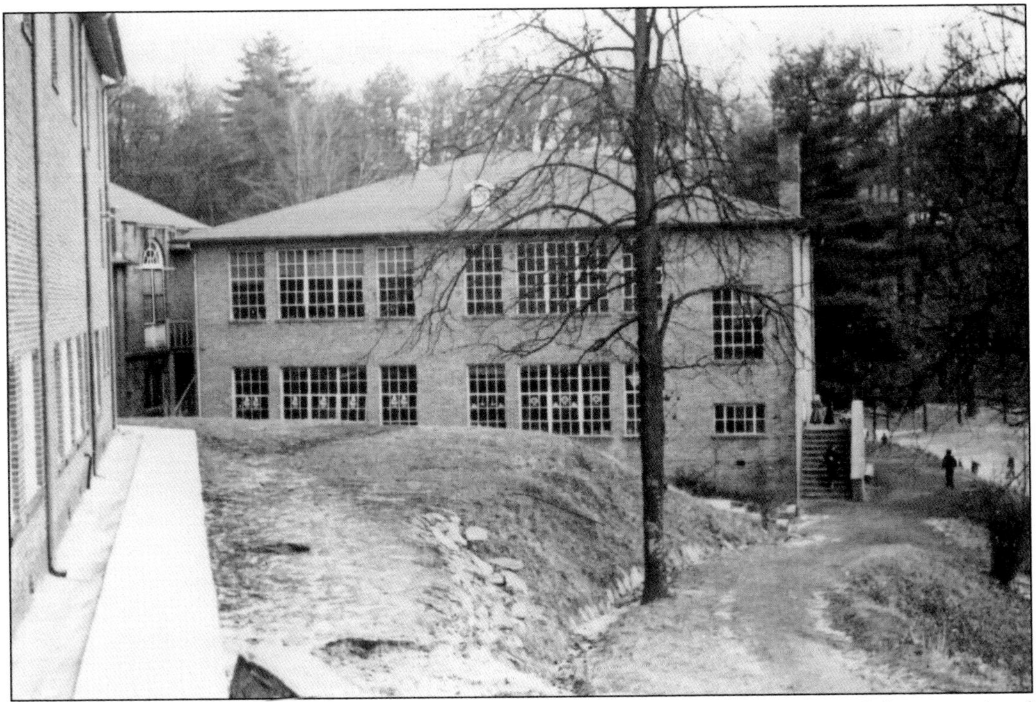

In the early 1920s, the Saluda Seminary gave way to the public school system, and the new school was constructed on the same grounds, using part of the main school structure originally built for the seminary. This was later torn down to build the current school. In the late 1930s, the Works Progress Administration (WPA) built the first gymnasium in Polk County on school grounds. Until 1974, the school provided an education from the first grade through high school. Today, it serves children from pre-kindergarten to fifth grade, and students may choose to attend either Polk or Henderson County schools after fifth grade. The above photograph is a view from the gymnasium of the old Saluda School building no longer in existence. The image below is the school in 1951. (Above, courtesy of Alex Salley; below, courtesy of Cindy Stephenson Tuttle.)

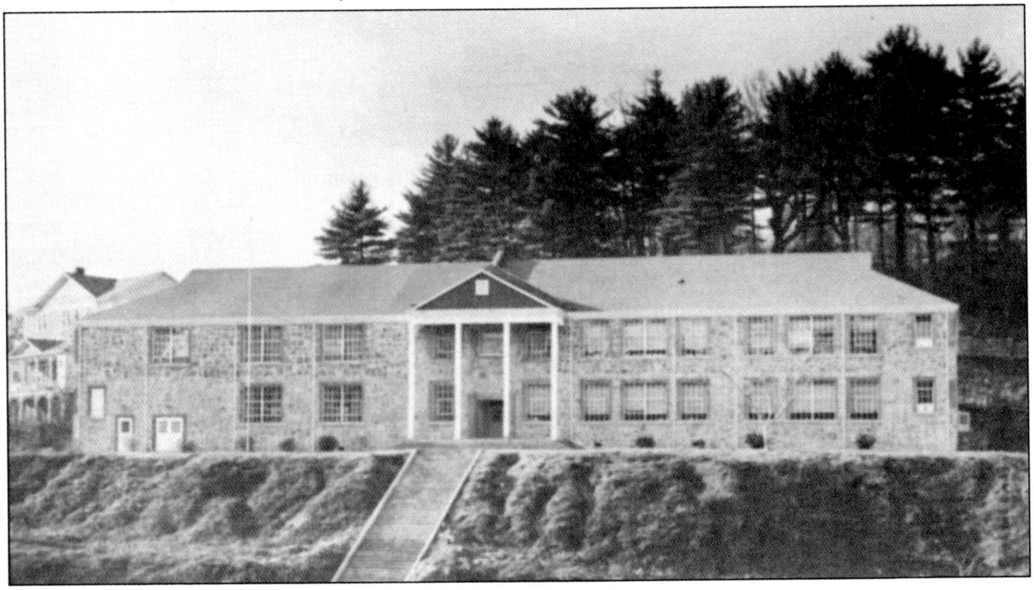

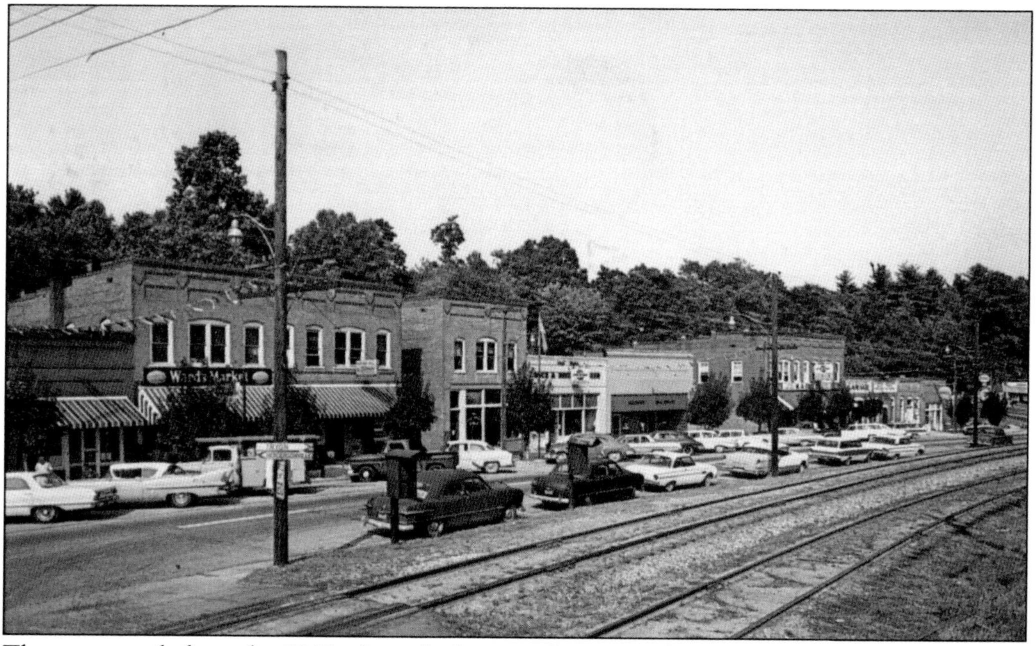

These postcards from the 1960s show the historic downtown business district as part of the US 176 main thoroughfare between Tryon and Hendersonville, before I-26 was opened in the 1970s. The district was placed in the National Register of Historic Places in April 1996, after Melody Gibson, a Saluda native, led the initiative. She became concerned due to the destruction of several historic buildings. Laura Phillips, an architectural historian, researched the district as required for the nomination and her efforts were coordinated with the work of the North Carolina Department of Archives and History. In was noted that of the 25 structures located in the district, 18 were contributing buildings, meaning they had not been altered to a degree that their character and authenticity had been lost. (Both, courtesy of Cindy Stephenson Tuttle.)

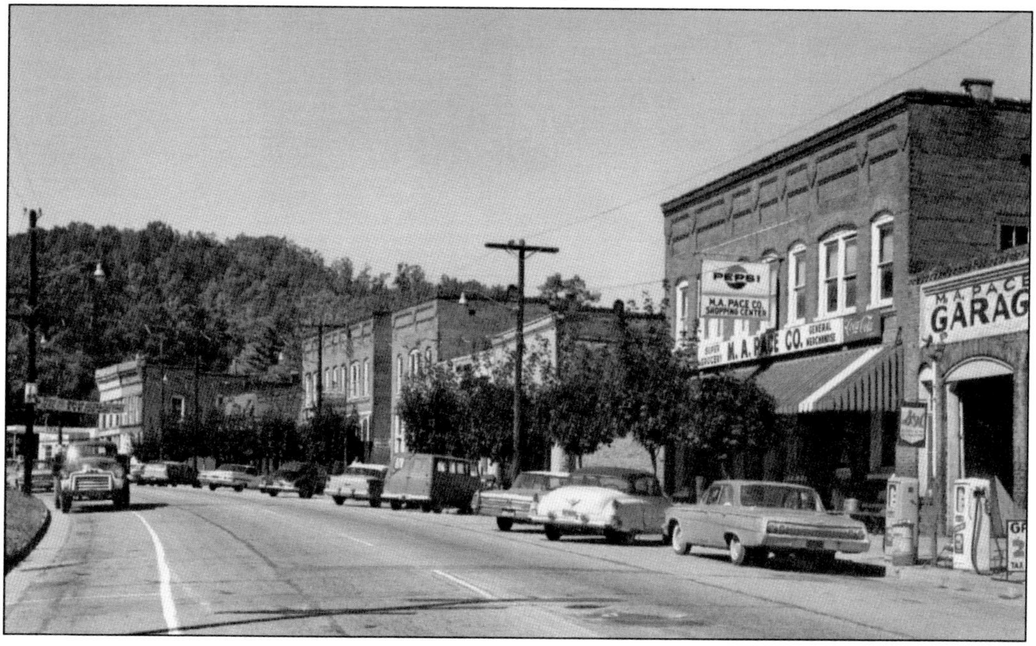

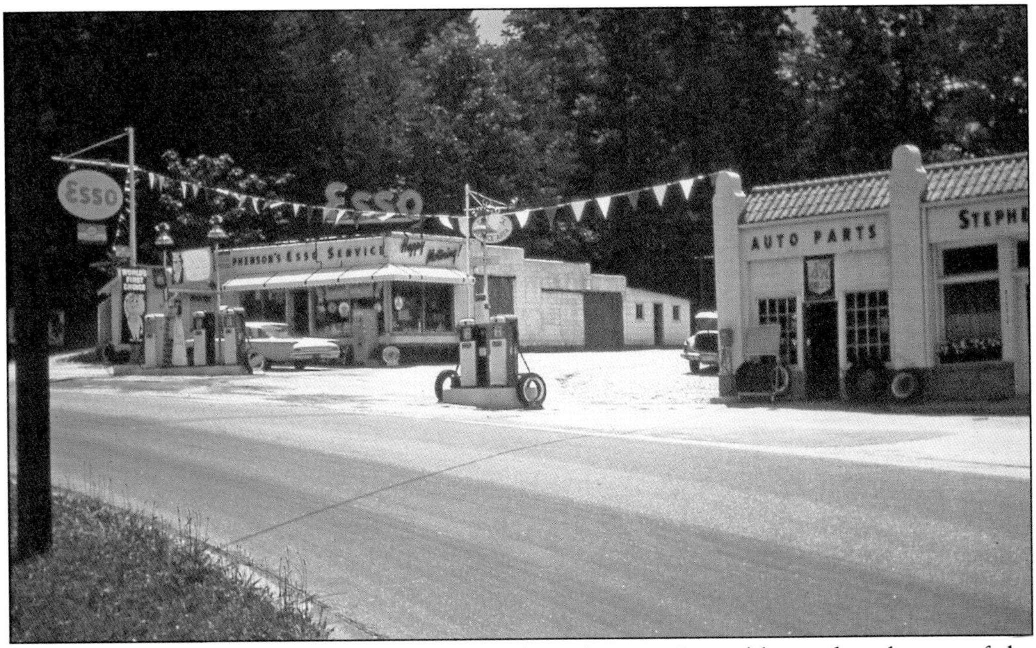

Stephenson's Esso was operated by J. Raymond Stephenson Sr. and located at the top of the Saluda Grade on Main Street. Originally located in the Whistle Stop building (right), which is the typical style of Standard Oil stations constructed in the 1930s, he built the newer station (left) in the 1950s. At one time, as many as five service stations were located downtown, but once I-26 was finished in 1976, highway traffic was diverted away from town and business. (Courtesy of Cindy Stephenson Tuttle.)

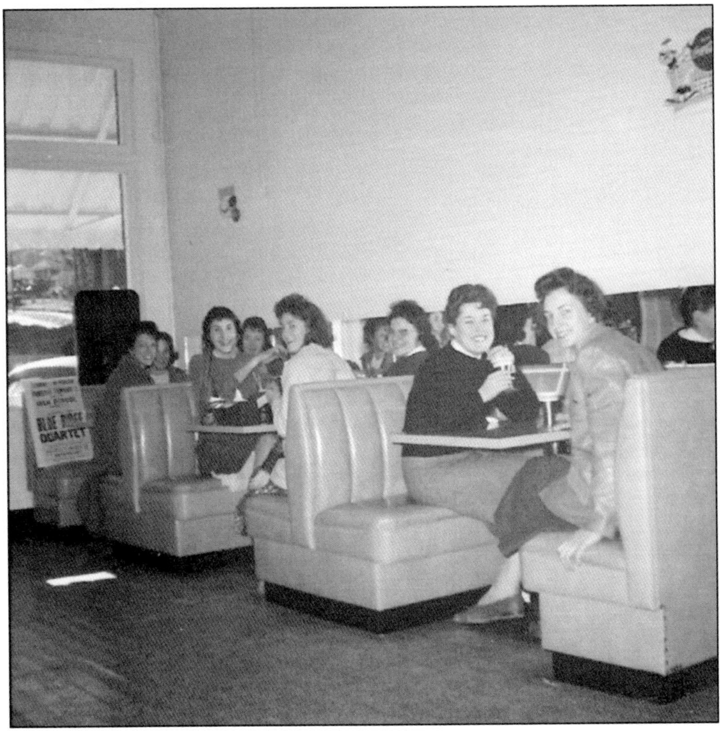

In the late 1950s, Lola Thompson Ward's husband, Roy, and their son Jack convinced her to add a grill to the Thompson's Store. Then and now it is a favorite hang-out and is appreciated for its fresh-cut meats, homemade sausage, and hometown hospitality. At one time or another, Thompson's Store and Ward's Grill delivered everything from heating oil to chili cheeseburgers. (Courtesy of R. Clark Thompson.)

Lucille Ann Stephenson is shown standing beside this stone water fountain that once provided drinking water on Main Street. It was moved to the Saluda Memorial Park in recent years. Carved on the fountain is a nod to the Woodmen of the World, founded by Joseph Cullen Root in 1890 after hearing about pioneer woodsmen clearing away the forest to provide for their families. The organization still provides financial services today. (Courtesy of Cindy Stephenson Tuttle.)

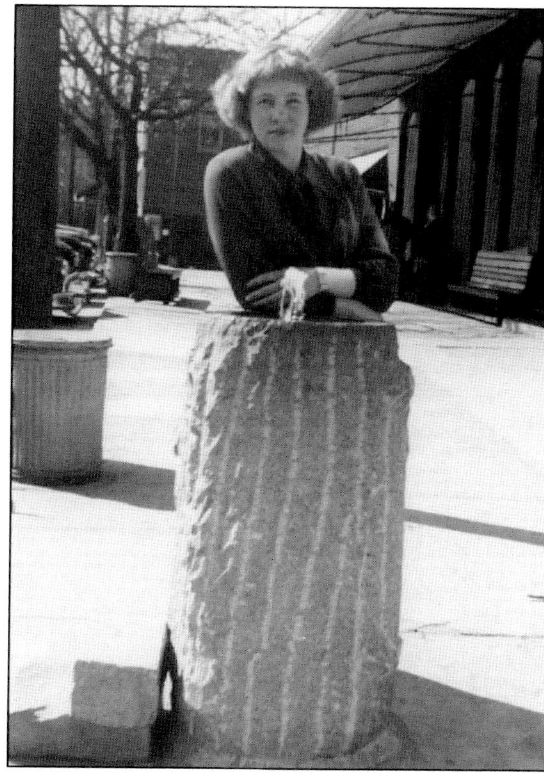

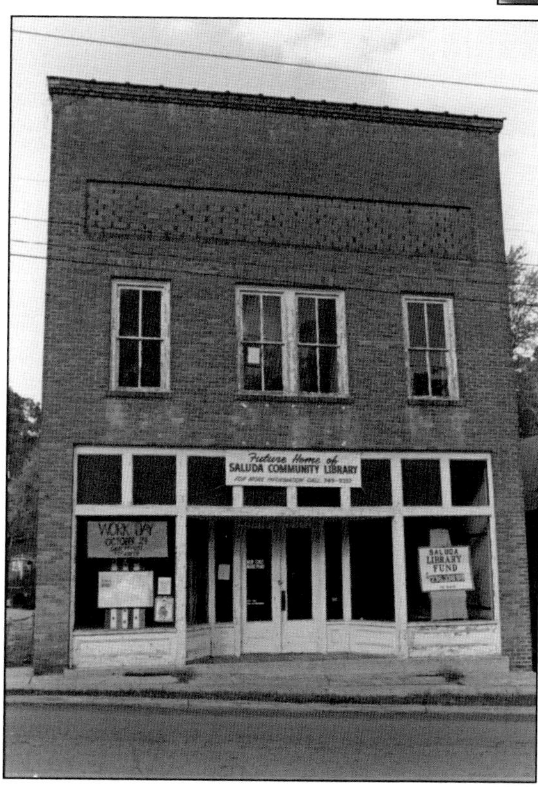

Melody Gibson of Saluda Community Help, Inc., started a library campaign with fundraisers, grants, and by sending letters. The 1919 brick building on Main Street was donated by the Nolan Pace family, and Scott Bessent donated $275,000 in honor of his father, Homer. Renovations began in 1999, and the grand opening was in December 2000. This was the first time Saluda had a library since the 1950s. (Courtesy of Chuck Hearon.)

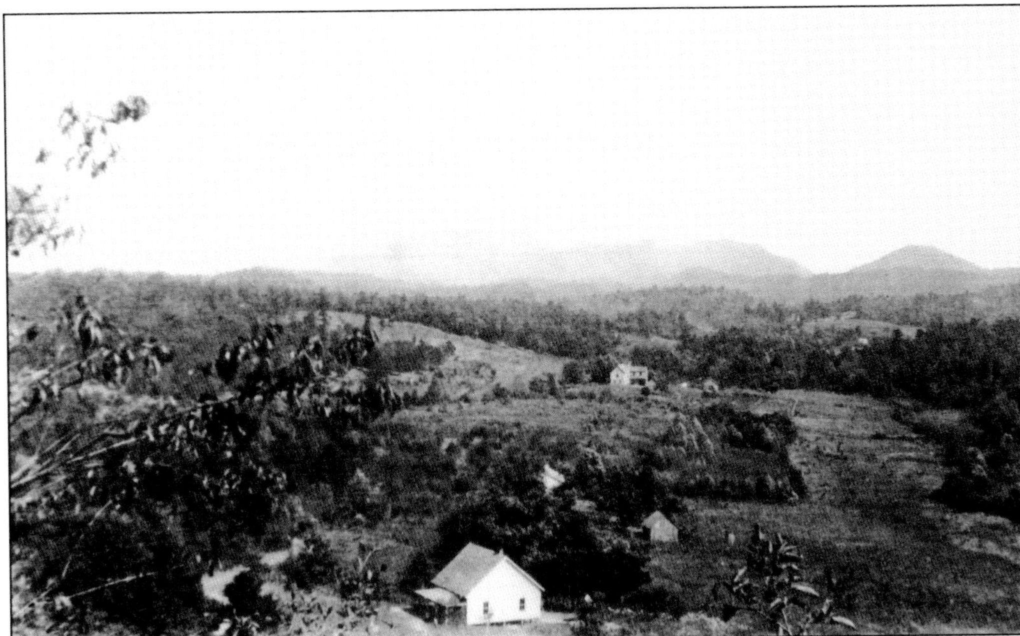

As early as the late 1950s, plans were in the works to build an interstate highway from Charleston, South Carolina, to Asheville. No one thought it would ever be finished, since it would have to go over Warrior Mountain. Based on the early experience with the railroad, this route was thought to be unstable due to the natural springs underground. The above photograph was taken in 1925 from Stackhouse Hill overlooking the Albert Salley house, prior to Interstate 26. In the center is the Ben Pace House, barn, well, and outbuildings. In the background is the James Pace Dairy. The original roadbed for the Howard Gap Road passes just to the left. The photograph below shows basically the same scene, but taken in the 1960s, it shows the Interstate 26 roadbed being cut into the landscape. (Both, courtesy of Alex Salley.)

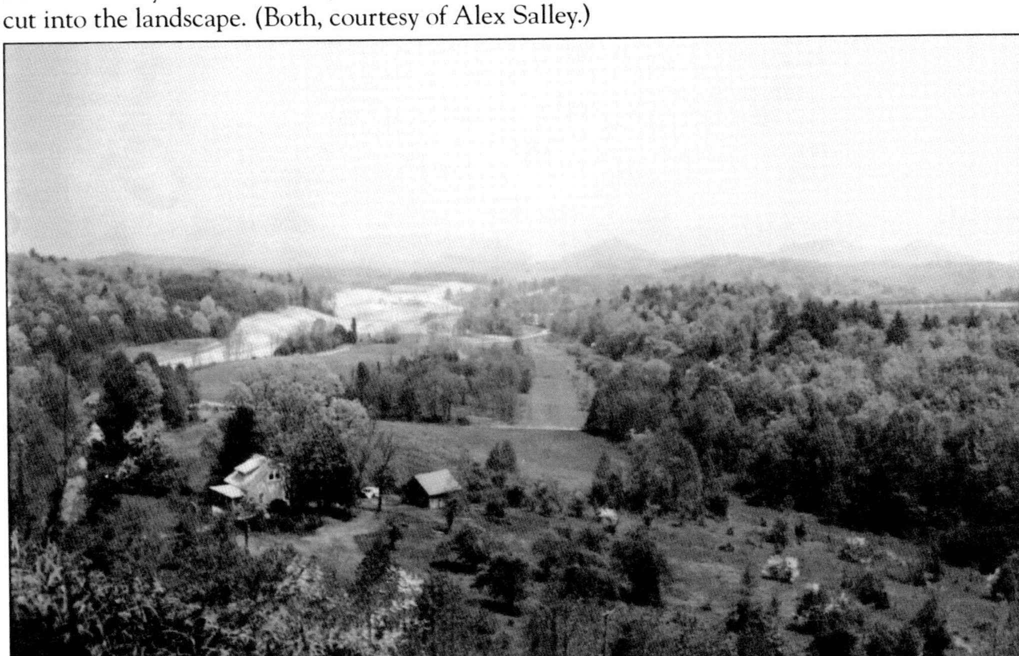

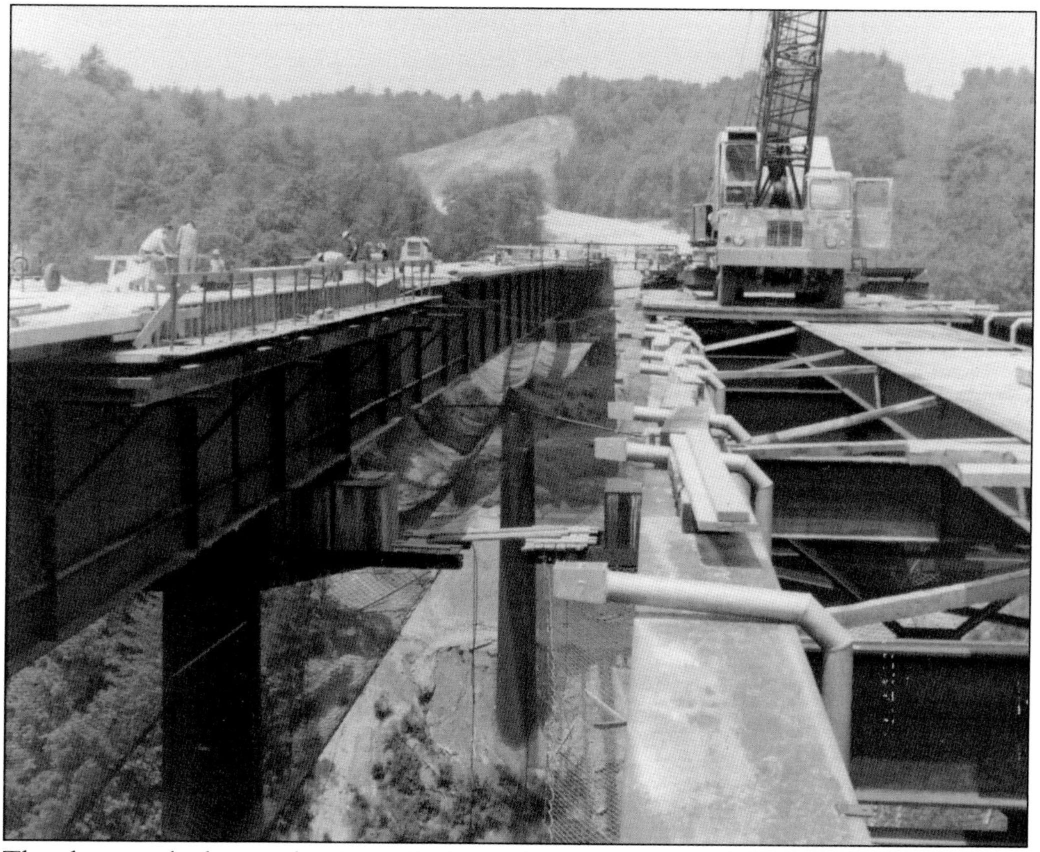

The photograph above, taken in 1967, shows the construction of the Peter Guice Memorial Bridge on Interstate 26, over the Green River. The current bridge is located directly above the original location of a toll bridge built by Peter Guice around 1820 to protect livestock and humans attempting to ford the raging waters of the Green River while traveling along the Howard Gap Trail. When the first bridge was washed away by rising waters, the second bridge was rebuilt by his son Joseph Guice. The second bridge was washed away after the great flood of 1916. The current bridge (below) was completed in 1972 at 225 feet above the Green River Gorge, the highest bridge in North Carolina. A historical marker is located at the nearby rest area on eastbound Interstate 26 between Asheville and Hendersonville. (Above, courtesy of Alex Salley; below, courtesy of Cindy Stephenson Tuttle.)

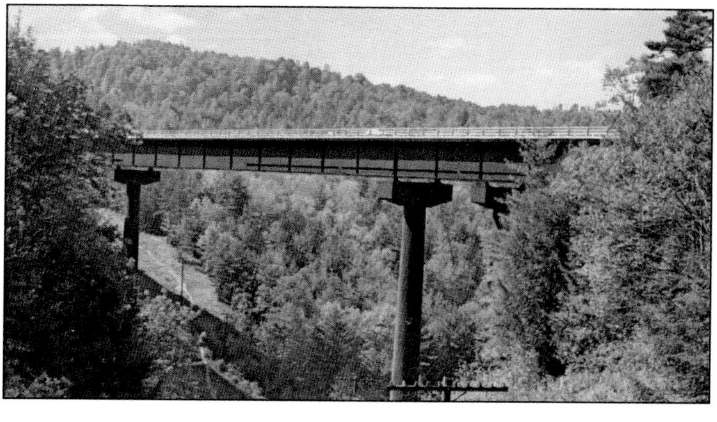

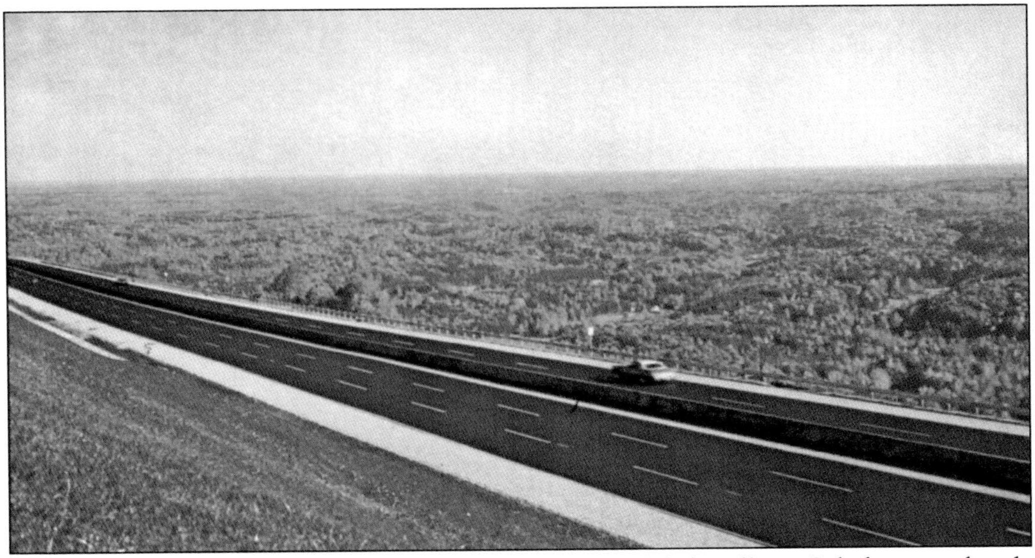

Stretches of I-26 between Charleston and Columbus and Asheville to Saluda were already complete, but it took eight years to finish the final 7.5-mile stretch between Columbus and Saluda. Holes were drilled in the rock to drain off the water of the underground springs, and step-bench grading was done to prevent landslides. On October 29, 1976, the finished road was dedicated. (Courtesy of Jim Boyle.)

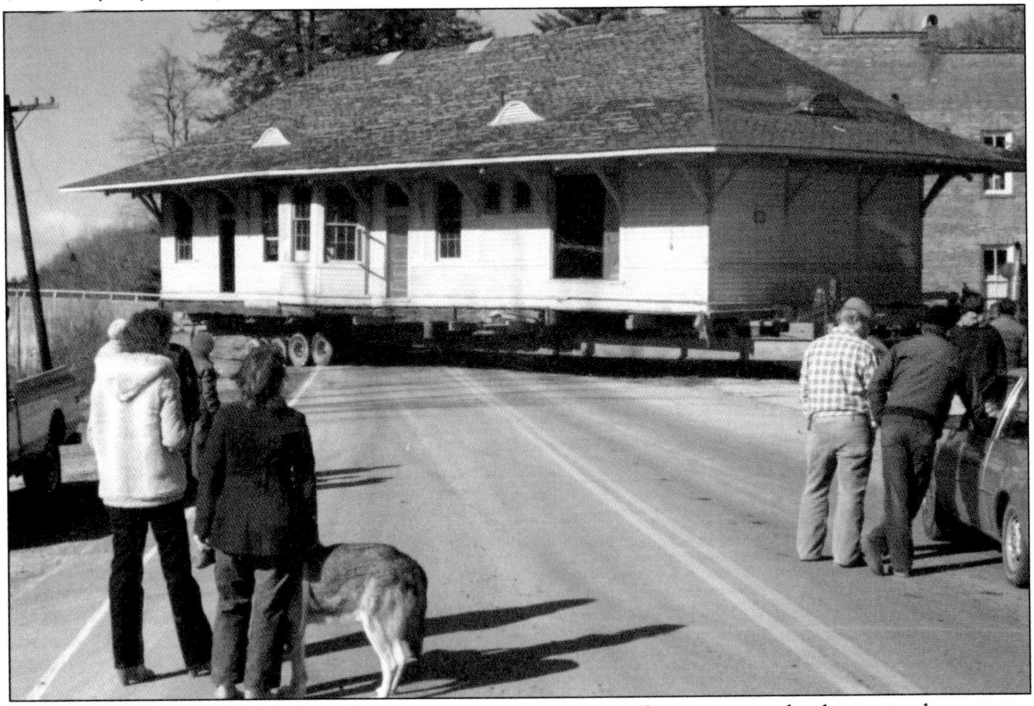

In 1983, the old railroad depot was moved to its current location in the historic downtown district. It was once located a quarter of a mile away, parallel to the north side of the tracks and west of the US 176. Pictured here, the depot is being moved after it was purchased from the city by Roy Eargle and Sam Talbot, who renovated it and made it available for retail shops. (Courtesy of J. Landwehr.)

Three

Historic Inns and Boardinghouses

People did not come to Saluda because of the railroad—it was merely their means of transportation to escape the unhealthy heat of the Lowcountry that pervaded the coastal plantations and inland cities perceived to cause deadly diseases.

After the Civil War, Saluda was able to capitalize on the fear of summer in the Lowcountry and the building of the railroad. In fact, Col. Andrew Tanner, the man in charge of the railroad's construction was the first to realize the potential of accommodations. He built the first hotel, to house his engineers, and named it the Mountain House. He also understood that entertainment was an important part of the package, so he added a billiards room, bowling alley, and pool tables.

Saluda also housed the accidental tourist. The railroad stopped when it crested the Saluda Grade, and further travel required another means of transportation over rough terrain. Foregoing a bumpy ride led to the opening of the Melrose Inn in 1893, and it soon overcame the Mountain House in popularity.

By the early 1900s, there were seven operating inns and hotels in Saluda that were populated by people wanting to escape the heat from the Lowcountry. Saluda's heyday from 1880 to 1930 saw the proliferation of over 30 boardinghouses, inns, and hotels in the community.

Saluda was more accessible when the first all-weather road was built in 1928. This was a double-edged sword, as this made locations at higher elevations easier to reach also. This road, in addition to the Great Depression in 1929, crippled Saluda's tourism. Some of the larger establishments survived, but then World War II took its toll. Fire and deterioration also led to the demise of many of the remaining places. A few were converted to private homes and are lovingly cared for today.

Specific hotels and inns are included in this chapter, but there are also many that did not have images available. However, these photographs and stories will give a good representation of how Saluda's visitors came to love this area.

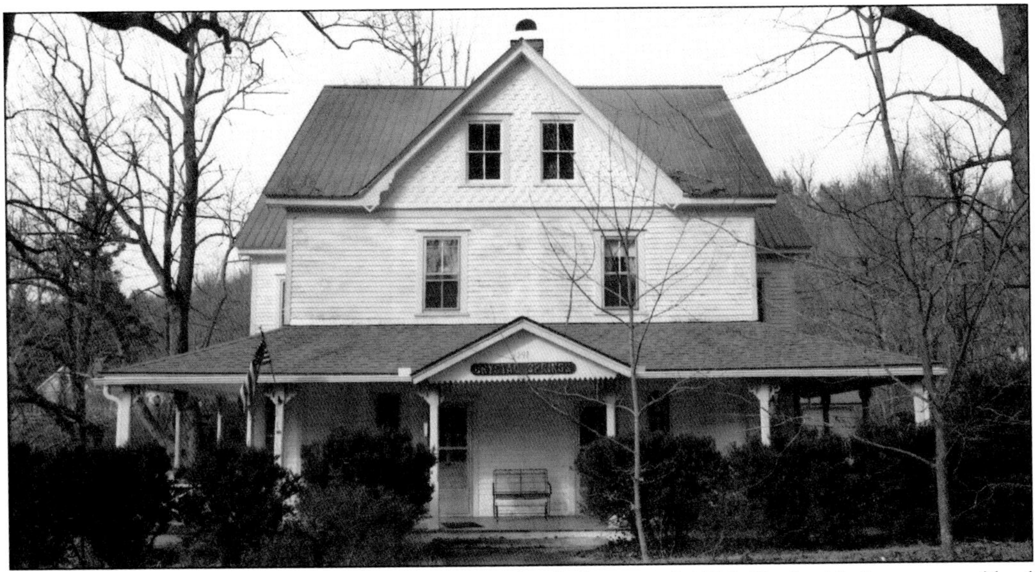

Charles Estes, a mill owner from Georgia, visited Saluda around 1899. He decided to stay and had Crystal Springs on Henderson Street constructed. Using a nearby spring, he created a system using a mechanism that created pressure, forcing water into wooden lines directly supplying Crystal Springs and the Melrose Inn with fresh running water, a first in Saluda. His great-granddaughter Martha Coates Ashley now owns the private home. (Courtesy of Martha Coates Ashley.)

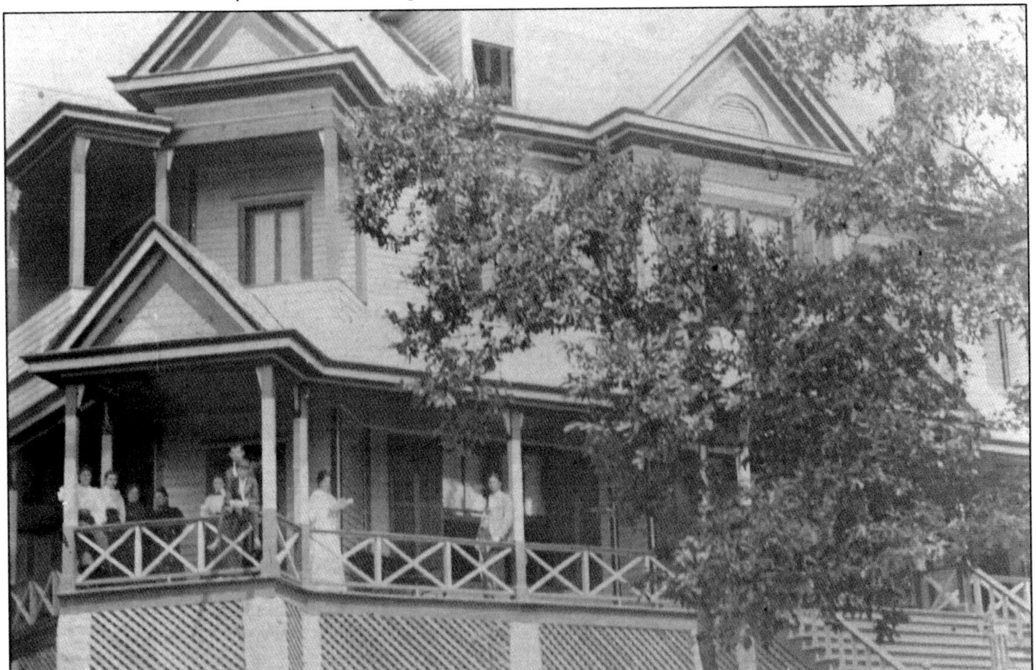

This photograph, taken by O.B. Garren, is of the Melrose Inn, once located on Henderson Street. It was erected in 1893 by two Charleston sisters, Agnes and Emma Heriot. Charles Estes stayed at the inn during his 1899 visit, which later benefited from his invention of indoor plumbing. The Melrose Inn was one of the many inns that burned at the start of the Great Depression. (Courtesy of Jim Boyle.)

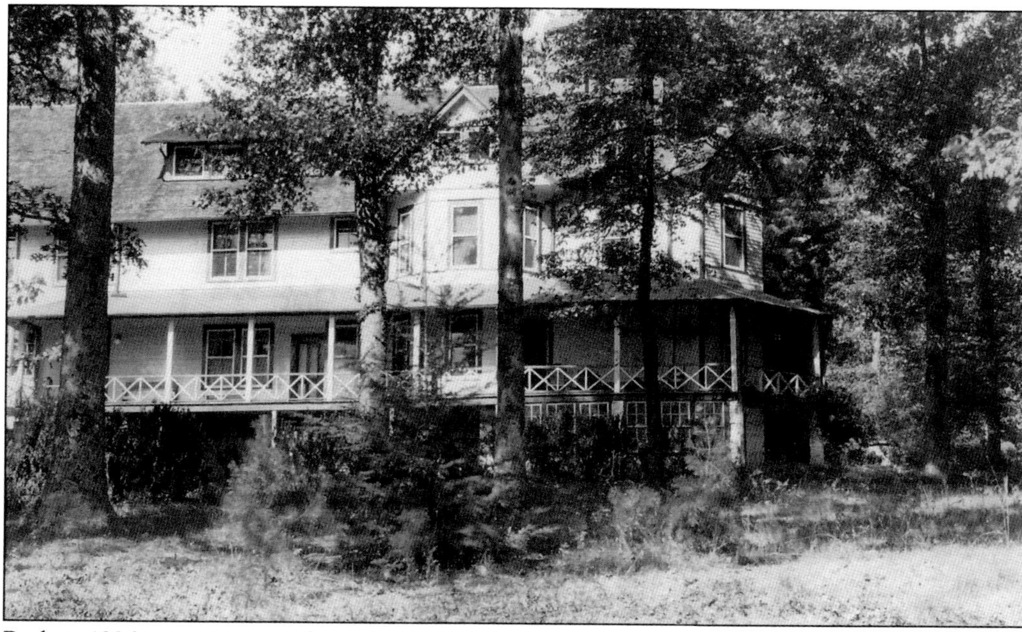

Built in 1896 as a private residence for Dr. E.B Goelet, this structure was converted to the Charlton Leland Inn by Louisa A. Leland from McClellanville, South Carolina, in 1914. These alterations, made by local builder Luther Thompson, were significant and included a 2.5-story rear addition. Placed in the National Register of Historic Places in 2006, it is presently owned by Richard and Joni Rauschenbach. (Courtesy of E. Cater Leland Jr.)

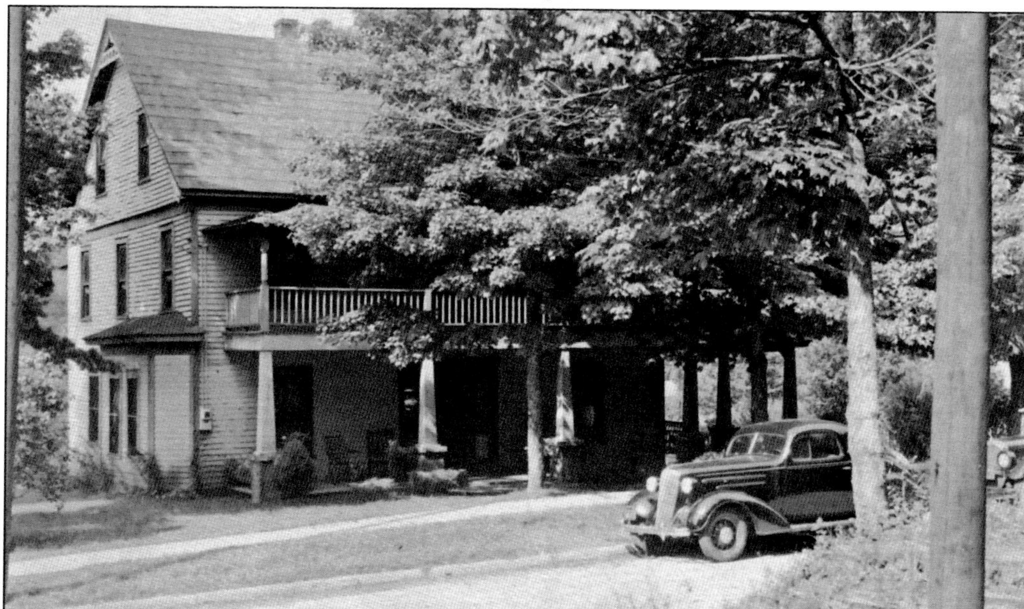

By the early 1910s, the Pines was one of the many boardinghouses in operation during the proliferation of guest inns. Operated by Mattie Hopkins, many boarding establishments in Saluda were run by women, and the Pines was no exception. The Pines was very popular with the railroad workers, particularly until the Mountain Home was built for the Brotherhood of Railway Clerks. (Courtesy of Charlene Pace.)

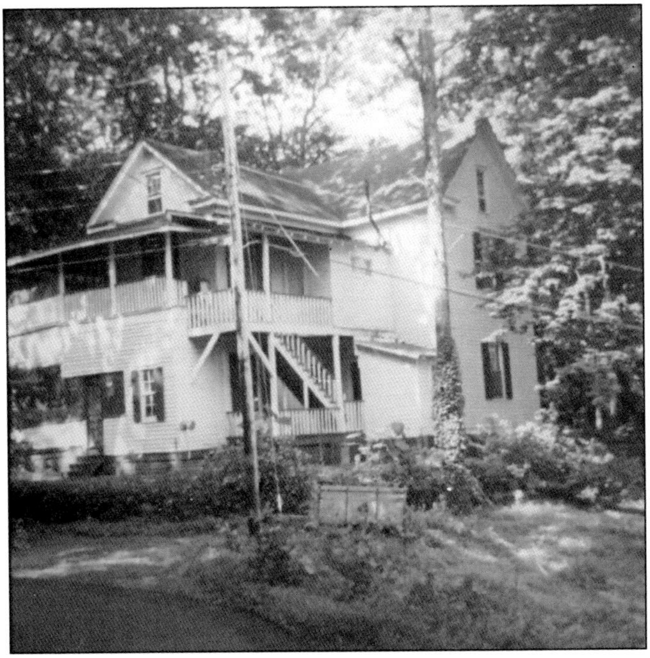

In 1887, Abigail Baynard Whaley built a large home above the Saluda Grade and had furniture shipped from Charleston for the comfort of her family and paying guests. Some of the old furniture still bears shipping labels and has been in the house since 1887. When Whaley died in 1905, Dr. Elton S. Osborne purchased the property as a private home, and it is now owned by Roger Gause. (Courtesy of Charlene Pace.)

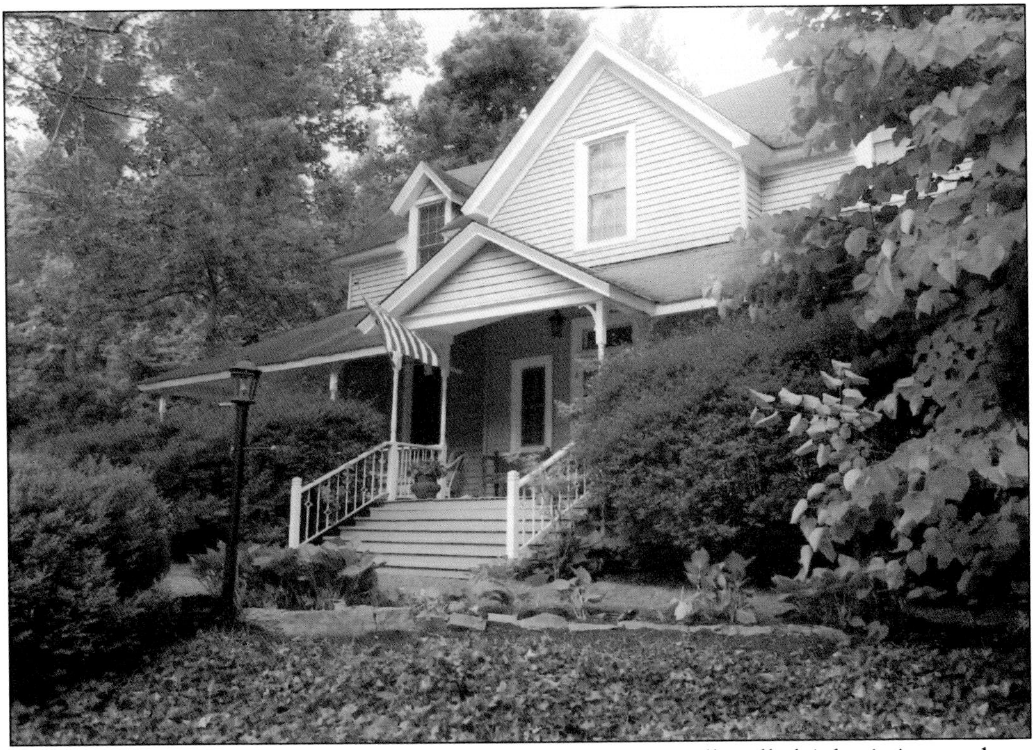

Thought to be built by O.B. Garren, Boxwood Terrace was originally called Aiken's Acre and was a private residence. It opened as a boardinghouse in the mid-1930s, operated by Mabel Moore, and is now privately owned by Marguerite and David Hankins. The Hankins are both accomplished artists. David works under the name of Jim Carson and is recognized for his Western-themed paintings. (Courtesy of Marguerite and David Hankins.)

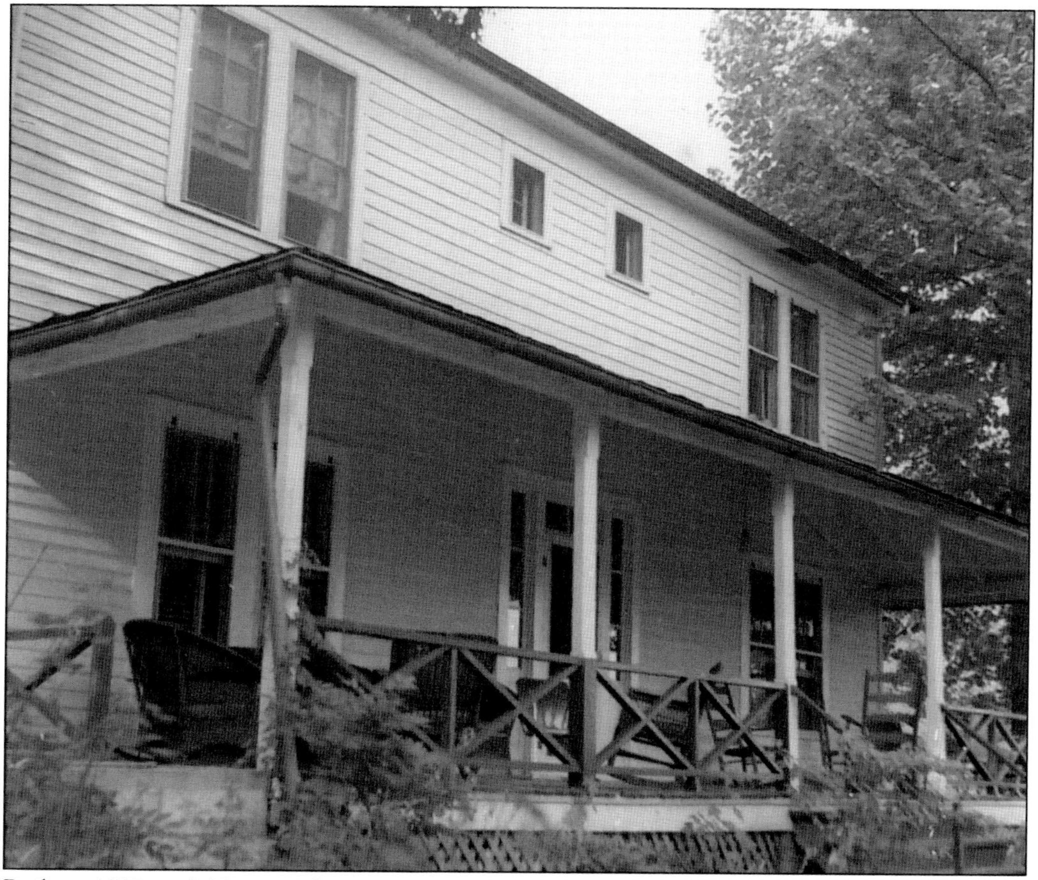

Built in 1901 on 3.49 acres, the property consisted of the Fairview House, a smaller house, and the Peter Pan cottage. Fairview House proved to have staying power under the management of Annie Locke and Rosa Box. The Locke-Box team ran the Fairview House as a summer place and Tryon Lodge as a winter boardinghouse. In the 1960s, the Saluda Fire Department burned the Peter Pan cottage as a fire training exercise. Roy and Mary Baisden purchased the Fairview House, smaller house, and cottage in 1948 and ran the Fairview House until around 1965. The Fairview House is no longer standing, but Fred and Terry Baisden own the smaller house and remodeled it into a private residence. (Both, courtesy of Fred and Terry Baisden.)

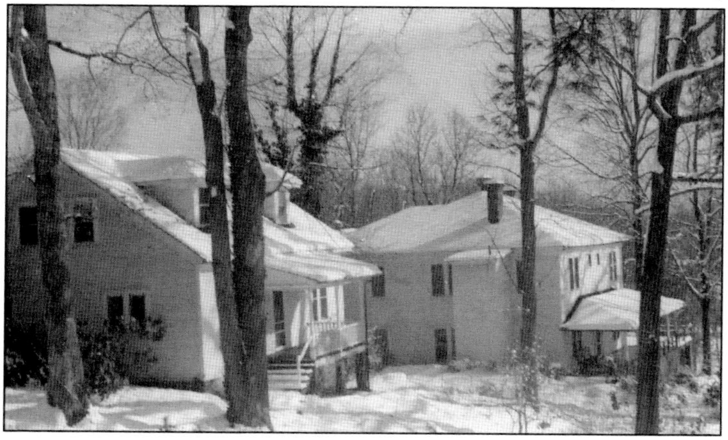

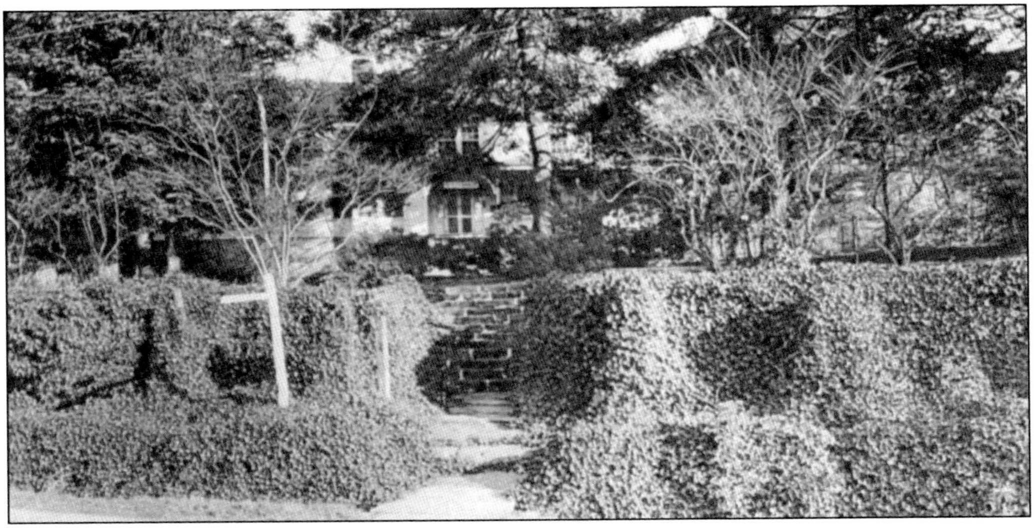

As depicted in this postcard, the Ivy Terrace lives up to its name with the eponymous vine creeping along its grounds and spilling over the rock steps out front as if to greet visitors. Located on US Route 176, it was owned and operated by L.L. Clippard as a boardinghouse in the early 1930s until the late 1940s. The Ivy Terrace is now a private residence, but the ivy continues to be a feature of the property. (Courtesy of Cindy Stephenson Tuttle.)

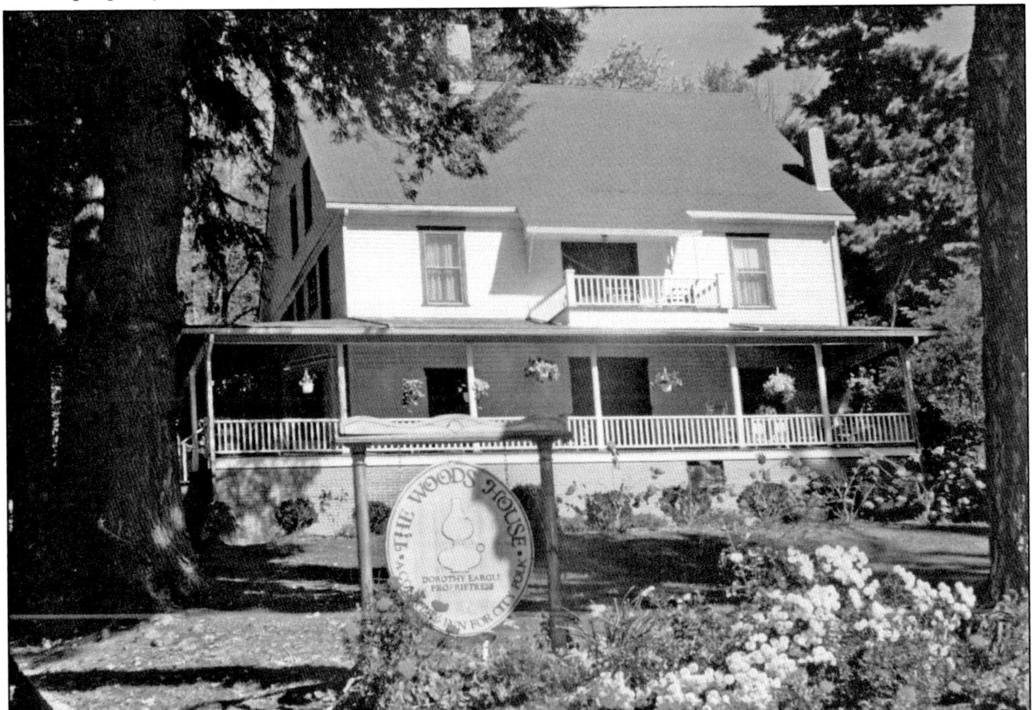

The Woods House operated as a boarding home for many years. Constructed in the style of local builder Luther Thompson, it is uncertain if he built the original structure, but it has been confirmed he remodeled it into a three-story house from its original two-story design. In 1977, the house was bought by Dottie and Roy Eargle, and they operated it as an inn until it closed in recent years. (Courtesy of J. Landwehr.)

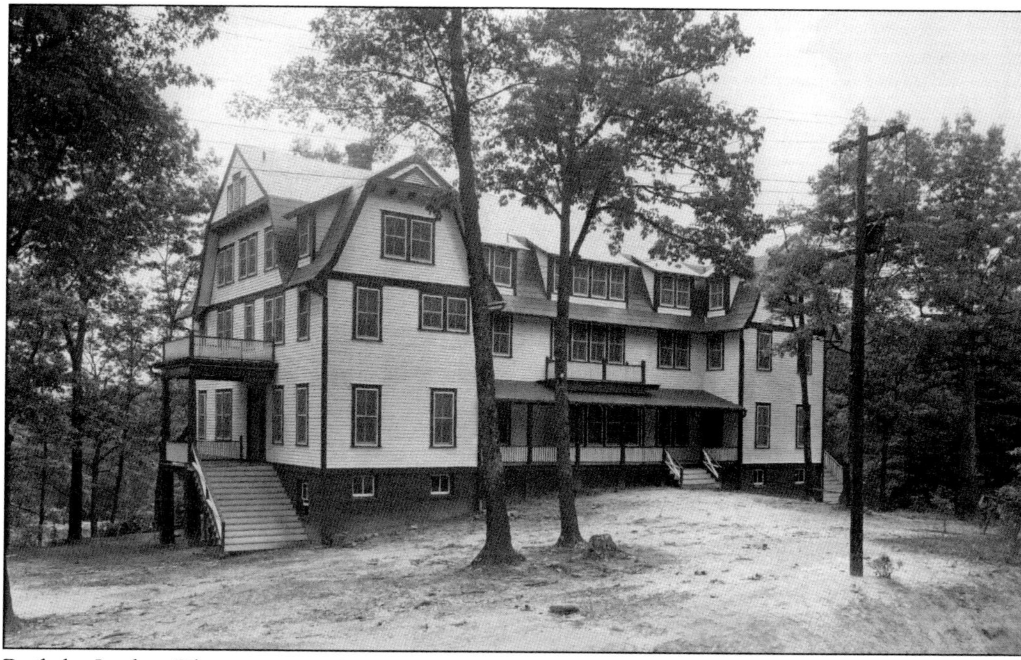

Built by Luther Thompson on Seminary Street in 1909, Ryder Hall was the girls' dormitory for Saluda Seminary. It opened in 1909 and by 1922 was converted to the St. Cloud Hotel and run under the direction of Alice "Fully" Fulton, who had been in charge of Crystal Springs. Fully, reportedly gregarious by nature, was a professional innkeeper in the community. Currently, it is the private residence of Judy and Charlie Brown. (Courtesy of the Polk County Historical Association.)

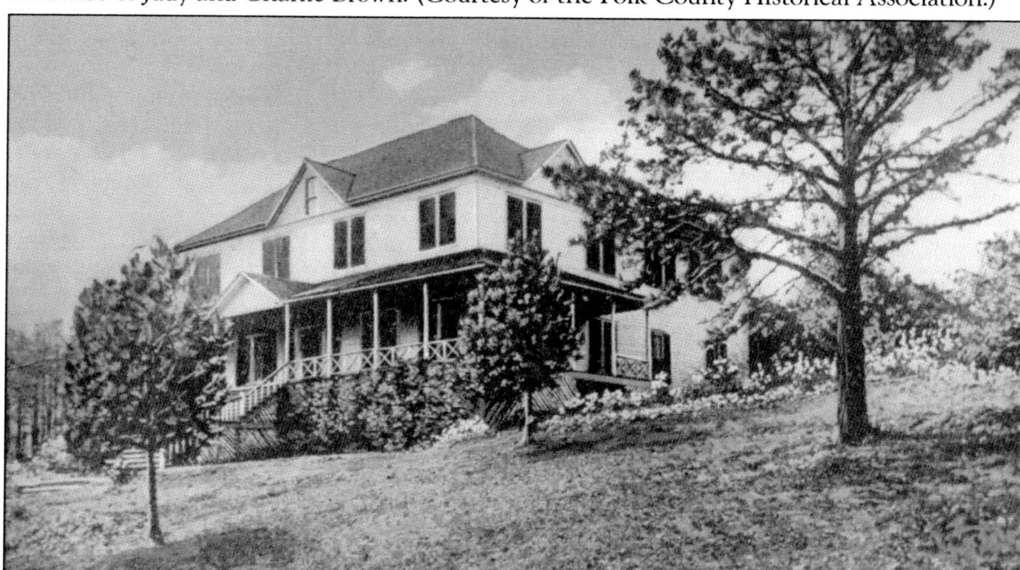

The Esseola Inn was home to Zelda Fitzgerald (wife of novelist F. Scott Fitzgerald) twice. She stayed as a child with her parents and then when she was an outpatient from Highland Hospital in Asheville. The Esseola Inn is no longer in existence, but the foundation can be seen from the interior of the lot, which is located at the intersection of Pine Street and Old Macedonia Road. (Courtesy of Marguerite and David Hankins.)

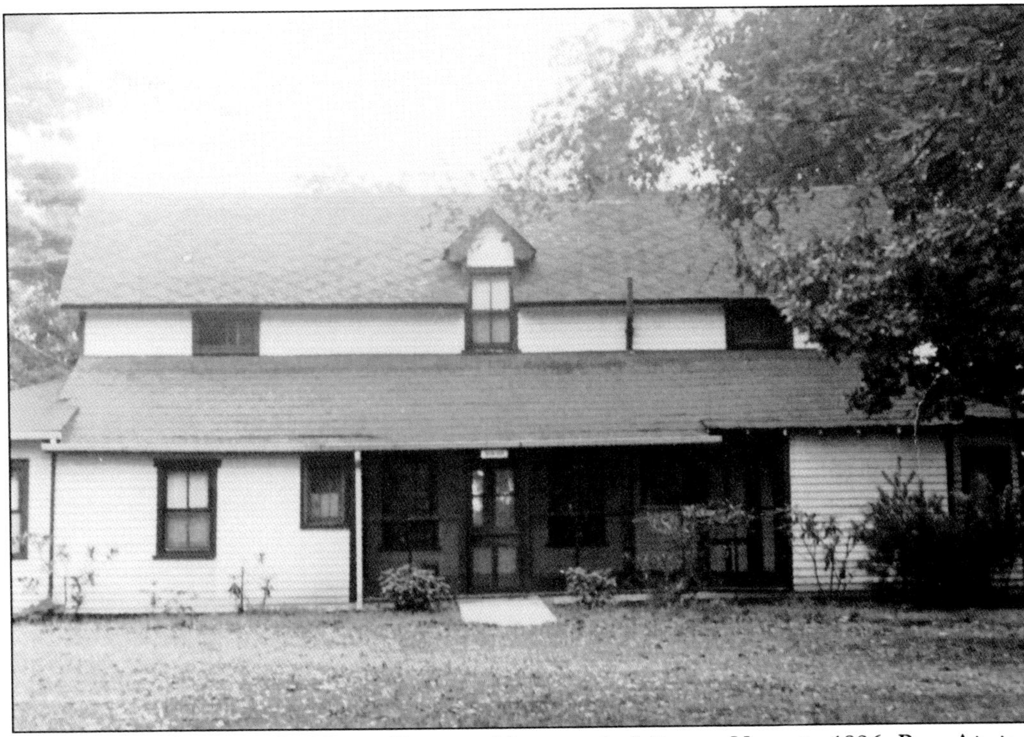

Built by a local artisan for Nettie Hane and her cousin Minette Hane in 1896, Bon Air is a two-story clapboard house that was built "seemingly without the benefit of a square and possibly without a level," according to Nettie Owings Sweet. The $850 it took to build the house came from Nettie Hane's nest egg, which was 50 bales of cotton hidden on Wadmalaw Island, South Carolina, after the war. Visitors enjoyed the home and then came as paying guests as it became a boardinghouse. When Dr. Lesesne Smith changed his career to become a pediatrician and touted the benefits of cool mountain air, Bon Air became a hospital in the summer and the founding building of what was to become Smith Hill. When the Smith Hill property was divided in 1960, Dr. Keitt Hane Smith and his wife became the owners. In 1998, their daughter Vivian "VeeVee" Smith Blackshear became the owner. (Above, courtesy of Nettie Owings Sweet; below, courtesy of Greaton Sellers.)

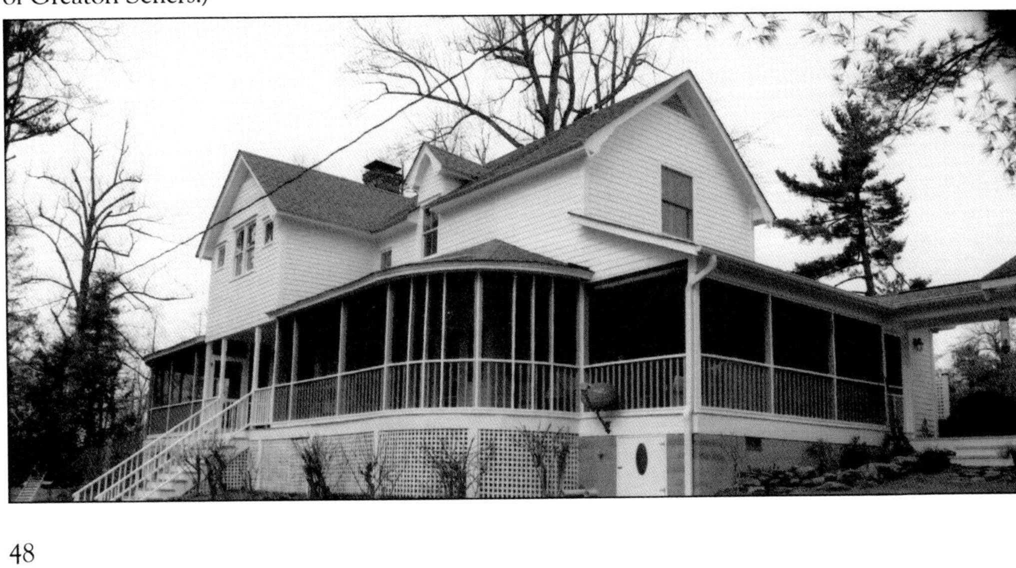

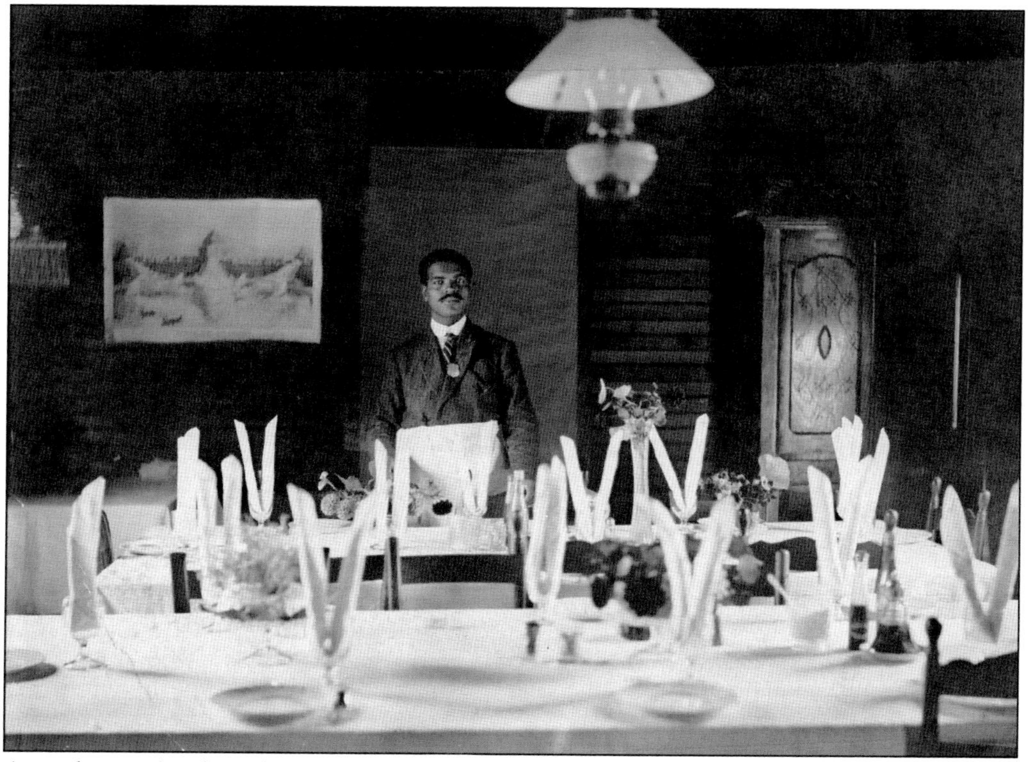

According to family oral history, this photograph, taken in 1915, is of a butler named William Killgo in the dining room of the Pace House, reflective of the elegance of the establishment. The inn had a long front porch with rocking chairs, tennis courts on the property, and in the back were five servant houses accommodating the workers that came up from the Lowcountry seeking work. (Courtesy of Cindy Stephenson Tuttle.)

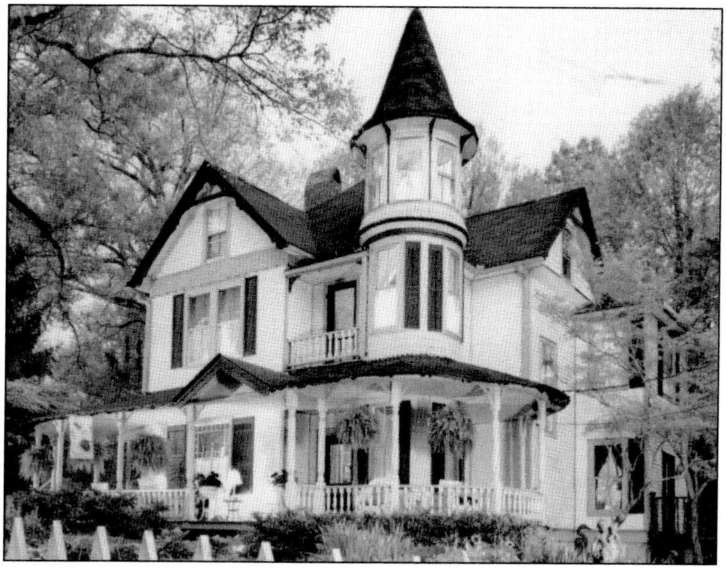

The Oaks was built on land originally purchased from the Pace family. A turreted Queen Anne Victorian, it was built in 1895 as a home for Dr. E.B. Goelet's daughter. It was sold to Wessie Roach Lane in 1906 and began a long history of accepting paying guests. Dale and Donna Potruski currently own the bed and breakfast that is known as the "beautiful Victorian up the hill." (Courtesy of the Oaks Bed and Breakfast.)

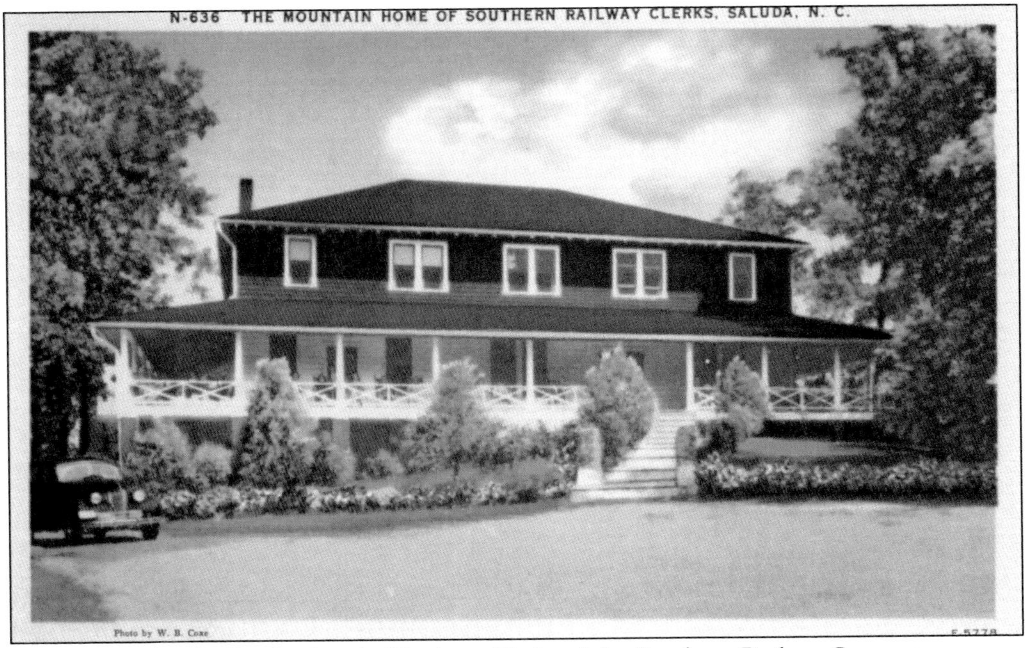

Built in 1926 by the Brotherhood of Railway Clerks of the Southern Railway System to serve as the organization's mountain home, this structure had fallen into disrepair and closed but was repeatedly rescued and restored by various innkeepers. It is now in the care of Marc and Marianne Blazar and is known as the Orchard Inn. The inn was placed in the National Register of Historic Places in 2000. (Courtesy of Mary Ann Hester.)

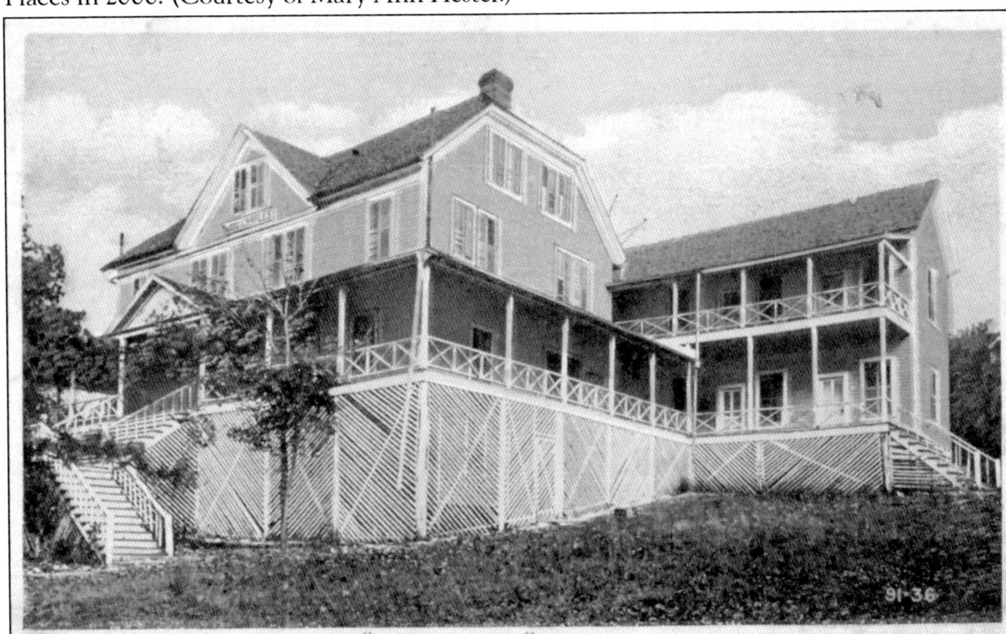

The Hotel Charles, erected in the early 1900s by Charles Estes, was one of the earliest hotels built on the bustling corners of Henderson and Charles Streets. It burned in the 1920s. Estes was also the brains behind the very successful Crystal Springs and introduced indoor plumbing to the Melrose Inn. (Courtesy of Cindy Stephenson Tuttle.)

Four

Arts, Culture, and Events

Saluda has always been a fun place to be. Even during hard times, folks found a way to swing a bat, sink a fishing line, or dance a jig. In the early days, old-time bands were the hallmark of dance celebrations where couples whirled about the dance floors. With the train came diversity and an introduction to cultures both far and near. But the newcomers and tourists were always welcomed at the dances and differences were, for a time, forgotten.

The arts in Saluda started as functional craft items. As W.D. Weatherford says in the foreword of *Artisans of the Appalachians*, "In the early pioneer days of the Appalachians, crafts provided wearing apparel and the furnishings and equipment for the homes since there was often no choice except to make what was needed." Among many, the artisans of Saluda included a wool dyer, fiddle maker, and a rug maker with national reputation. With the early formation of the men's library society, it was proven the literary arts were held in high esteem. This continued to be true when in 1908, the first official library was opened to the public, a women's book club was formed, and in recent years, the Saluda Public Library opened in a beautifully renovated historic building.

Despite not having a town newspaper, interesting and informative homegrown magazines and newsletters have always kept everyone informed, from the *Saluda Magazine* of the 1930s to today's *Saluda Lifestyles*. Parades, festivals, and the excuse for a community celebration were and are frequent. Where else has the tradition of a coon hunt turned into an event so popular as today's annual Coon Dog Day? Today, the annual Saluda Arts Festival brings regional fine artists and crafters and live demonstrations throughout the day.

The great outdoors have always been a favorite destination, where waterfalls abound and trout fishing remains a favorite. The variety of rapids in the Green River provide adventure and challenge for even the most extreme kayaker to a lazy river ride for the tube enthusiast. There is something for everyone in Saluda.

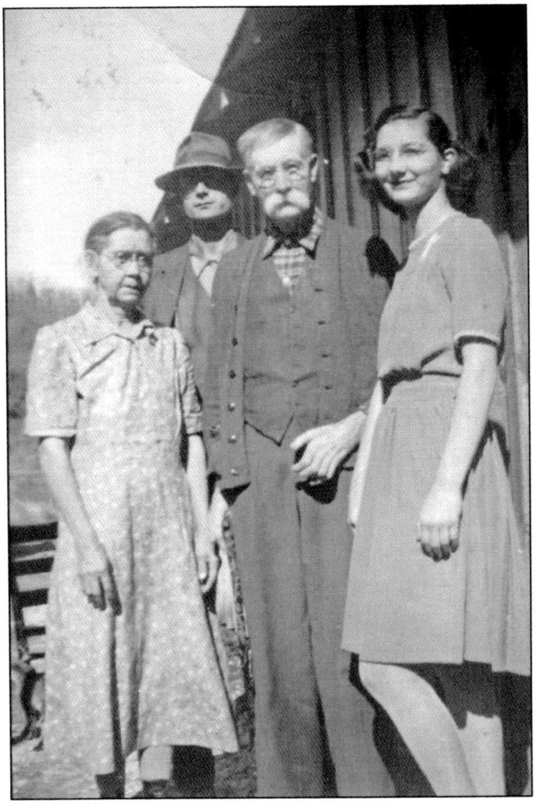

Marion Gordon, known as the "Fiddle Maker," also made chairs and stools. His violins, as he called them, sold for $10 to $20 apiece. His wife, Matilda Coggins Gordon, carded and hand spun fibers, making them into crocheted pieces and hooked rugs. Pictured here are, from left to right, Matilda, John Gordon (son), Marion, and Pauline Gordon Corn (granddaughter). John ran Gordon's General Merchandise, located where Ward's Grill is today. (Courtesy of Pauline Gordon Corn.)

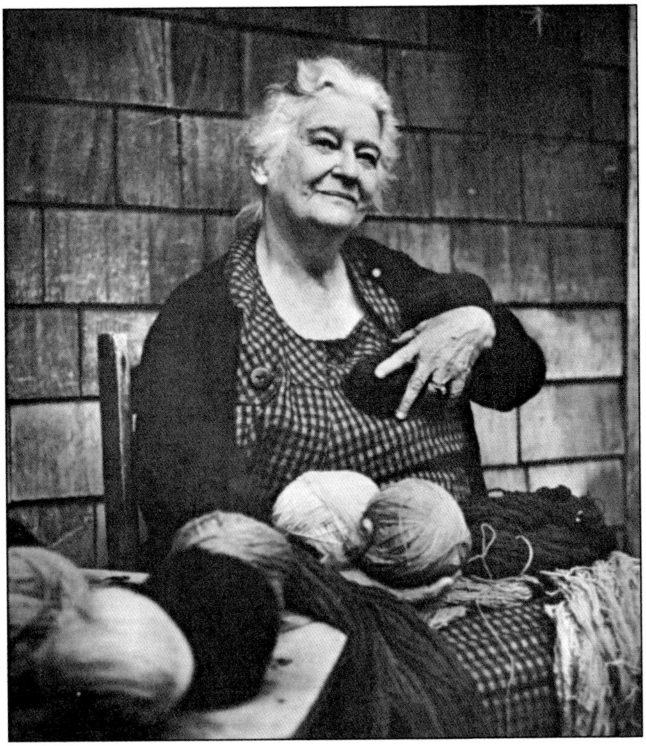

Wilmer Stone Viner studied political science at Vassar but declared it boring. While working at a school in Kentucky, she developed an ardent interest in natural dye plants and processes. Pursuing this interest, she had friends knit sweaters and gloves for the children. She had spent her summers in Saluda, so she and her husband, H.E.S. Stone, returned and opened the Weave Shop. They wrote *The Catherine Pettit Book on Vegetable Dyes*. (Courtesy of *Artisans of the Appalachians*.)

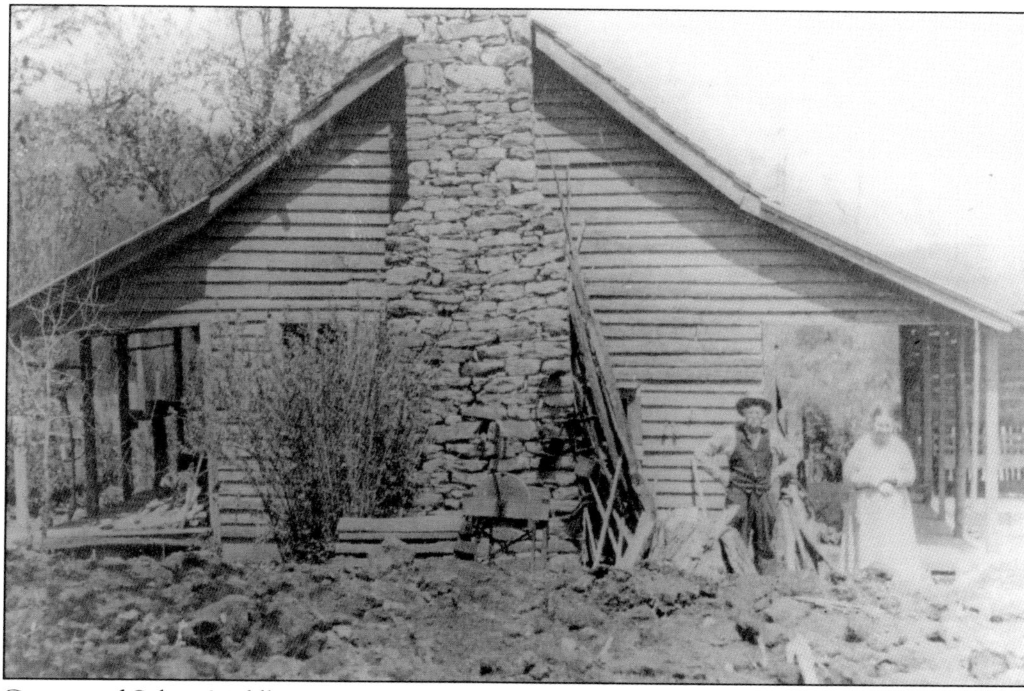

George and Salena Middleton Metcalf were both known for their skills as basket weavers. In 1934, they were visited by John Jacob Niles, known as the "Father of the Modern Folk Movement," who spent his adulthood searching for the most well-loved songs of the southern Appalachia. During his visit, Salena sang the "Murdered Brother" for him, which he documented in his book *The Ballad Book of John Jacob Niles*. (Courtesy of the Polk County Historical Association.)

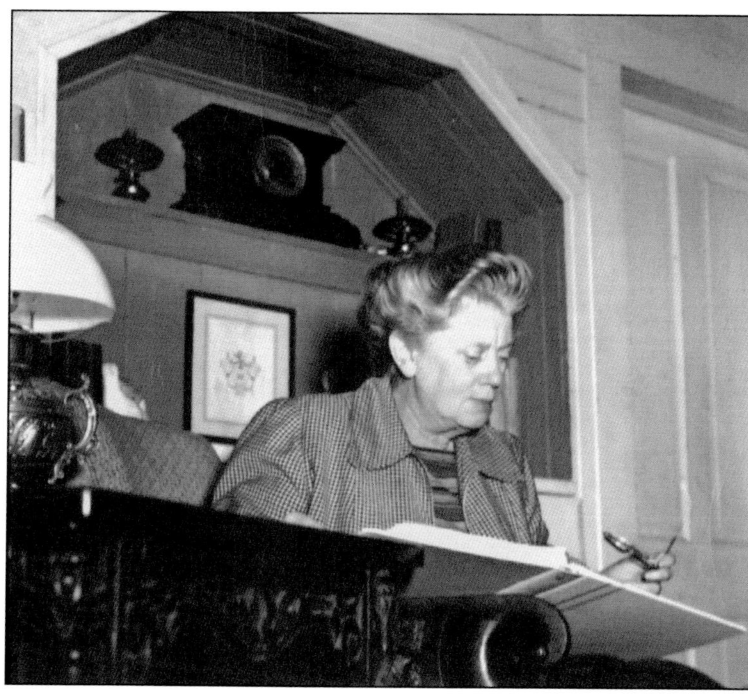

Lillian Mills Mosseller began making rugs in 1925 and was a pioneer in the hooked rug industry. She and her son Ronnie made rugs that now reside in the permanent collection of the Metropolitan Museum. In 1945, when Franklin Roosevelt had his fatal stroke in Warm Springs, Georgia, it is said that he was seated in his wheelchair upon a Mosseller rug specifically made for him. (Courtesy of Ronnie Mosseller.)

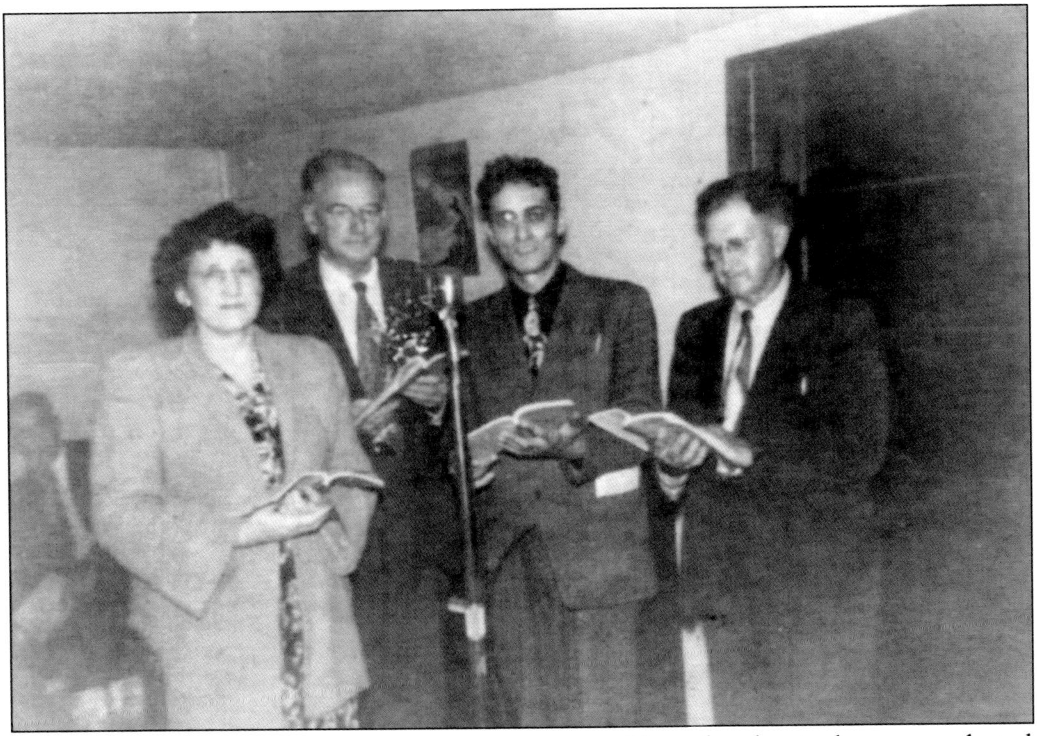

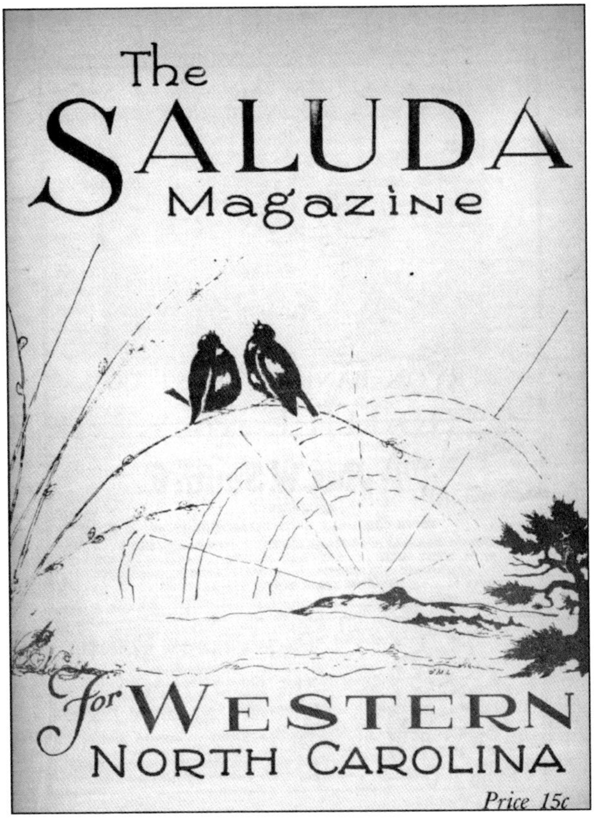

Many churches in the area conducted singing schools through the Vaughn Music Company and often used the shape-note method to teach a song. Pictured here are, from left to right, Alice Johnson, a Mr. Poole, Roy Johnson Sr., and Herbert Pace. Both Pace and Roy Johnson Sr. were teachers, and the highlight each year was homecoming at Mountain Page Church. (Courtesy of Roy Lee Johnson Jr.)

Susan Leland Craig operated a small printing business, Excelsior Printers, and helped with the operation of her family's business, the Charlton Leland Hotel. In 1936, she began printing the *Saluda Magazine* and assumed the role of editor. The magazine ended in 1938, after eight issues were published. These magazines were reprinted in 1979 and remain a source of information about Saluda's historical past. (Courtesy of Cindy Stephenson Tuttle.)

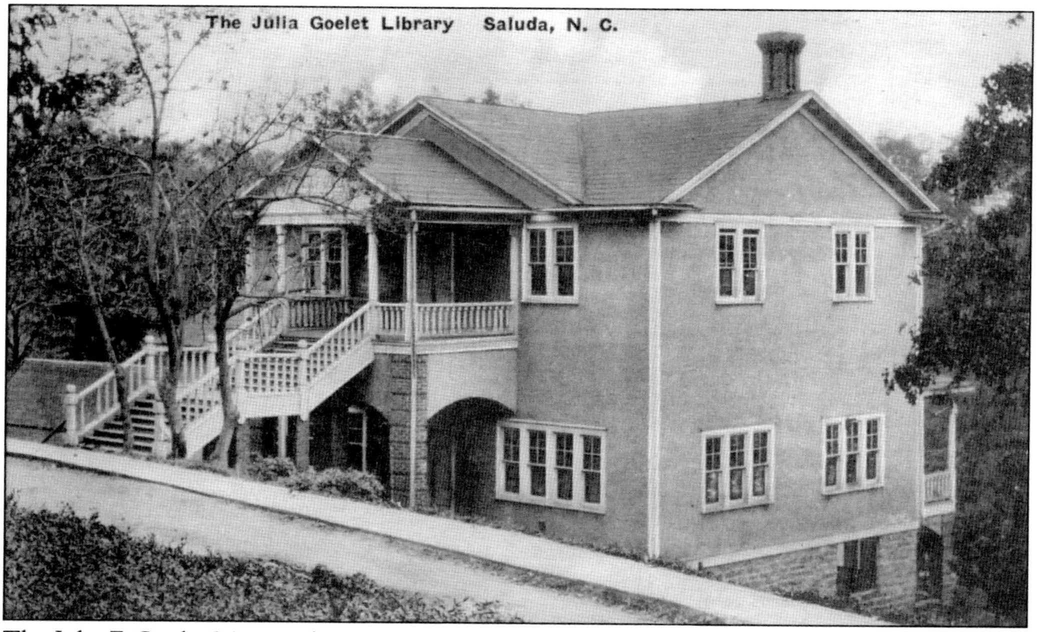

The Julia F. Goelet Memorial Library, pictured on this postcard, provides proof that priorities were in order during Saluda's early years. After an old building burned down that housed the men's library society, Julia Goelet went to work to see that a new library was constructed. Though she did not live to see its completion in 1908, under her leadership the library grew to 6,000 volumes that were used for educational and entertainment purposes. (Courtesy of Cindy Stephenson Tuttle.)

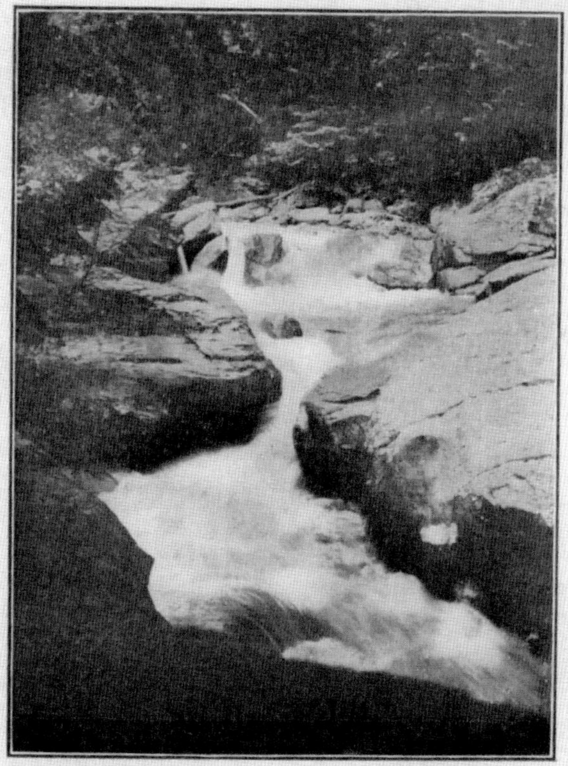

GREEN RIVER NARROWS, NEAR SALUDA, N. C.

The Green River has dished up challenges and entertainment since man first walked its banks. Located within the Green River Game Lands, the river provides plenty of water activities for the meek and even the most daring. Pictured in this postcard are the Narrows, located deep in the Green River Gorge. Offering Class V whitewater rapids, the Narrows have become the ultimate challenge for extreme kayakers. (Courtesy of Cindy Stephenson Tuttle.)

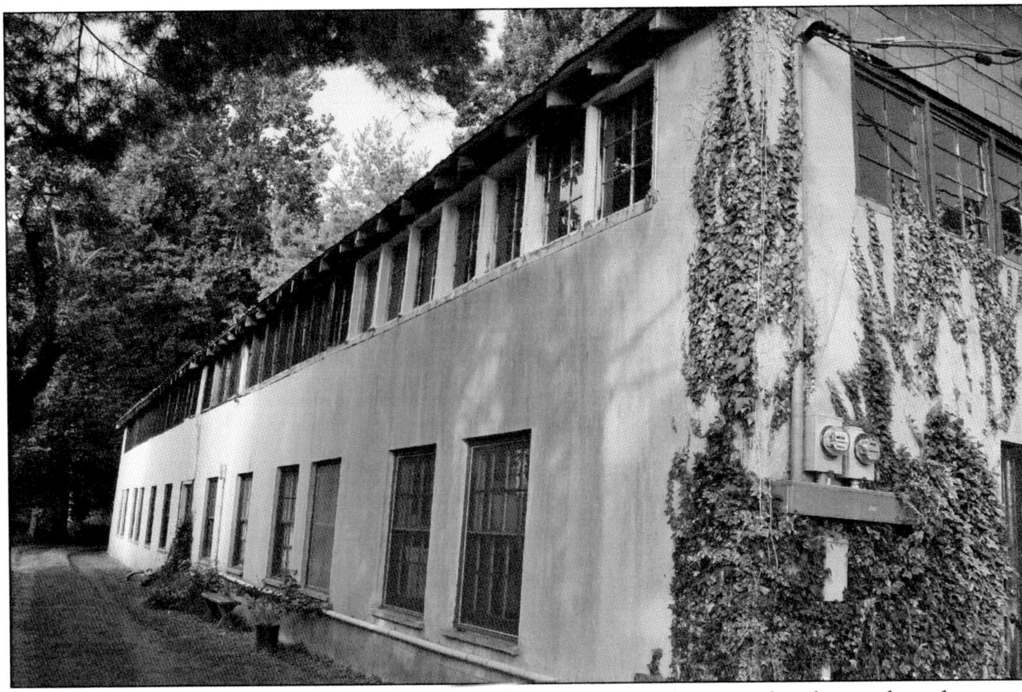

Built in the 1960s, the Chicken House was only used as a working poultry house for a few years before Leslie Bensen, a photographer for *Life* magazine and a noted artist, bought it. He converted one end of the building into a large studio with a huge window and built a massive fireplace. Bought by Ruth Anderson in 1993, it is now a haven for artists and craftspeople. (Courtesy of Greaton Sellers.)

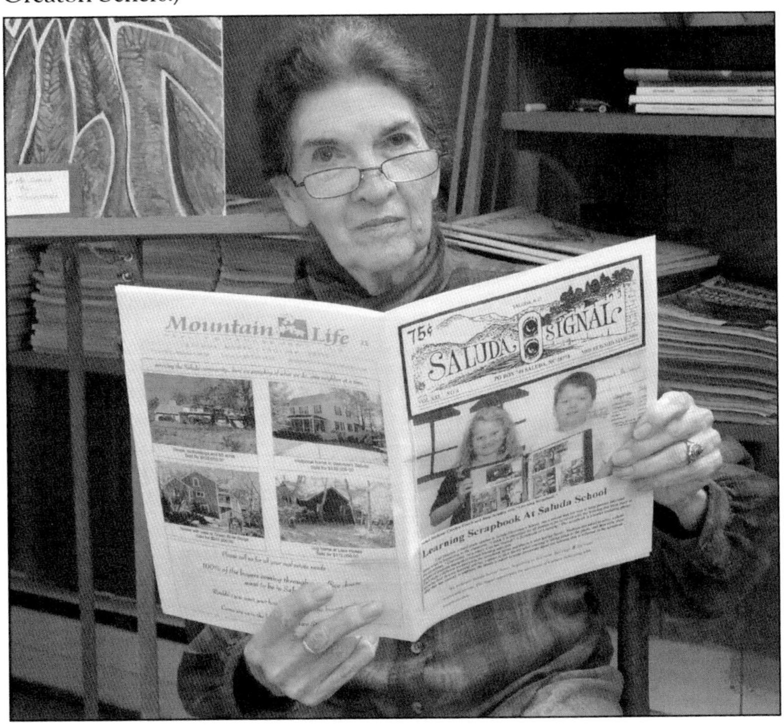

Ruth Anderson, owner of the Chicken House, saw a need for a local Saluda newspaper, so in the mid-1980s, she started the *Saluda Signal*. It was for residents and summer folk and had over 950 subscribers. Even when many folks had turned to computers, Anderson insisted the *Saluda Signal* look as if she cut and pasted on her kitchen table, which was true. It ceased publication in 2006. (Courtesy of Greaton Sellers.)

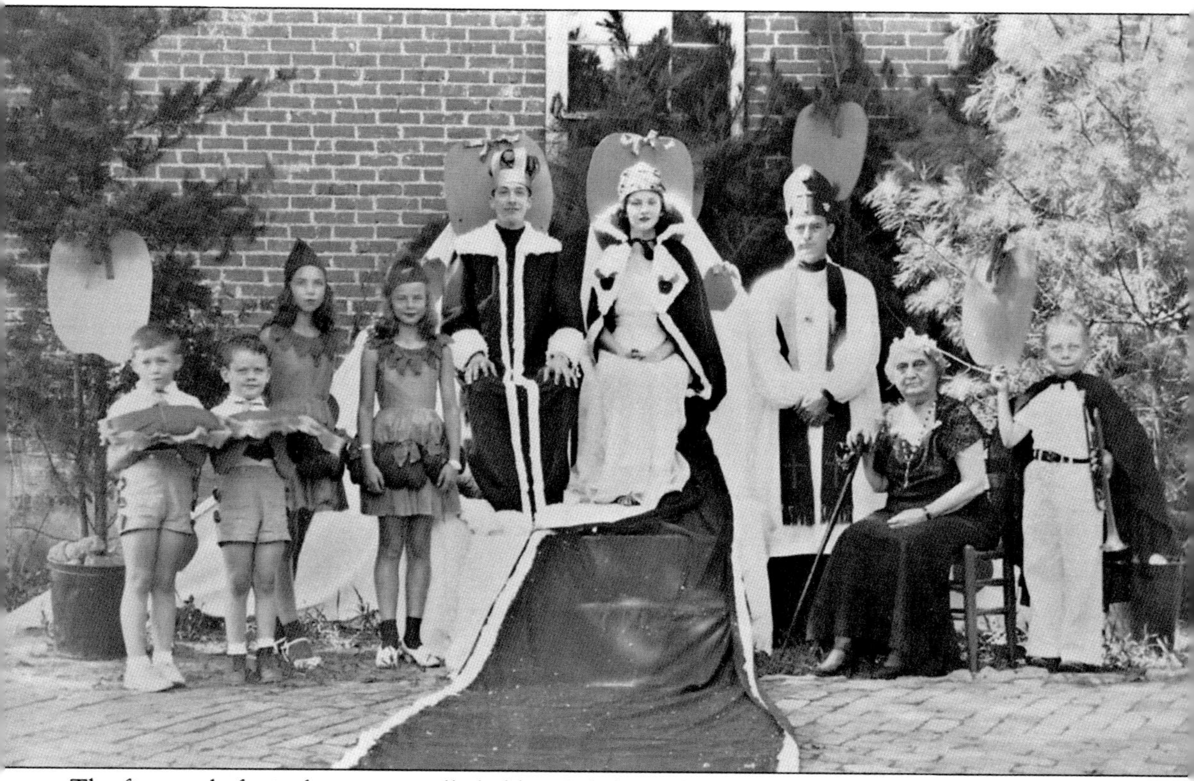

The first apple festival was originally held in Saluda in the 1930s under the guidance of Henry P. Corwith, a horticulturist who owned Overbrook Orchard, a modern, experimental orchard located off Ozone Drive. Saluda apples were recognized for their outstanding quality, flavor, and color. In the 1930s, it was documented that trees planted not long after the Revolutionary War were still bearing fruit with delicious flavor. One such tree had a trunk approximately three feet in diameter. A royal court, including kings and queens, was crowned as part of the festivities. The advent of World War II put a halt on the festival, which was later passed to Hendersonville, where it continues today. This is a photograph of the royal court from 1939; from left to right are Joseph Raymond Stephenson Jr. and Jimmy Pace (crown bearers), Martha Coates Ashley and Adelaide Haffenden (train bearers), Fairchild Sonner (king), Elizabeth Cooper (queen), Gene Brandon (archbishop), a Mrs. Bushnell (queen mother), and Charles Haffenden (herald). (Courtesy of the City of Saluda.)

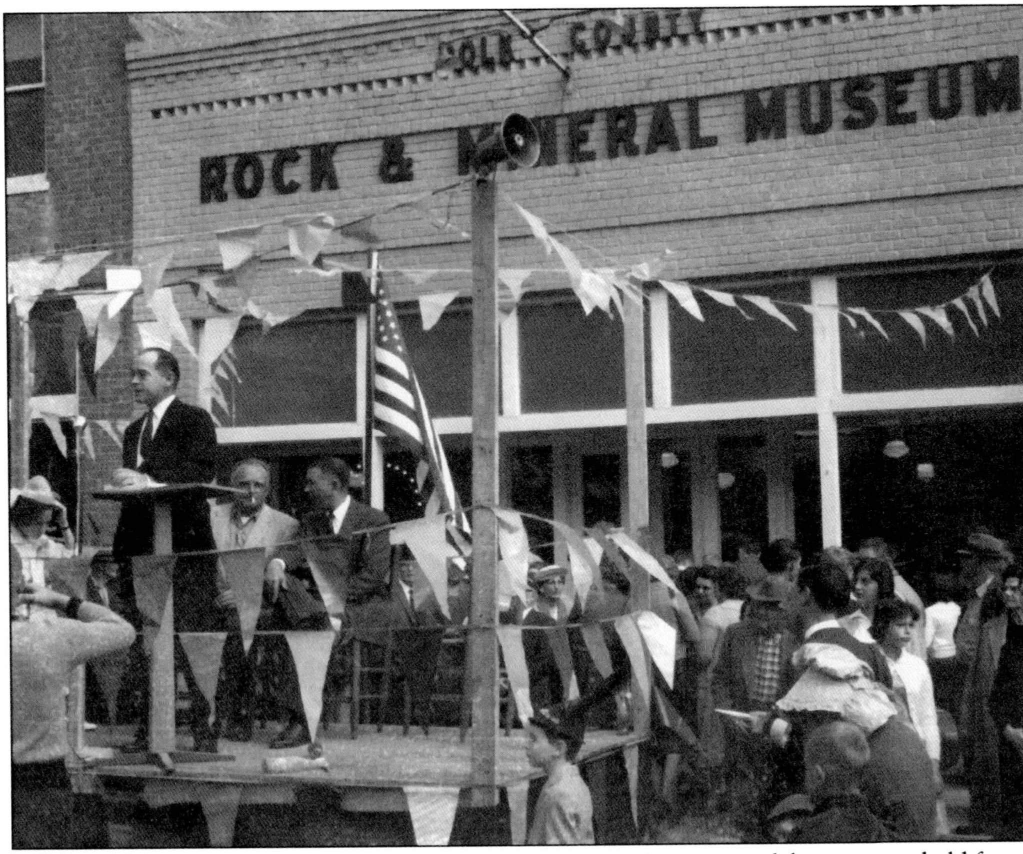

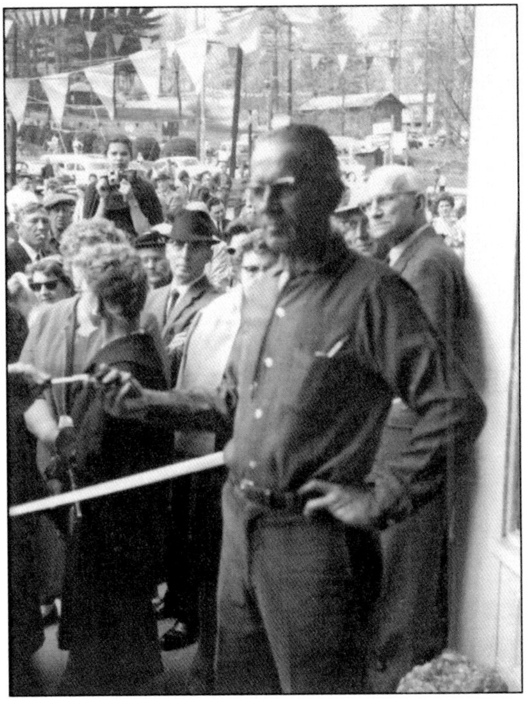

In March 1962, a celebration was held for the grand opening of the Polk County Rock and Mineral Museum, the first rock museum to be made up entirely from one man's collection in North Carolina. Prior to the ribbon-cutting ceremony, a parade was held and speeches were made by state legislators and other dignitaries. William Crawford "W.C." Ashley, pictured left, had only been collecting for nine years, but his exhibit had more than 1,000 specimens by the opening day. In the 1930s, Ashley was the building supervisor for the WPA in Polk County, during the time the current Saluda School was built. After retiring from this line of work, he pursued his hobby of searching for and collecting gems and minerals and was often referred to as a rock hound. This hobby led to the opening of the museum. (Both, courtesy of Martha Coates Ashley.)

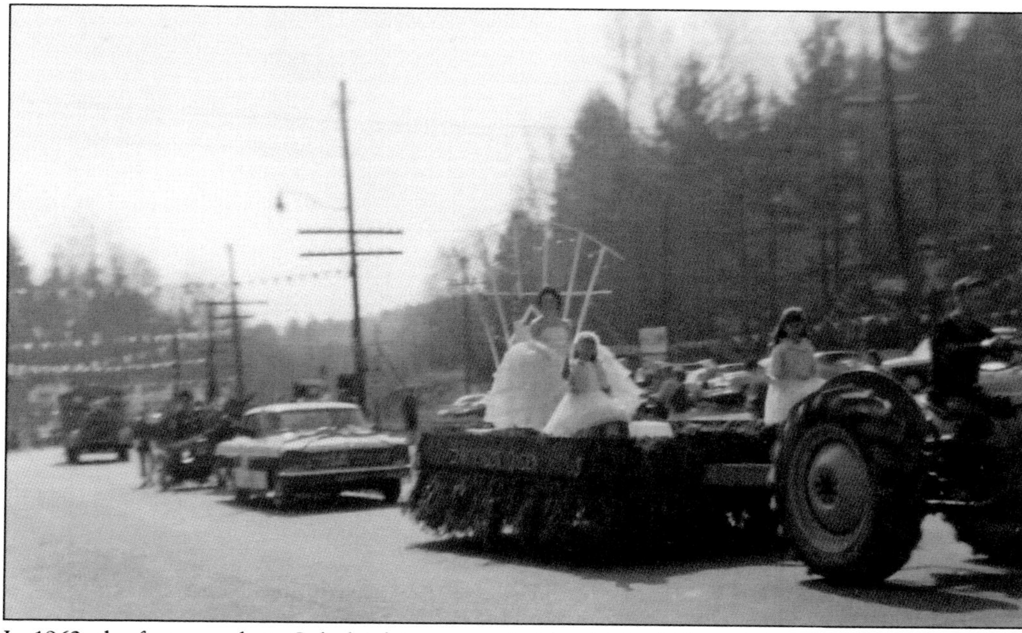

In 1962, the first parade in Saluda's history was held to kick-off the celebration of the opening of the Polk County Rock and Mineral Museum. A Hendersonville VFW color guard led the parade with the Tryon High School Band, 17 floats, and marching units taking part. John T. Coates Jr. was the grand marshal, and prizes were awarded for the best floats. A chicken barbeque was prepared by the Blue Ridge Coon Club for the cost of $1 for a half chicken, and the Mountaineer String Band provided additional entertainment. The entire event was sponsored by the Saluda Mountaineers Association, with John M. Morse Jr. acting as president. Morse reported to the *Spartanburg Herald* in December 1962 that 10,000 visitors registered at the museum that summer, representing 32 states and 12 foreign countries. (Both, courtesy of Roy L. Johnson Jr.)

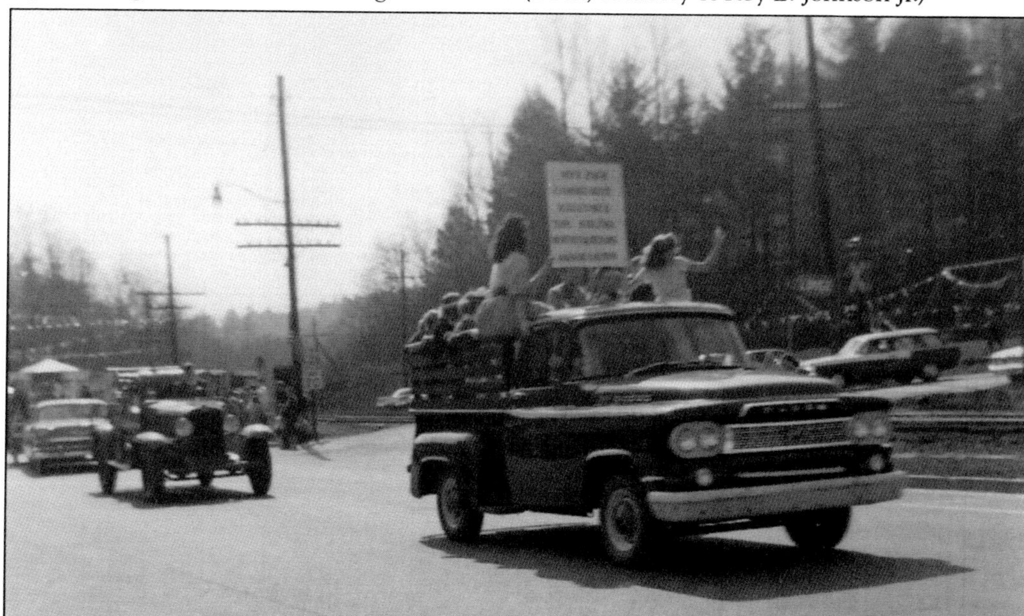

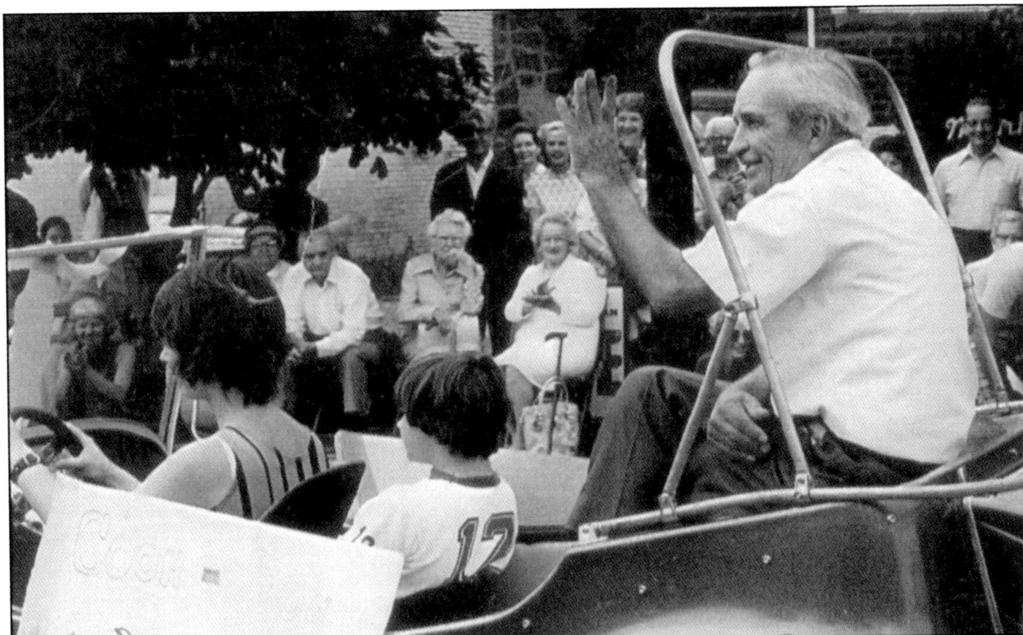

The Blue Ridge Coon Club was organized by 1957, with George Johnson as the first president. The club was organized due to concerns that the local raccoon population had dwindled and needed to be replenished so the hunt could continue. Pictured here, Johnson participates in a Coon Dog Day parade as Coon Dog Day king. (Courtesy of Charlene Pace.)

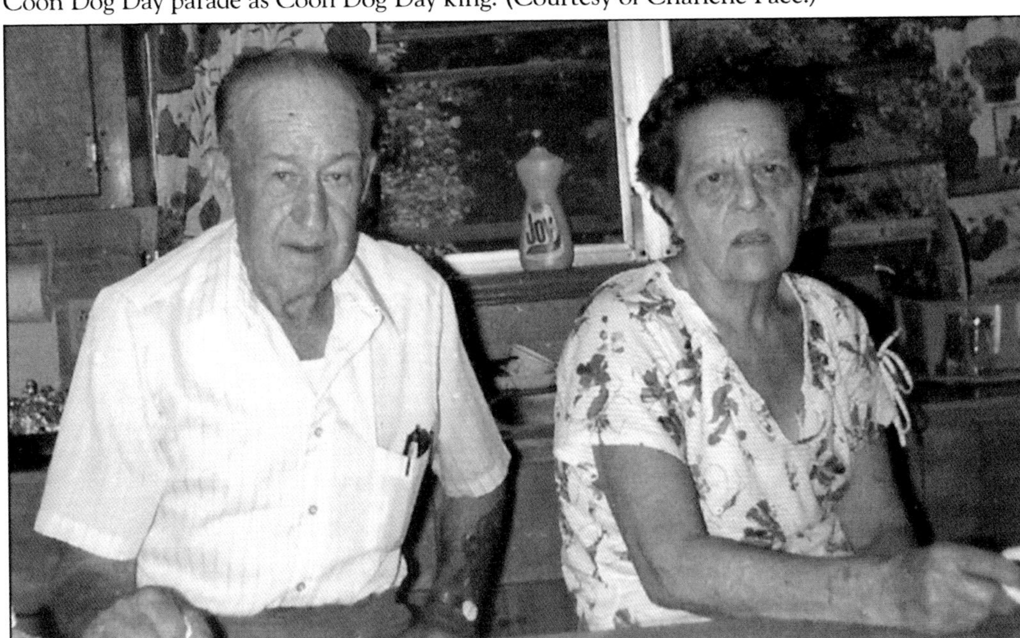

Walter Dewitt Summey, pictured here with his wife, Frances Arkansas Case Summey, was a member of the Blue Ridge Coon Club and worked alongside George Johnson to create the first Coon Dog Day event. Frances punch hooked rugs and worked for a time with the Mossellers, helping to make rugs that are now in the Smithsonian, and one was used in the movie *Gone With the Wind*. (Courtesy of Janet Clayton.)

The Blue Ridge Coon Club had been having successful chicken dinners and dog shows for many years, which were always held the Saturday after the Fourth of July. When the club saw the success of the Old Prospectors parade, they decided to add a parade to their event. In 1963, the Blue Ridge Coon Club hosted the first Coon Dog Day Parade. Pictured here are images from the 1966 Annual Dog Show and Chicken Dinner, better known as the Coon Dog Day Parade. (Both, courtesy of Cindy Stephenson Tuttle.)

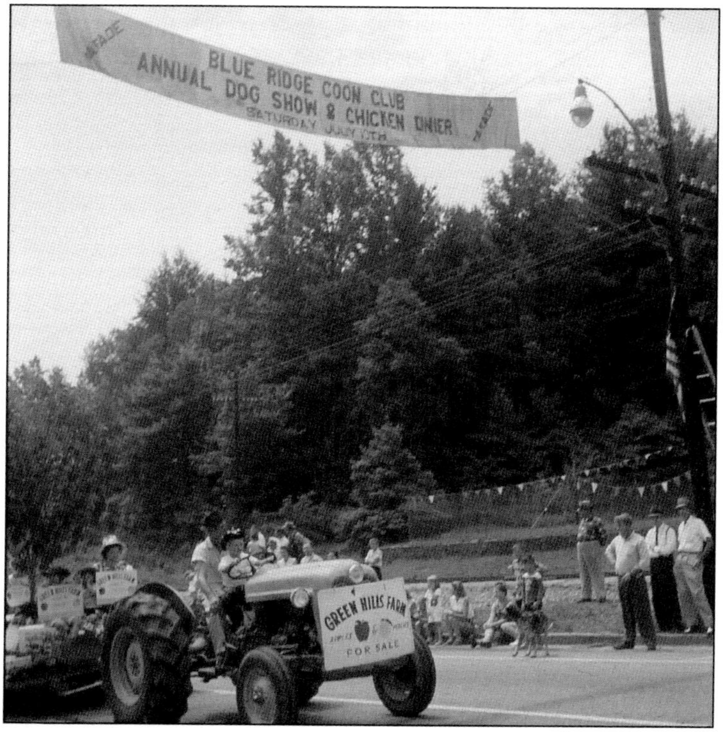

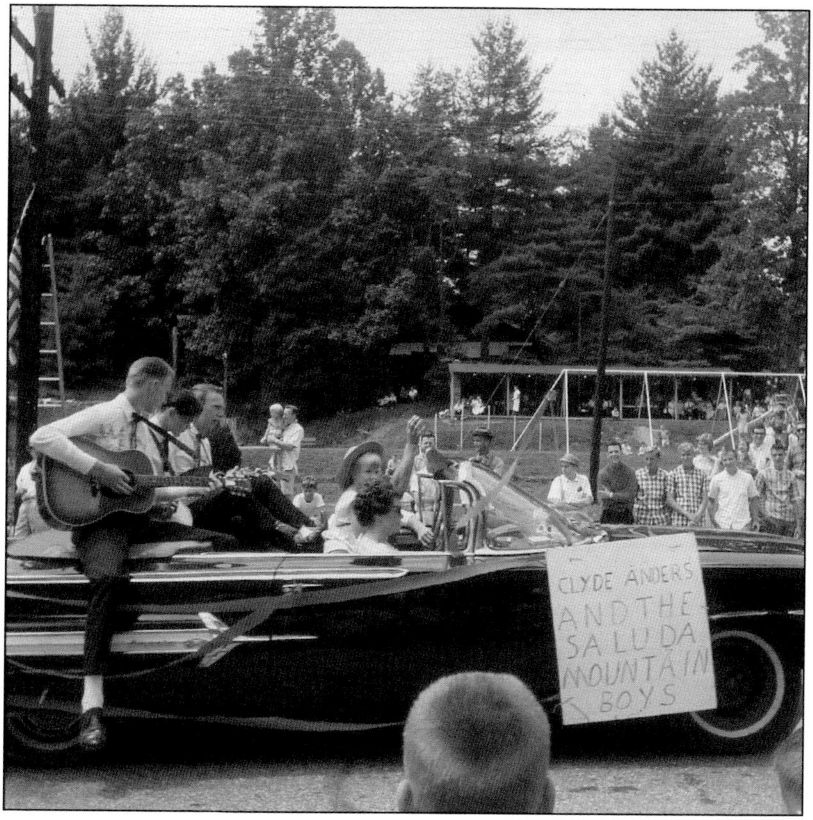

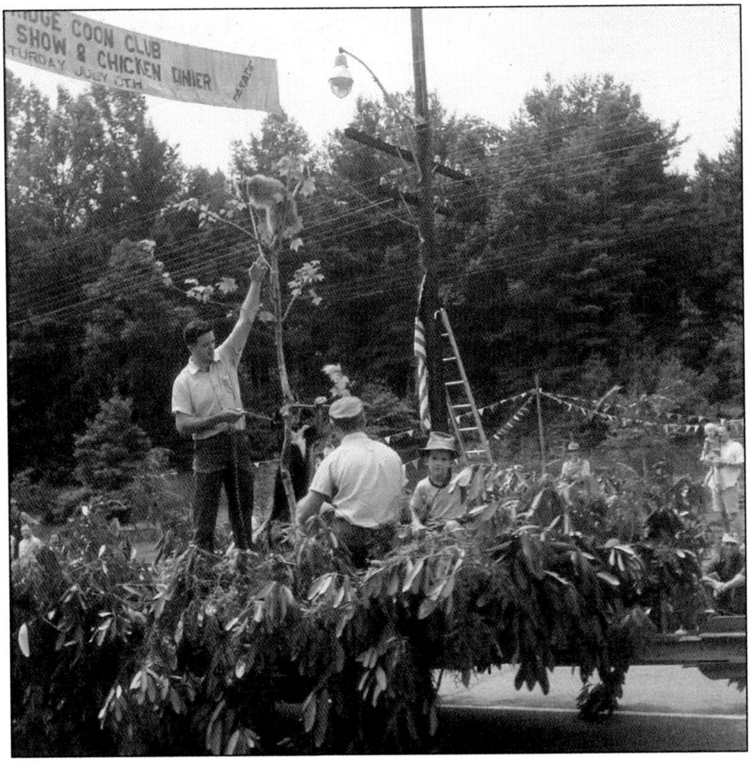

Today, the tradition of a Coon Dog Day float continues, complete with a raccoon up in a tree and a coon dog baying below with the owner struggling to restrain him from getting to the critter. The only difference between today and the early days is that now times are a little more humane, with no live raccoons used on the float. This image from 1966 does portray a live raccoon on the float, though. (Courtesy of Cindy Stephenson Tuttle.)

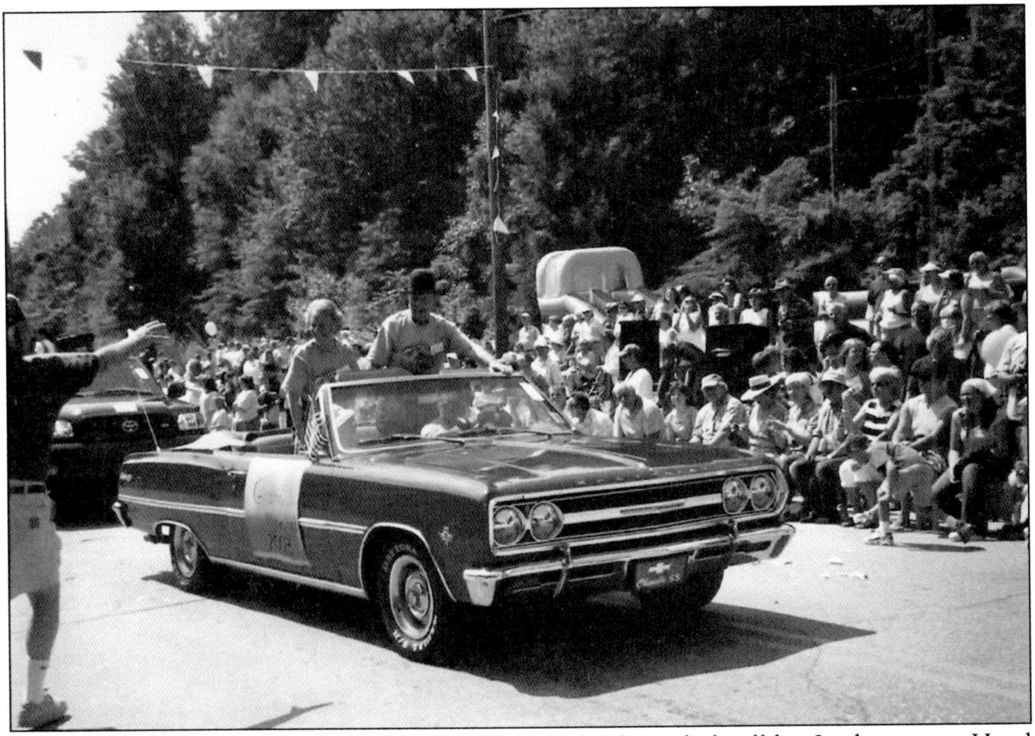

Saluda folks always look forward to seeing who the grand marshal will be. In this image, Hazel and Horace Pace were the grand marshals in 2003. (Courtesy of Charlene Pace.)

Selecting the Coon Dog Day Royalty Court is a favorite tradition and very competitive. Donation jars are placed around town, and the one with the most votes wins. A penny counts for one vote. This photograph from around 1964 is of Coon Dog Day queen Patricia Russell and an unidentified driver. (Courtesy of Janet Clayton.)

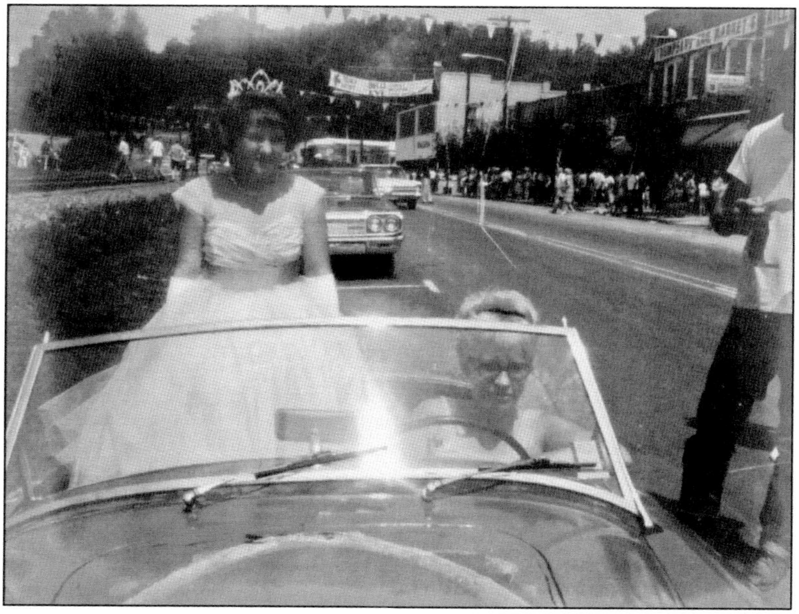

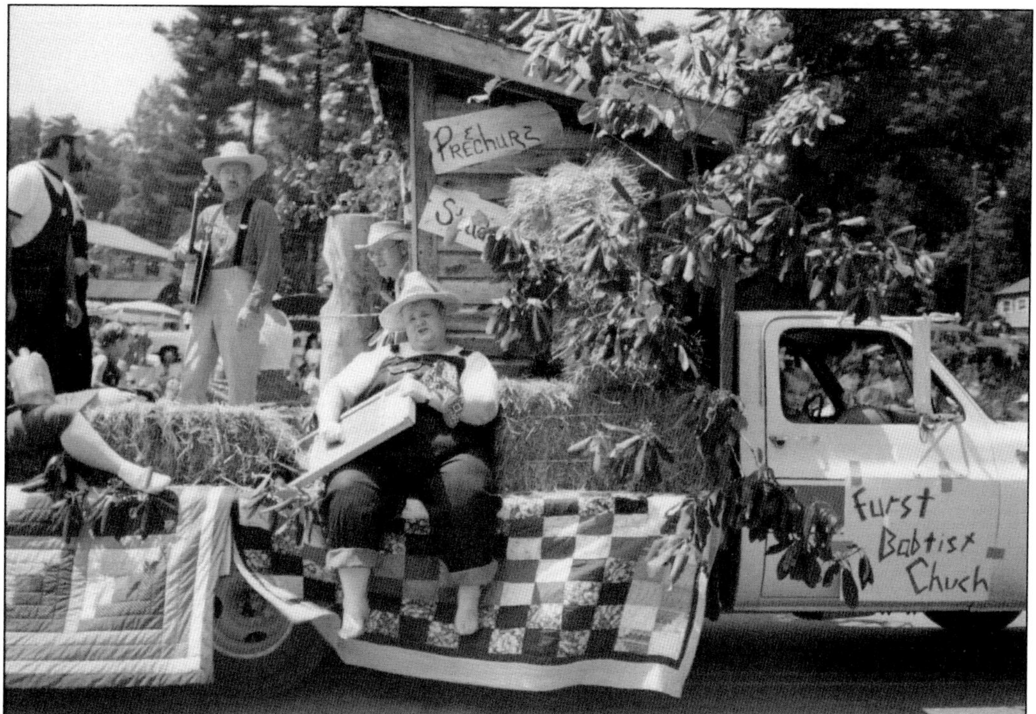

Aside from the coon dog, the raccoon, and the coon hunter, the hillbilly is another favorite character who shows up in many forms during Coon Dog Day. In 1989, Ron Poole played up his character to the hilt while riding on the First Baptist Church float, drawing lots of laughs from the audience. Humor is a must for those participating or attending the annual Coon Dog Day events. (Courtesy of R. Clark Thompson.)

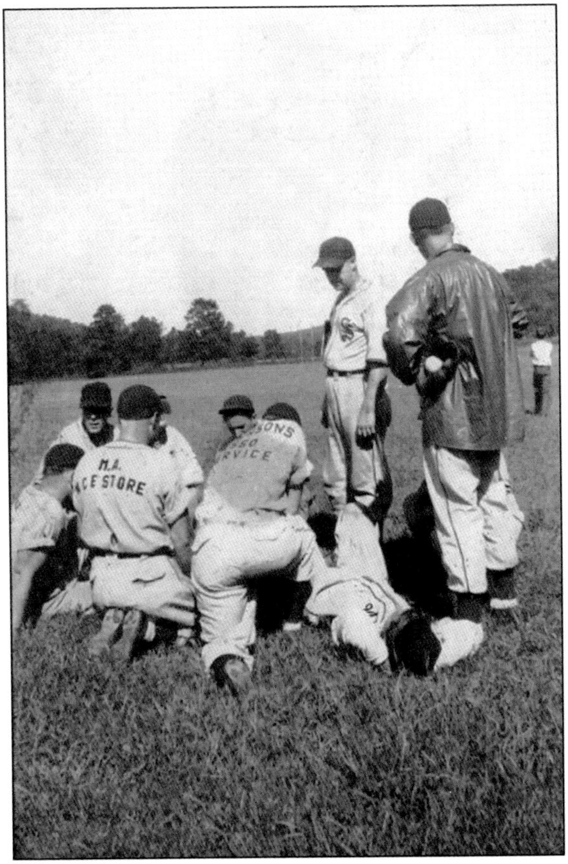

Baseball was a popular pastime, and local leagues were formed, inspiring tales of great, talented players from Saluda. This photograph shows one of the early Saluda teams, sponsored by local businesses M.A. Pace Store and Stephenson's Esso Service. (From the album of Lola Ward, courtesy of Judy Ward.)

In 1921, the Saluda Civic League filed a complaint with the city because of "abominable dancing and drunkenness in the city." In 1923, the league decided Saluda's young people needed a place to gather, so with the help of the Harmon Foundation in New York City they built a playground, picnic area, tennis courts, and pavilion for public use, which came to fruition in 1929. Pictured here, the clay tennis courts are being prepared for use. (Courtesy of Martha Coates Ashley.)

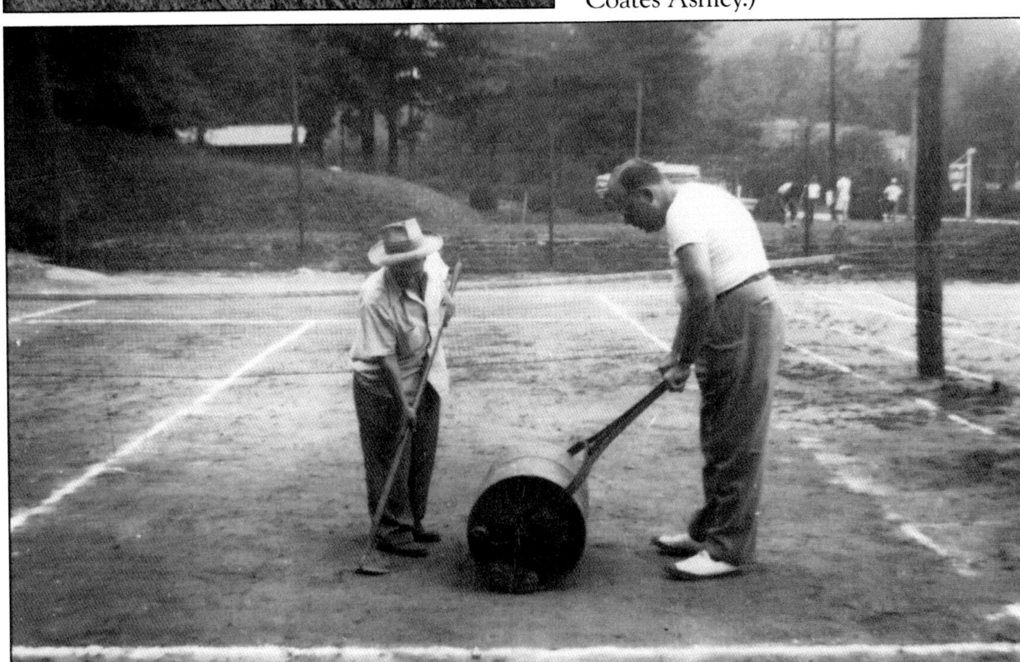

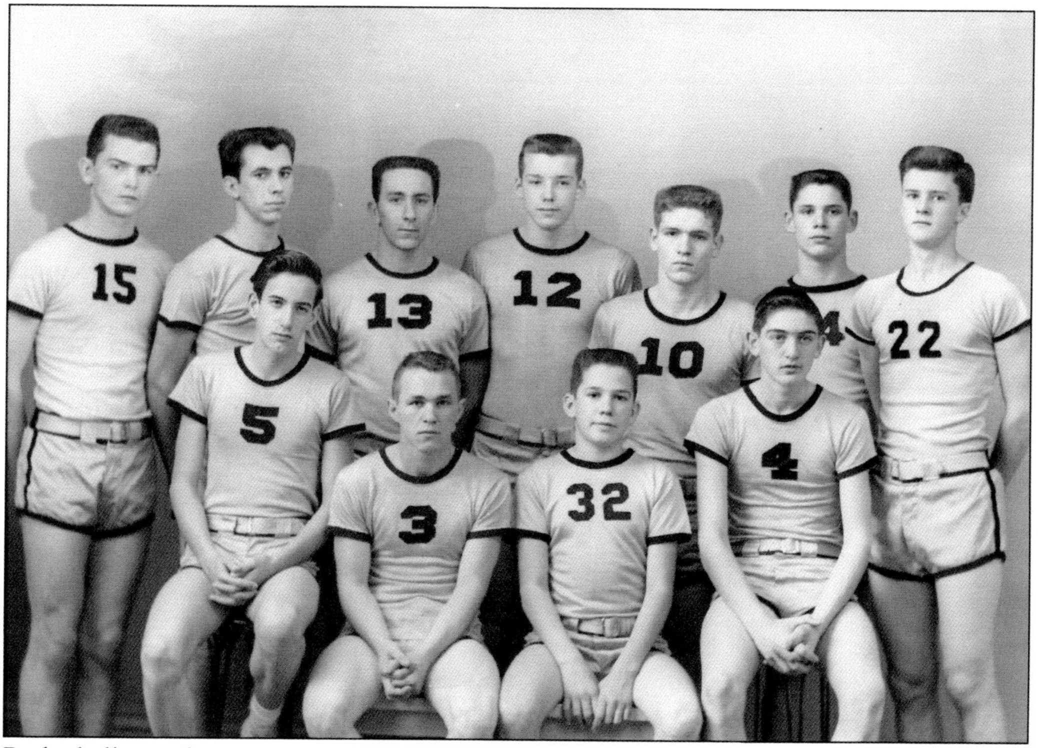

Basketball was the major sport of Saluda High School, especially since they were not large enough to have a football team. The 1958–1959 Saluda High School team won the Polk County Basketball Championship. Pictured here are, from left to right, (first row) Marshall Hill, Ralph Pace, Stephen Pace, and David Fowler; (second row) Jerry K. Pace, Allen Pace, Harold Foster, Cater Leland, Frankie Ashley, Jerry Pace, and Stanley Byers. Coach Clyde Smith was not in the picture. (Courtesy of E. Cater Leland Jr.)

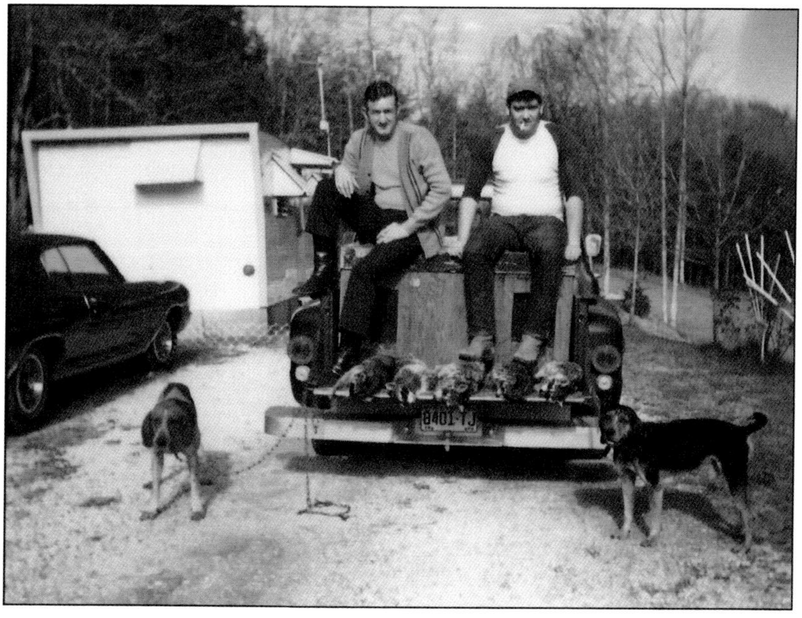

Hunting has always been a favorite pastime in the hills around Saluda, especially raccoon hunting. In this photograph taken in 1967, coon hunters Bobby Campbell (left) and Jay Summey, with their prized coon dogs, are obviously pleased by the success of their most recent hunt. (Courtesy of Janet Clayton.)

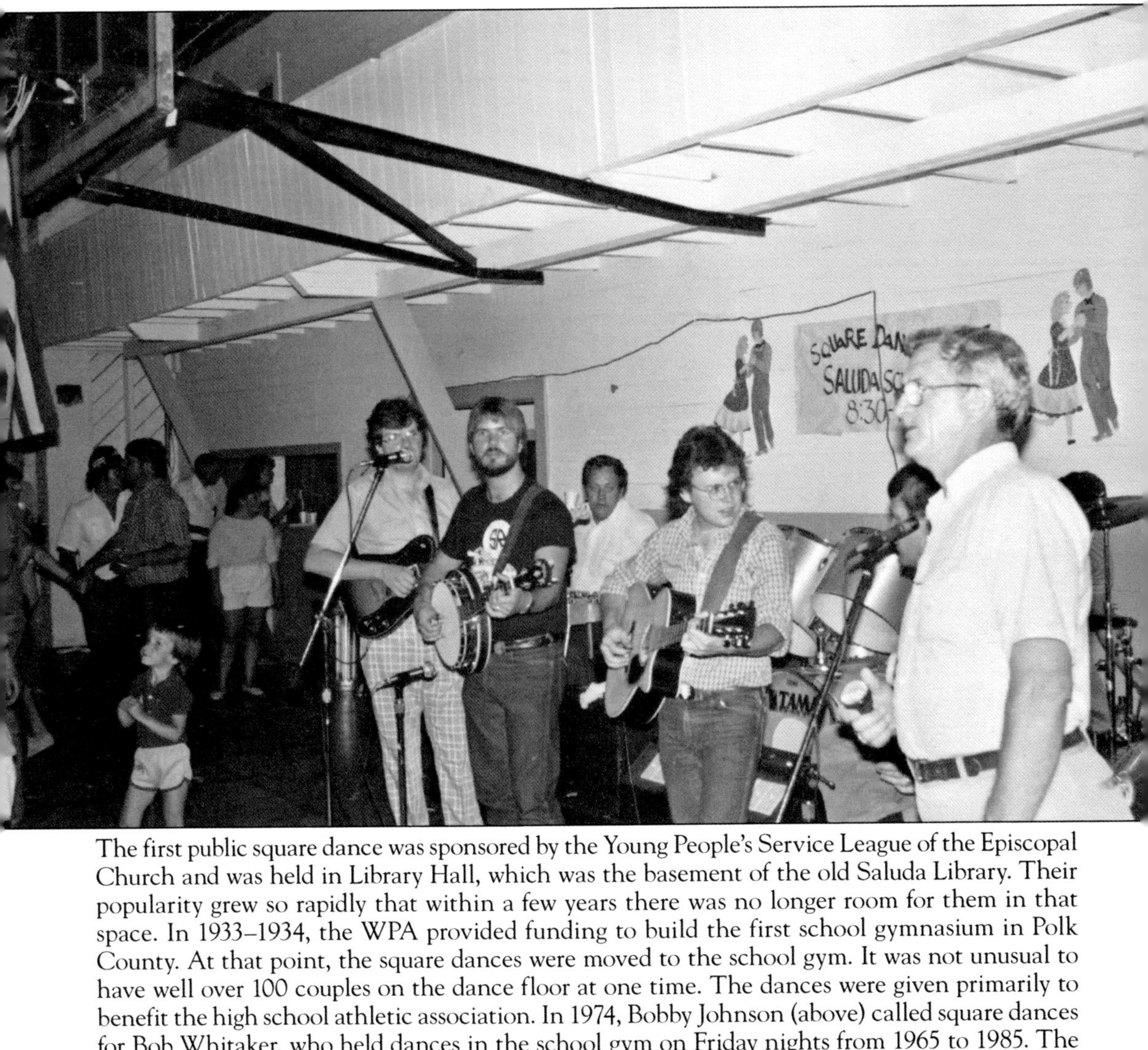

The first public square dance was sponsored by the Young People's Service League of the Episcopal Church and was held in Library Hall, which was the basement of the old Saluda Library. Their popularity grew so rapidly that within a few years there was no longer room for them in that space. In 1933–1934, the WPA provided funding to build the first school gymnasium in Polk County. At that point, the square dances were moved to the school gym. It was not unusual to have well over 100 couples on the dance floor at one time. The dances were given primarily to benefit the high school athletic association. In 1974, Bobby Johnson (above) called square dances for Bob Whitaker, who held dances in the school gym on Friday nights from 1965 to 1985. The band (above) was called the Buddy Dance Band, and they played on a regular basis. The style of dance was called mountain square dancing, with calls like "right hand over and how do you do? Left hand over and how are you?" (Courtesy of Bob Whitaker.)

Pictured here are Bob Whitaker and the Rhythm Note Band. When he was not calling, Whitaker (far left) played with his buddies. It was not unusual to have 200 folks for clogging and square dancing on Friday nights, with ages from seven to 75. It was a family affair, with parents and children welcome. The gym was always decorated appropriately with a favorite being a real wagon wheel suspended from the ceiling with streamers. (Courtesy of Bob Whitaker.)

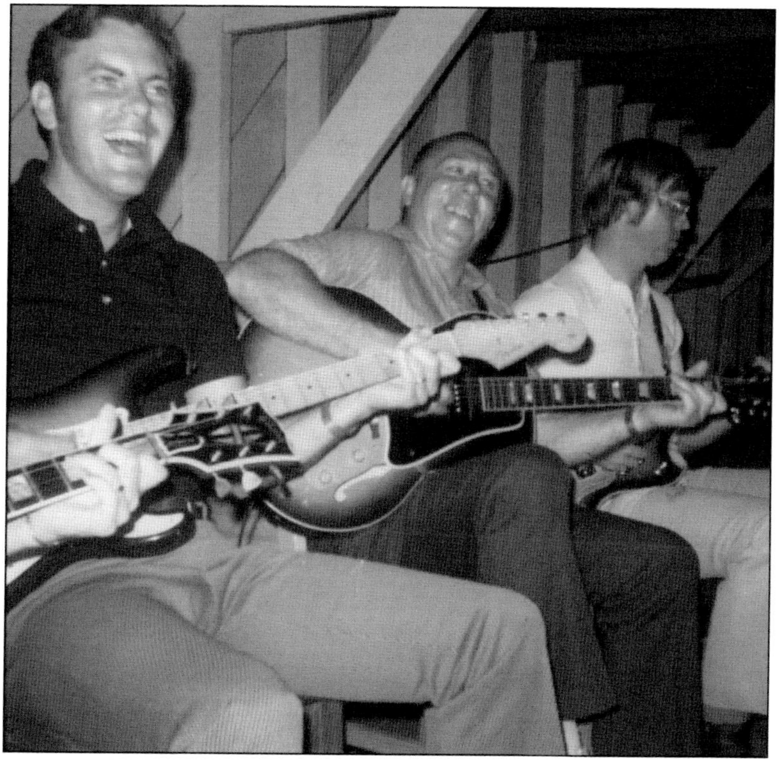

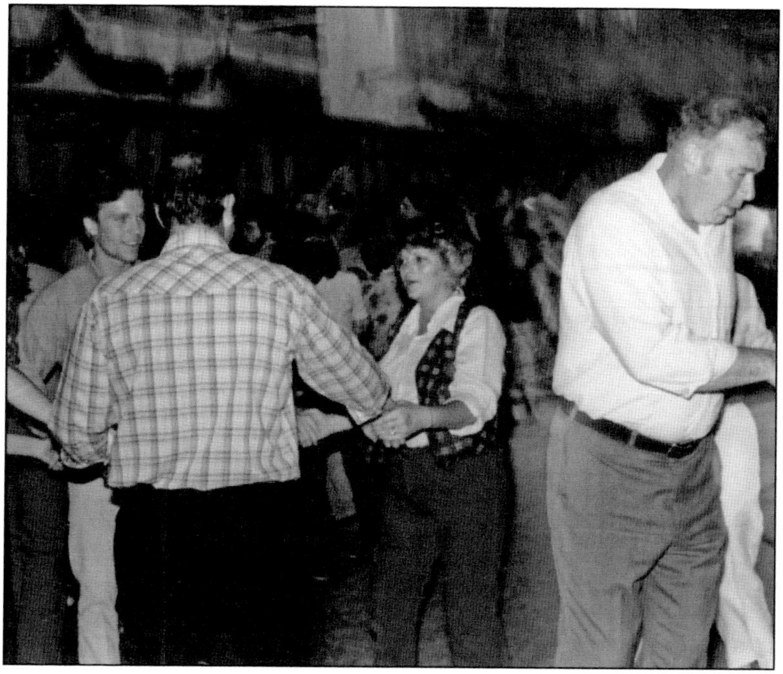

The gentleman in profile is Lloyd Thompson, who was well known in Saluda. These popular Friday night dances started when school let out on Memorial Day and continued until school started after Labor Day. For the last dance, caller Bob Whitaker always started with "swing your cornered lady all the way 'round," which of course meant one's girlfriend. (Courtesy of Bob Whitaker.)

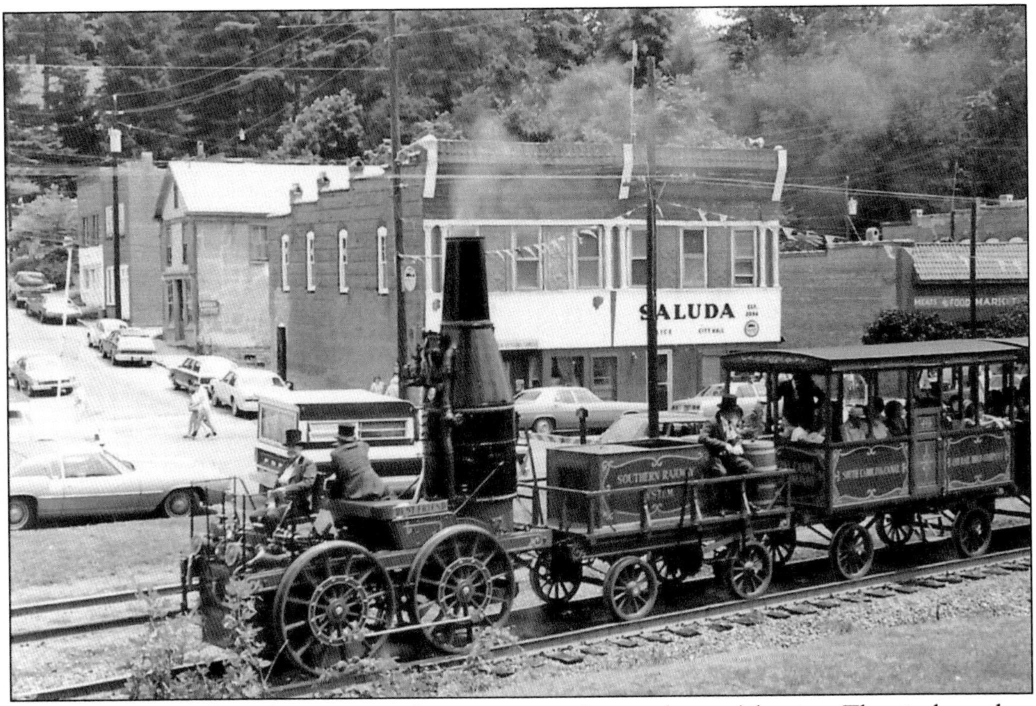

In 1981, Saluda celebrated its centennial anniversary with a yearlong celebration. The city hosted an open house in February 1981 featuring old-timey photographs, refreshments, and lots of fellowship. Cakes made to look like two trains were created by Mary Phillips and Margaret Pace Burrell and featured passenger, coal, wood, and freight cars made from various delicious ingredients. A two-day celebration was held in August 1981 featuring crafts, exhibits, and demonstrations; rides on the Best Friend of Charleston (above); barbecue prepared by the volunteer firemen; homemade cake and ice cream; and an evening square dance (below). On the final day, there was a community worship service, a picnic on the grounds, and an old-fashioned gospel sing. (Both, courtesy of the City of Saluda.)

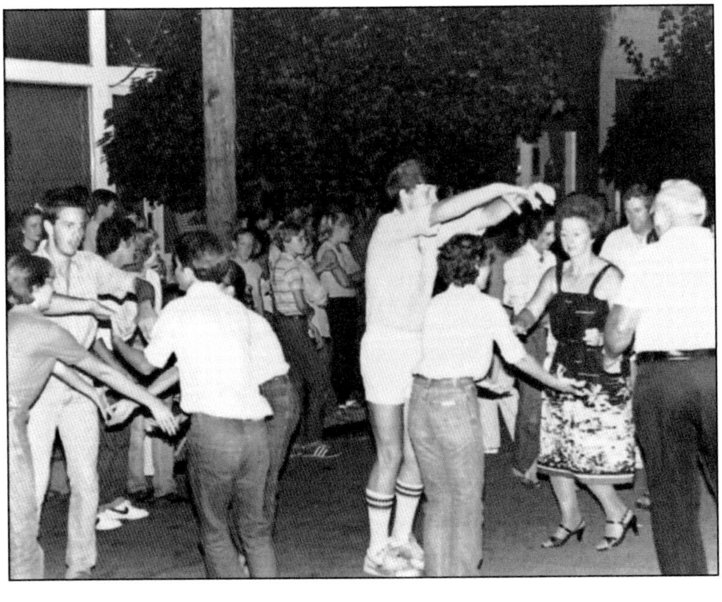

Five

Saluda's Medical Community

With the railroad came the people, and even though the fresh air was restorative, there was still a need for physicians. Dr. E.B. Goelet was the first to practice in Saluda, and he also owned the local drugstore. Other physicians who practiced in Saluda at this time were Dr. Shankle and a Dr. Cooksey. Dr. Joseph Fauntleroy, who practiced on Judd's Peak, was a much-loved figure, as he would go to homes on horseback to help and often stayed with patients until they were out of danger.

After Dr. Goelet's death in 1908, Dr. E.M. Salley moved from Tryon to Saluda to fill the gap. He also had a real estate business, as he needed a second source of income. Dr. Hooper was in Saluda at the same time and had an office and apartment above the M.A. Pace store, practicing in Saluda until his death in the 1920s.

But it was Dr. Lesesne Smith who put Saluda on the medical map, not only in the South, but across the country. A summer resident of Saluda, he was a pediatrician from Spartanburg, South Carolina, who saw that mountain children had fewer summer fevers, which killed so many infants. In 1914, he began a private children's sanitarium, open in the summer, to treat his patients and also those from the Lowcountry that were ill. The first hospital building, called Bon Air, was a converted boardinghouse. He also bought up land around it for patients' families and staff.

The *Spartanburg Herald* "expressed some hope that some way might be provided by which those who were unable to pay hospital prices might receive benefit of mountain climate." Dr. Smith volunteered his services, and 14 Carolinians formed a hospital committee. The Spartanburg Baby Hospital was born, and "a sick baby is all you have to have to enter here."

Dr. Smith also realized that a postgraduate school was needed to keep up with the newest medical trends, so in 1921 he and Dr. F.R. Richardson opened the Southern Pediatric Seminar, which operated for the next 38 years.

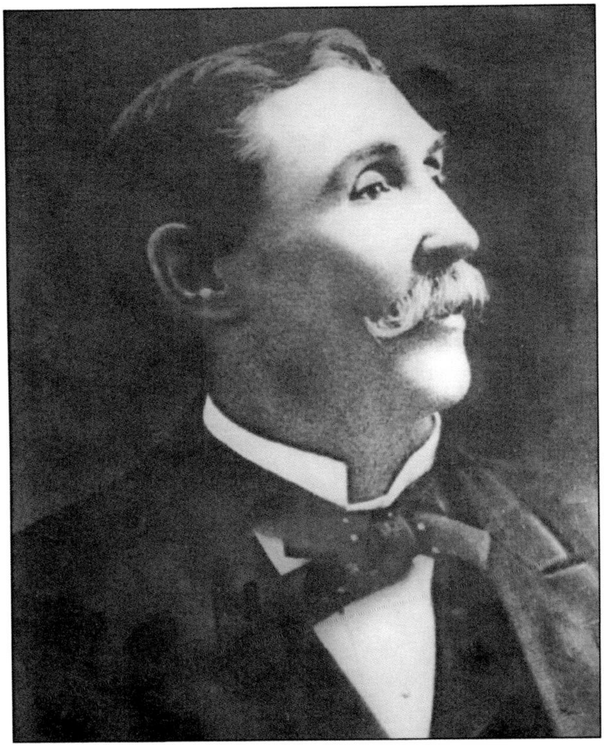

Dr. E.B. Goelet was the first medical doctor in Saluda, and he also owned and operated the first drugstore in town. Dr. Goelet was famous for driving his buggy night and day, delivering babies and treating illnesses. He was a pillar of the Episcopal Church along with his sister Julia Goelet, who established a mission building, which is now the parish hall for the Episcopal Church of the Transfiguration. (Courtesy of the Polk County Unity Lodge No. 482.)

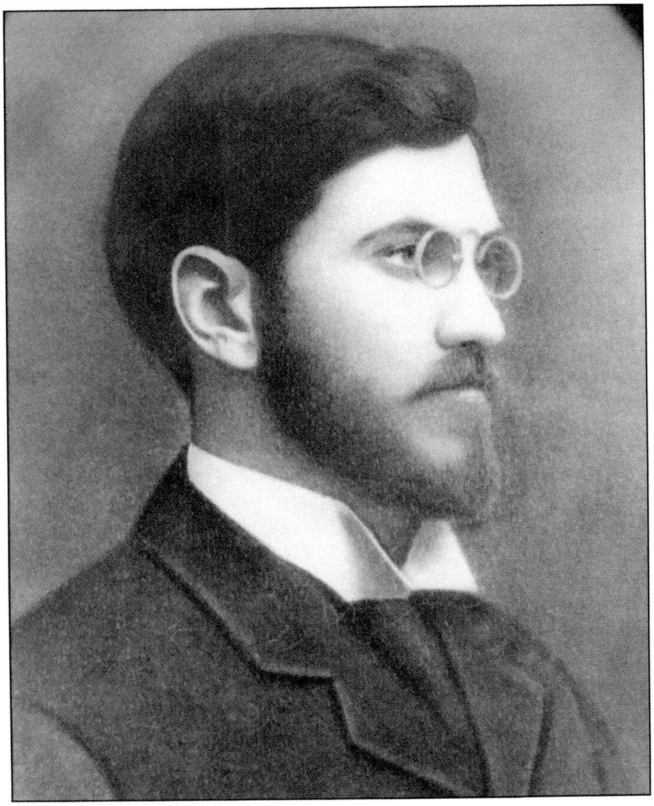

After Dr. E.B. Goelet's death in 1908, Orangeburg, South Carolina, native Dr. E.M. Salley moved from Tryon to Saluda, where he had practiced for many years. His second-floor office on Main Street was above what was then the local post office. Like many physicians, he had a second career, real estate, to augment his income. He moved his practice to Hendersonville in 1934. (Courtesy of the Polk County Unity Lodge No. 482.)

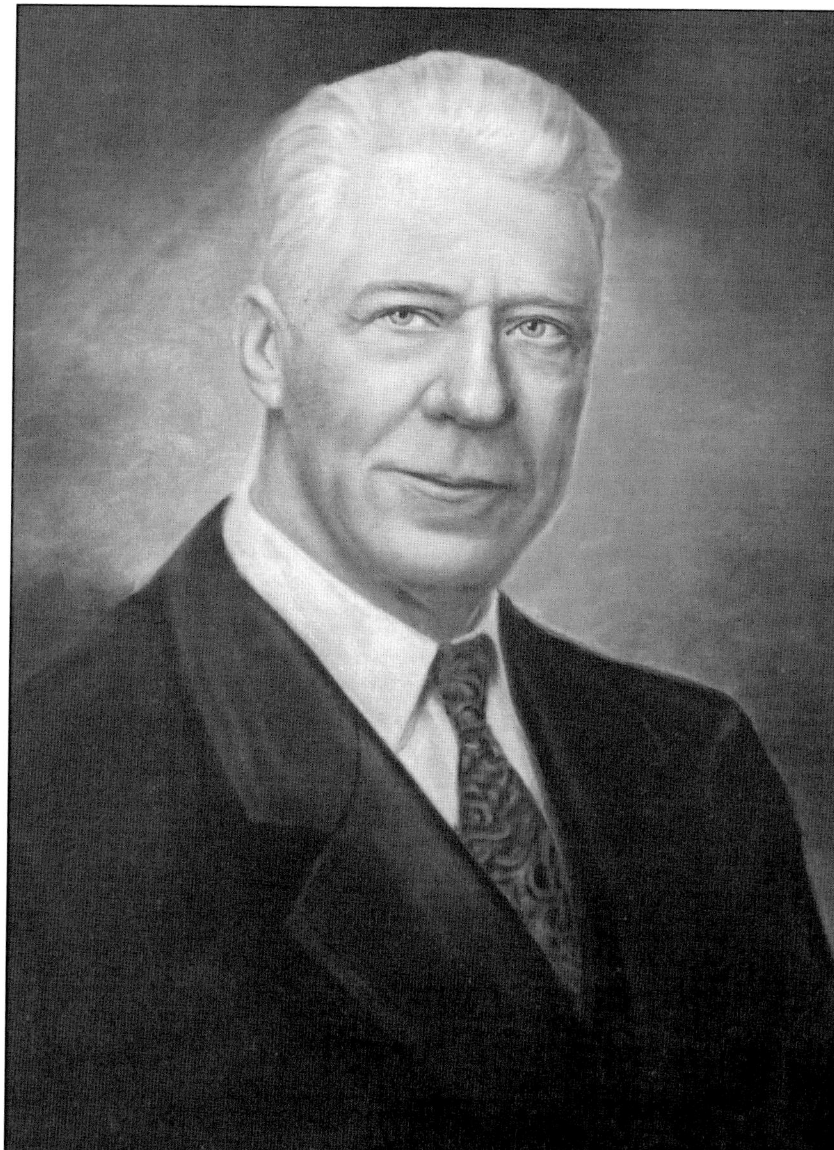

Dr. D. Lesesne Smith's general practice in Spartanburg was healthy but not satisfying. So in 1913, he went to Harvard Medical School and became one of the first pediatricians in the South. With a high rate of infant mortality in the southern Appalachian Mountains, he reasoned that using his skills he could reduce the number of deaths in Saluda and the surrounding mountainous communities. In 1914, he established the Infants' and Children's Sanitarium (ICS), which was open from June 1 to September 1. The first summer, 18 babies were treated, and the sanitarium grew to 12 cottages where mothers and babies stayed together. Another entity under Dr. Smith's supervision was the Spartanburg Baby Hospital, where babies could be seen for free. Out of these two hospitals in 1921, Dr. Smith developed the Southern Pediatric Seminar, from which physicians received "a post-graduate summer course in methods of diagnosis, prevention and treatment of diseases of children." Until it closed in 1958, the seminars put Saluda on the medical map of the country, as physicians came to learn how to care for their smallest patients. (Courtesy of VeeVee Blackshear.)

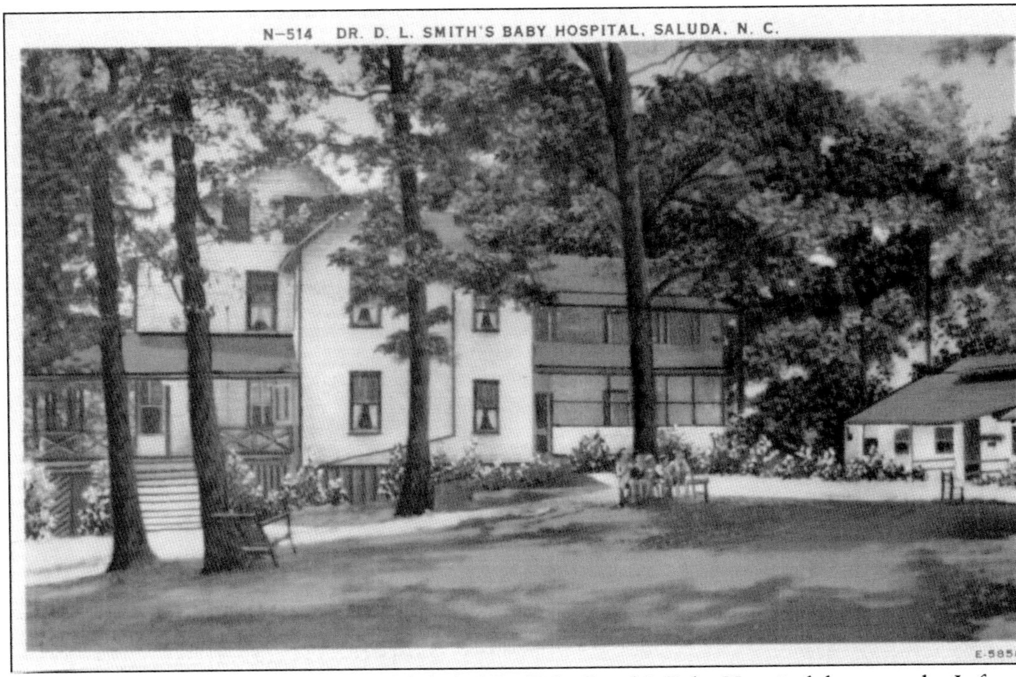

The structure shown in this postcard, labeled Dr. D.L. Smith's Baby Hospital, became the Infants' and Children's Sanitarium's main building. Prior to the inception of the sanitarium, Dr. Smith's wife owned two houses in Saluda, providing him a base from which to operate. From an original eight-room cottage, the sanitarium grew to 12 cottages, a central dining room, a diet kitchen, an assembly hall, and examination and treatment rooms. The building is no longer standing. (Courtesy of Cindy Stephenson Tuttle.)

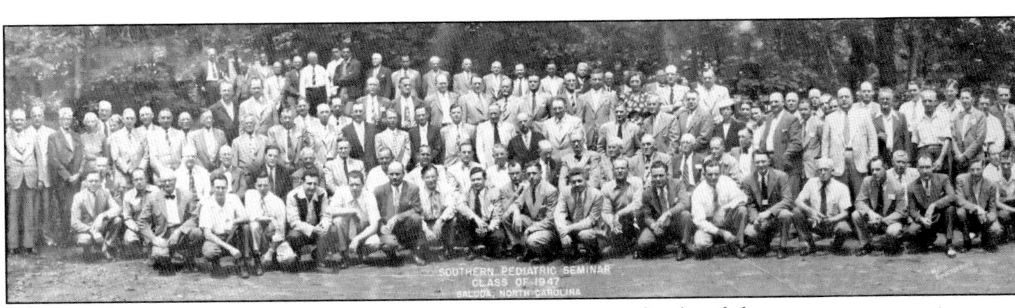

Describing itself as a postgraduate summer course in methods of diagnosis, prevention, and treatment of diseases of children, the Southern Pediatric Seminar started in 1921 with three students. The class of 1947 (above) had over 50 physicians enrolled in the six hours of lectures a day for three weeks during the summer. During its 38 years of operation, it is estimated that more than 3,000 doctors attended the seminars. (Courtesy of Clara Smith Carter.)

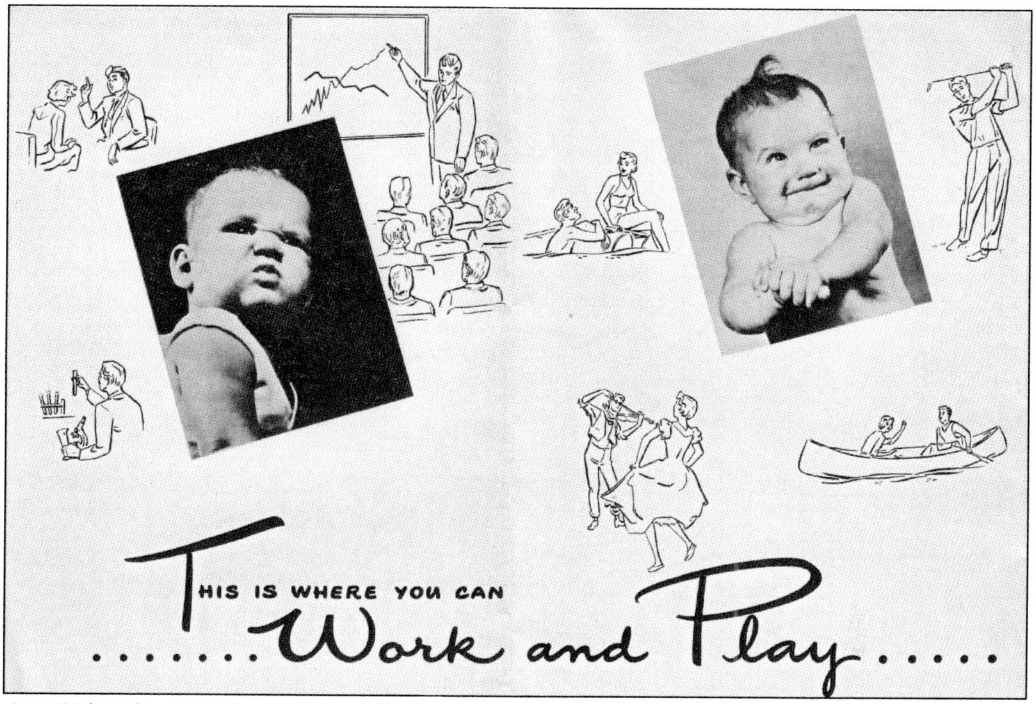

A 1952 brochure on the Southern Pediatric Seminar touted, "This is the kind of vacation that combines business and pleasure . . . having fun and learning in a pleasant atmosphere of informality and relaxation." The brochure showed the three-week class schedule, the special lecturers, and the family possibilities in area known as the Land of the Sky. (Courtesy of Clara Smith Carter.)

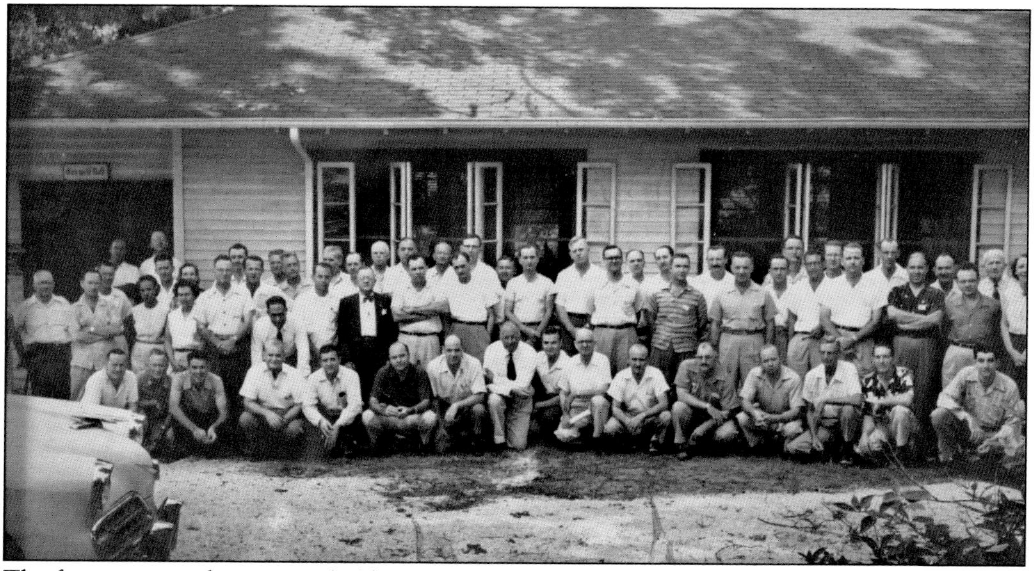

The first seminar classes were held in a tent rented from a revivalist. The seminar hall, Cornell Hall, was built and named in honor of Dr. William P. Cornell. Designed for student chairs, it had a raised platform for the lecturer. The atmosphere was still informal, as spittoons were available. It is now a private home owned by Mike and Lynn Cass. (Courtesy of Clara Smith Carter.)

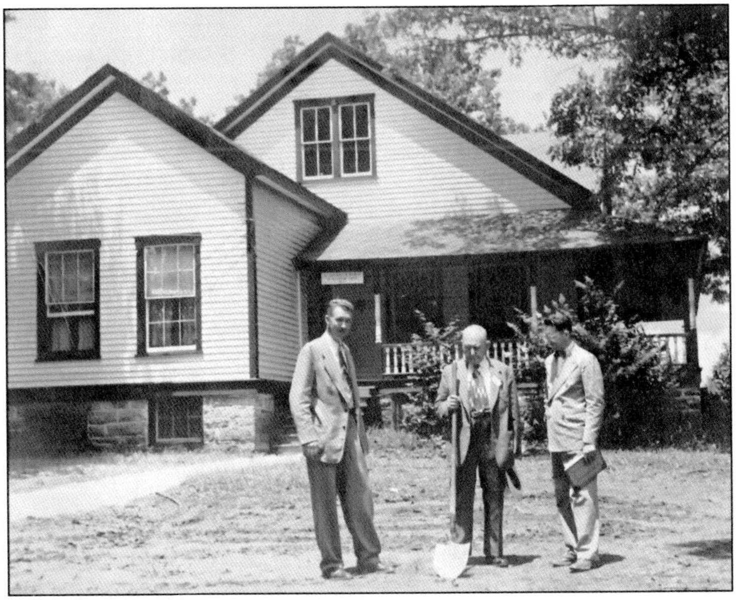

From left to right, Dr. Lesesne Smith, Dr. Owen Wilson (head of pediatrics at Vanderbilt University), and Dr. M. H. Owings stand in front of the Hamer House. The first house on Smith Hill, it was built by Colonel Sloan of Charleston as a summer home. Babies and nurses stayed here as part of the Infants' and Children's Sanitarium, and it is now the private residence of Clara Smith Carter. (Courtesy of Clara Smith Carter.)

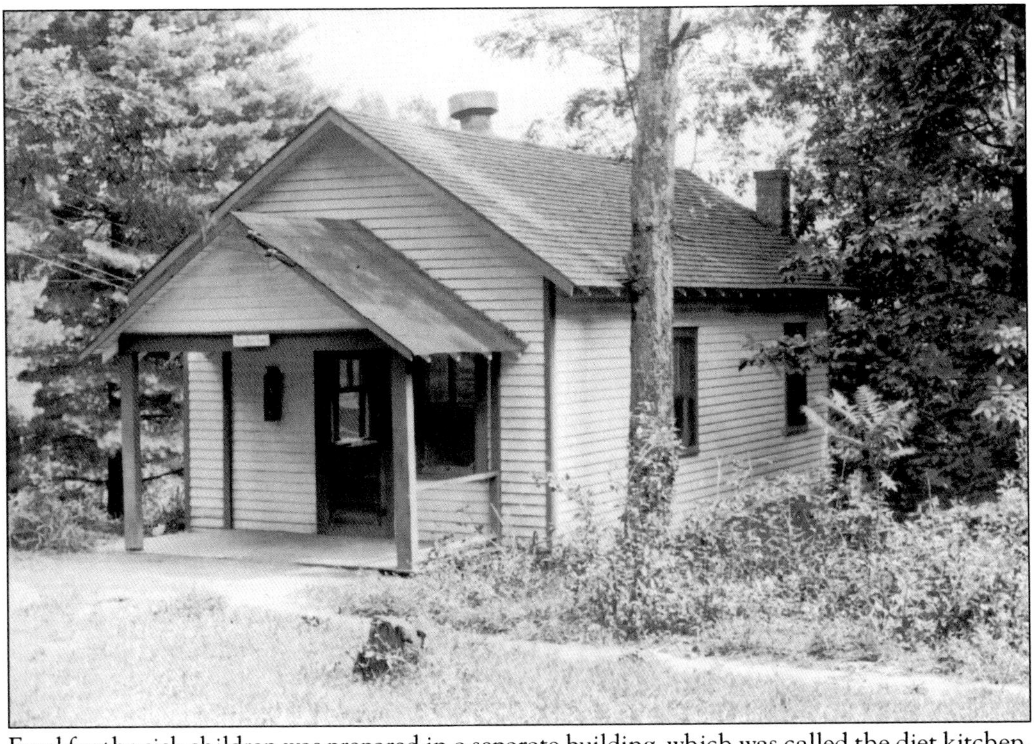

Food for the sick children was prepared in a separate building, which was called the diet kitchen. It consisted of two rooms and a screen porch. There were stoves, sinks, a pantry, and, most importantly, refrigeration for baby milk. It was staffed by economics majors from Winthrop College. Many years after its use as the diet kitchen, the building was added on to and became the residence of Ammie Owings Weymer. (Courtesy of Nettie Owings Sweet.)

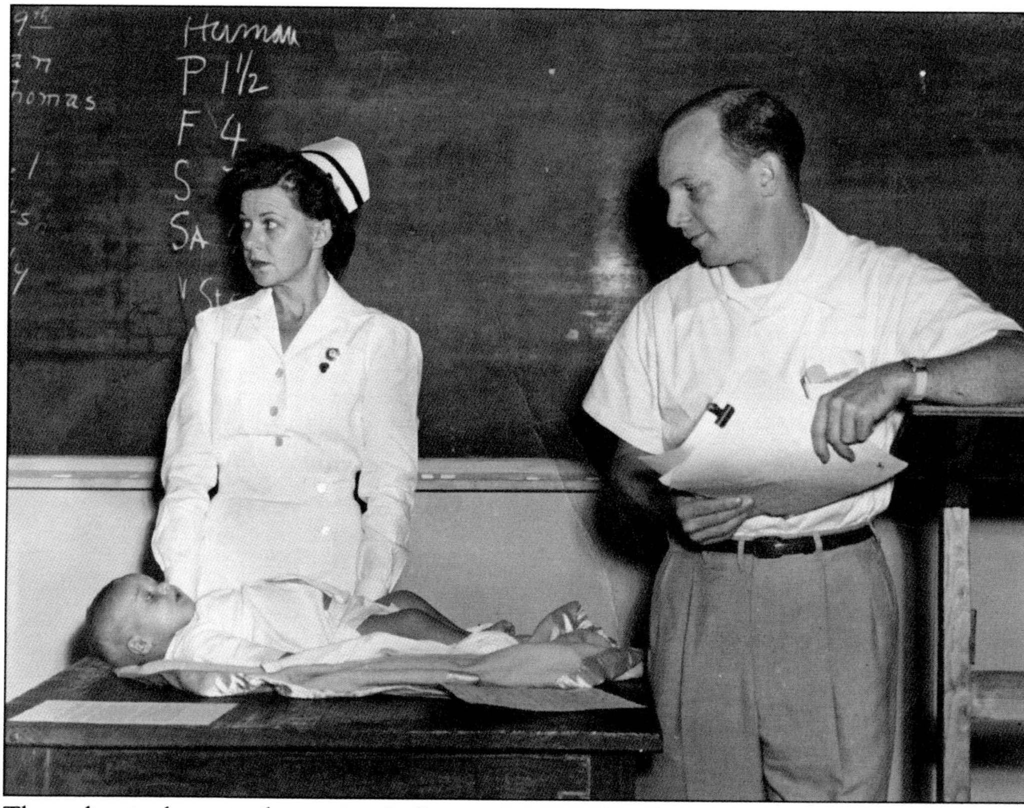

The pediatric classes in the seminar hall gave physicians hands-on instructions in the care of sick infants. As the brochure said, "One hour a day is devoted to the presentation of clinical cases and material is chosen from the 50 beds available in the Spartanburg Baby Hospital." Thousands of sick babies and physicians benefited from this approach. (Courtesy of Clara Smith Carter.)

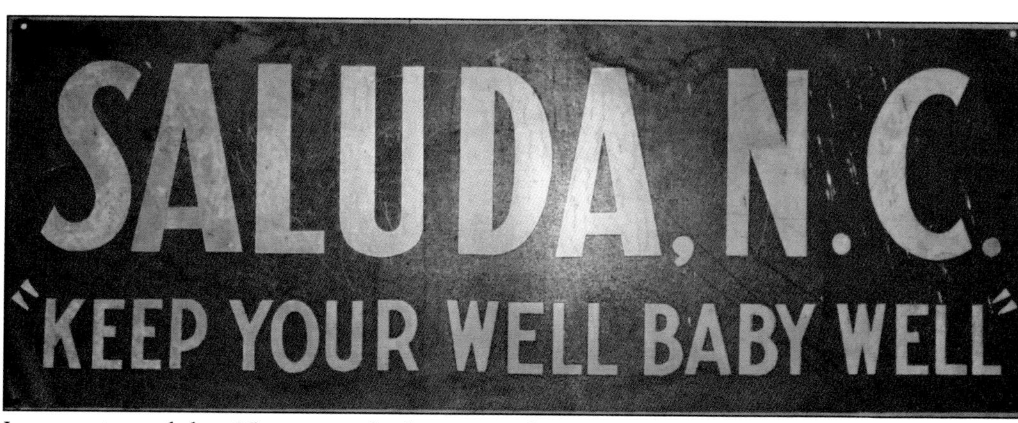

It was estimated that 95 percent of sickness in infants was due to improper care and feeding. Dr. Smith's slogan for the Infants' and Children's Sanitarium was, "Keep Your Well Baby Well." An advertisement from the 1930s highlighted the cool and invigorating climate, reasonable rates, and educational courses for mothers. (Courtesy of Clara Smith Carter.)

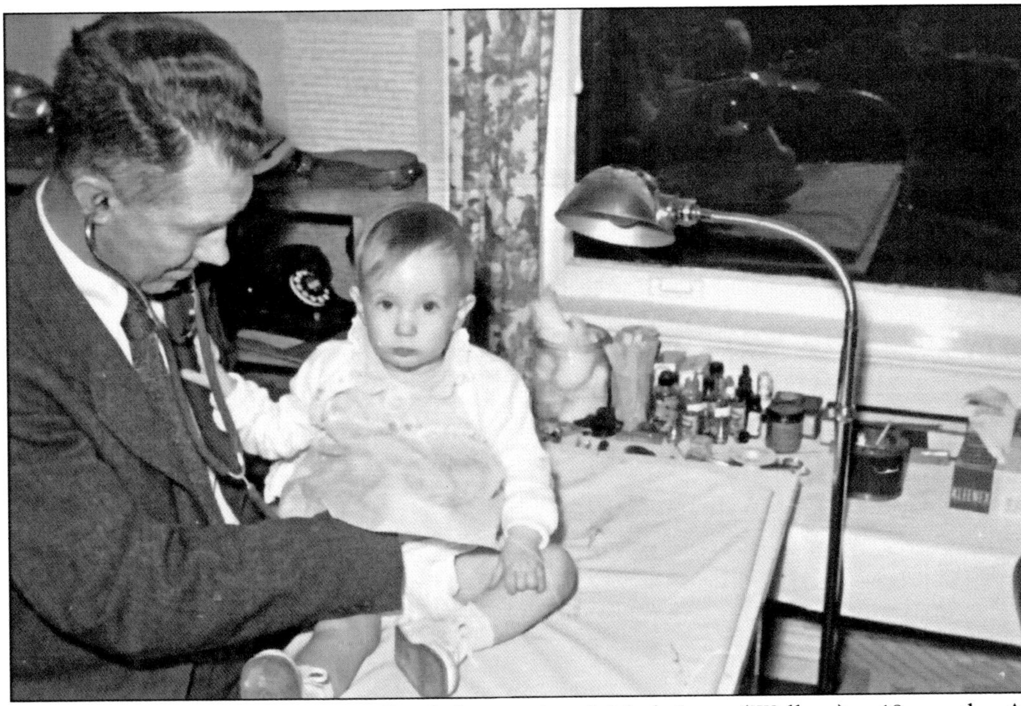

In this photograph, Dr. D. Lesesne Smith Jr. examines Melody Lowe (Wallace) at 18 months. As an expert in health care for the young, Dr. Smith knew that climate and diet affected children. So he controlled what they ate and developed nutritious feeding formulas for infants. He refused to take any profit for this innovation. Under the guidance of the nursing staff, mothers of children from ages four to six were also given a class in nutrition. (Courtesy of Clara Smith Carter)

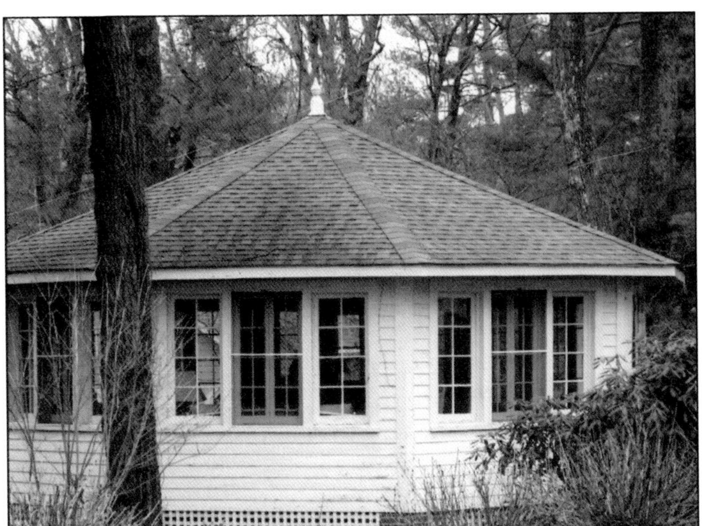

This octagonal building was the children's dining room and the last structure to be developed for the sanitarium. Nurses fed the children, and no mothers were allowed. This meant that Dr. Smith could control the diets of children who had eating problems. In fact, all of the houses that were part of the sanitarium had their kitchens removed. The building now belongs to VeeVee Blackshear as part of Bon Air. (Courtesy of Greaton Sellers.)

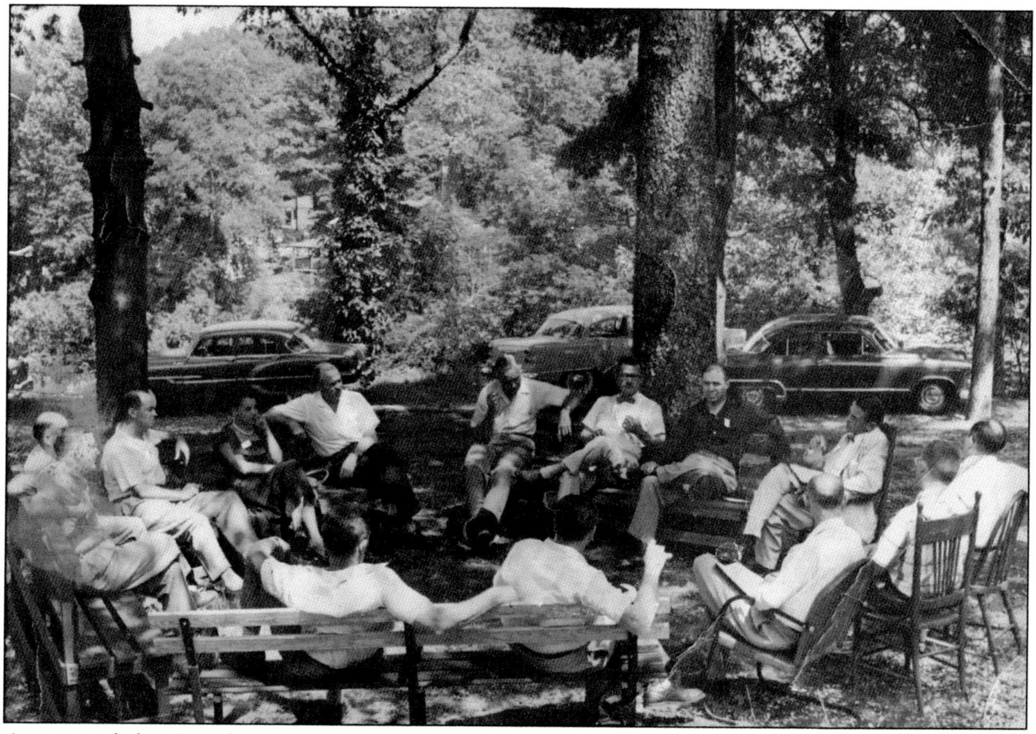

As one of the Southern Pediatric Seminar brochures says, "This combines business with pleasure . . . having fun and learning in a pleasant atmosphere of informality and relaxation . . . the atmosphere is always congenial, friendly and conducive to better understanding." The lectures, indoors and outside, were given by renown specialists from Southern universities that volunteered their services. (Courtesy of VeeVee Blackshear.)

Detail Hall was named for the drug representatives, who during this period were called detail men. They set up the equivalent of a trade show under this shelter (right). Visible are some of the products they sold and the conversations that went with it. It was also another chance to get some fresh air during the day. (Courtesy of Clara Smith Carter.)

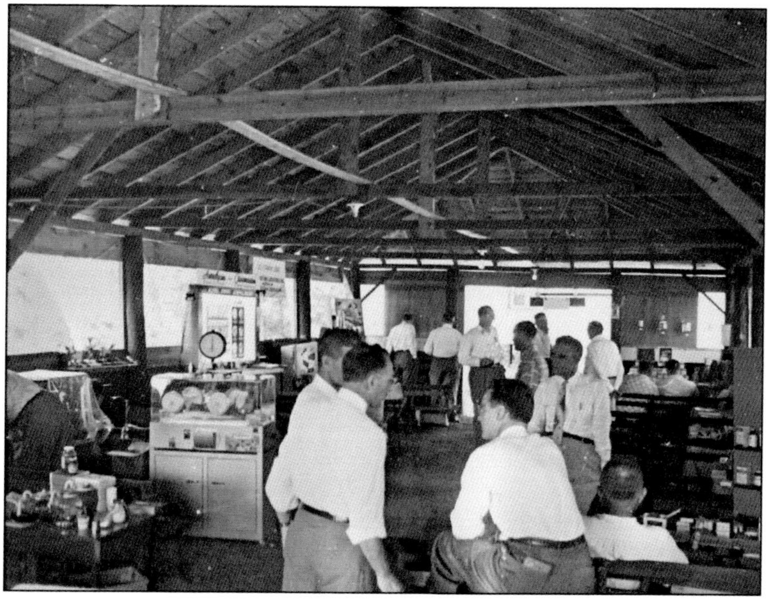

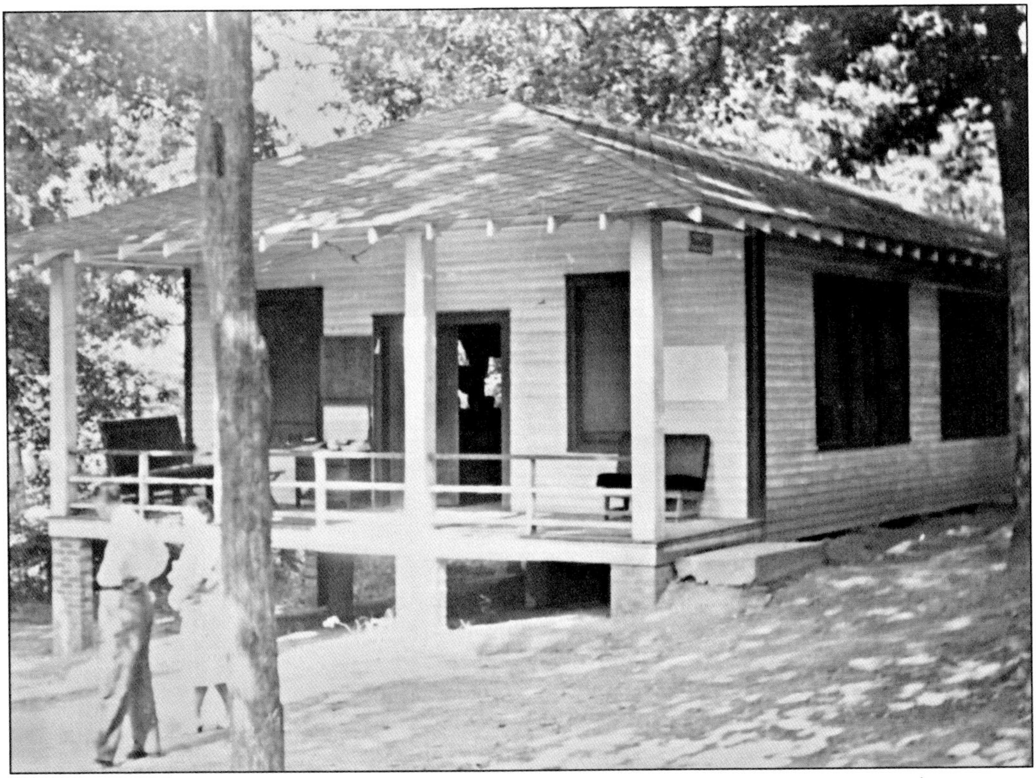

Cottages were constructed to accommodate the growing needs of the sanitarium and seminars. Today, many of the original structures still stand and are private residences, some still owned by the Smith family. Above is Cornell Hall, which was used for lectures and demonstrations for the doctors who came to Saluda for the pediatric seminars. Below are Staton Hall (left) and Cameron Hall (right), both of which were used as housing for the visiting lecturers. (Both, courtesy Clara Smith Carter.)

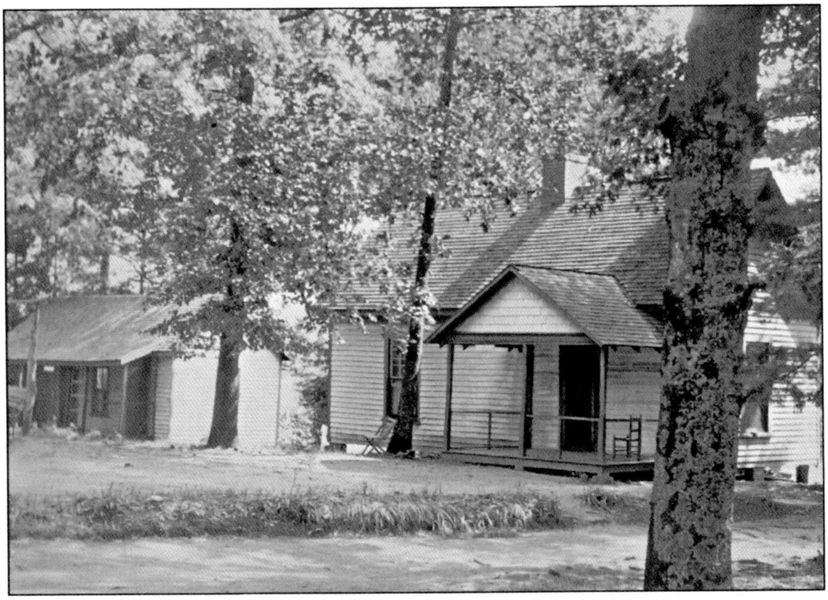

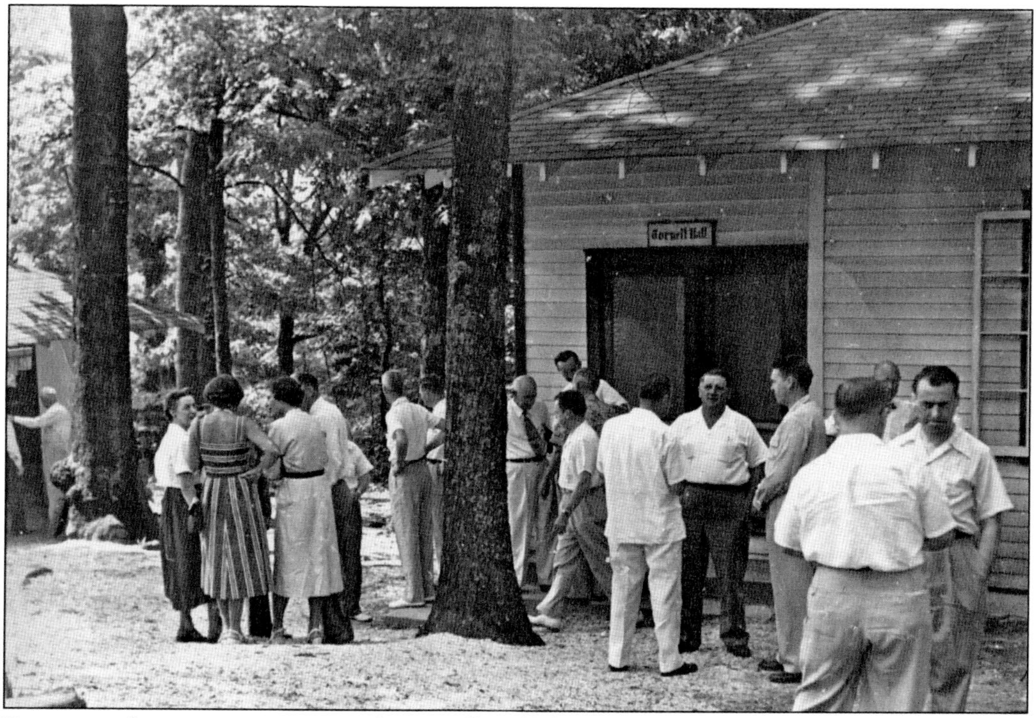

Doctors and nurses converse outside Cornell Hall during a break. Working hard during the day, physicians had fun at night playing bridge, dancing, and telling jokes and stories. One house was even named the Bull Pen, as wild tales and laughter could be heard all over Smith Hill from this building. (Courtesy of Clara Smith Carter.)

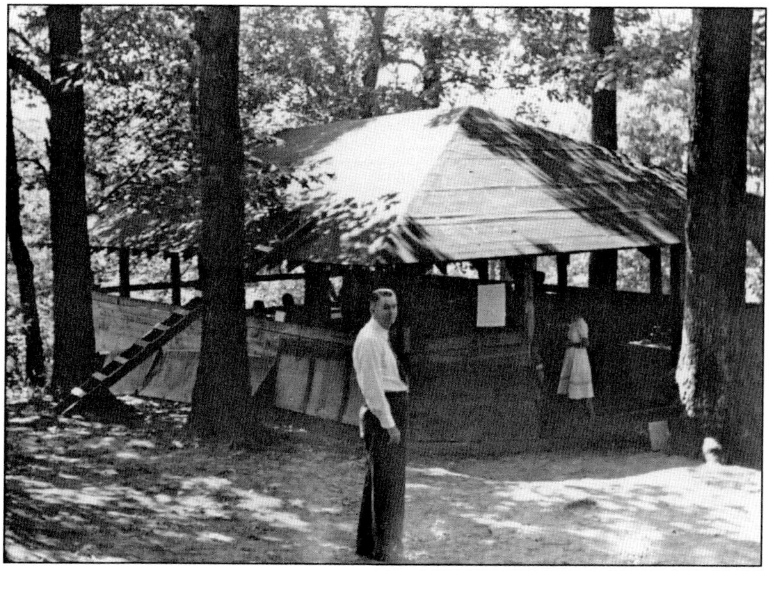

Except for a nominal registration fee, the only income the seminar had was from the commercial houses that exhibited their products. This structure, named for one of the detail representatives, E.M. Stevens from Illinois, provided the perfect spot for the detail men to play checkers or bridge when the physicians were attending lectures. (Courtesy of Clara Smith Carter.)

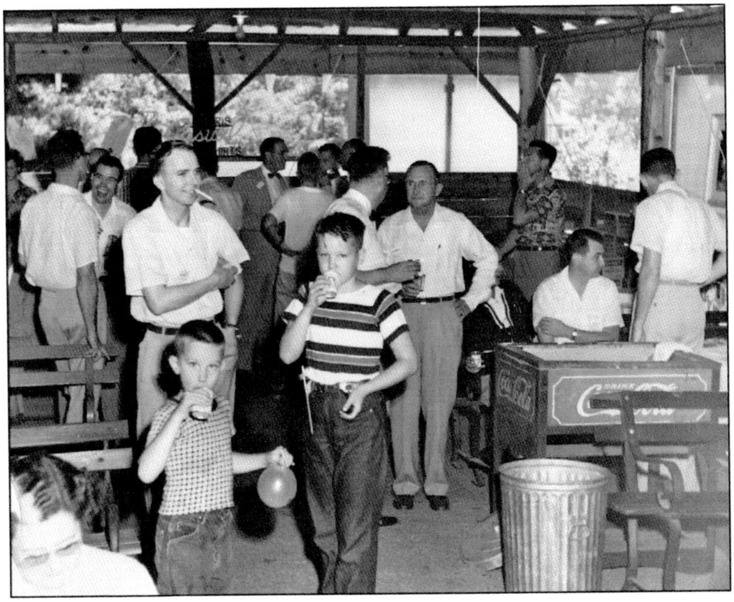

As grandchildren of Dr. Smith, Nettie Owings Sweet, Ammie Owings Weymer, Alice Smith Phillips, and Clara Smith Carter all worked in the Detail Hall selling cokes, candy, gum, and cigarettes. Every grandchild worked during the seminar weeks selling items, cleaning the grounds, or being a guinea pig in the baby clinic. According to these grandchildren, it was a wonderful childhood to be a part of this venture. (Courtesy of Clara Smith Carter.)

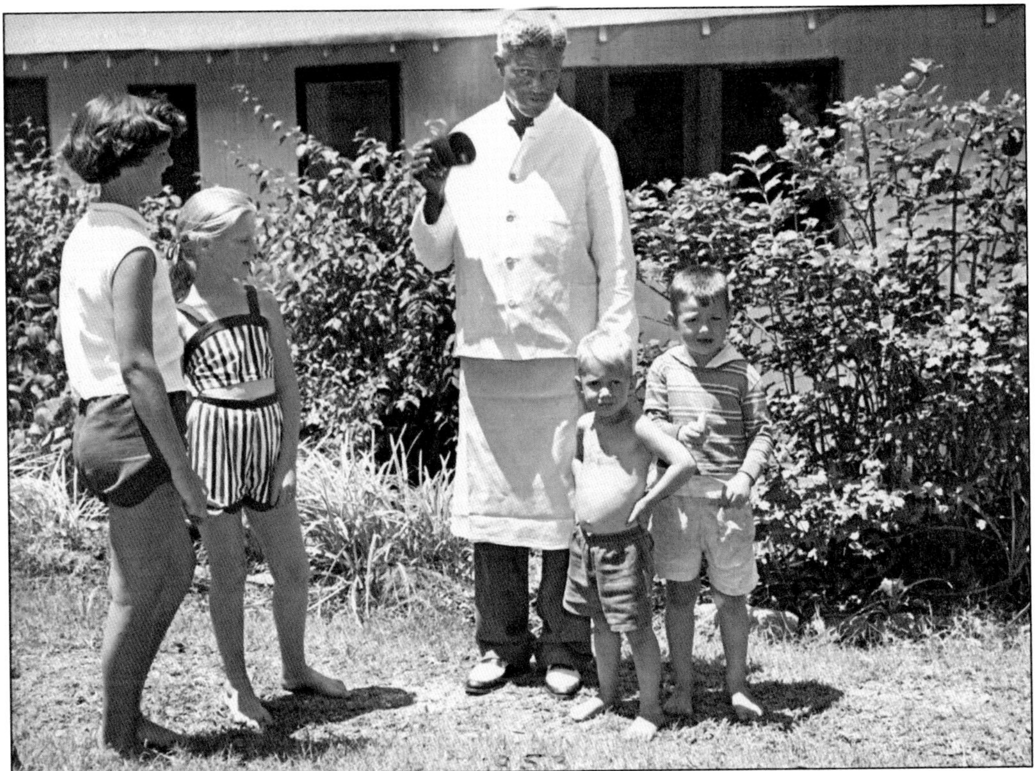

The sanitarium, hospital, and seminars were so special, they encouraged loyalty from faculty and all the workers. Kenneth Jeter, the headwaiter, rang the cowbell that awakened everyone at 7:00 a.m. He was also a favorite of the Smith grandchildren, from left to right, Clara Smith Carter, Ammie Owings Weymer, Marvin Owings, and Ravenel Smith. (Courtesy of Ammie Owings Weymer.)

Six

Saluda's Community of Faith

Faith played a major role in Saluda's history, much as it did in the history of the entire country. Early immigrants came to the United States to practice religious freedom, which formed the backbone of the nation. By the Civil War, thousands of Scotch Irish had moved into western North Carolina, having left their home country to escape religious persecution. They migrated to North Carolina because land was abundant and inexpensive. The Germans also journeyed to the region, and like the Scotch Irish were descendants of Pennsylvania, Maryland, and Virginia's early settlers who had traveled the Great Wagon Road into the Piedmont. With them they brought their traditions, including their religions. In the southern Appalachian Mountains, there were three very distinct ethnic groups that led to a diverse culture—the Native Americans, Africans, and Europeans.

According to old deeds between 1785 and 1788, early settlers built a church on the outskirts of what eventually became Saluda, in Henderson County. A cemetery was established beside it. This church, the old Mountain Page Baptist Church or the old Mountain Meeting Place, was the first church in what became the Saluda township and was the heart of the community for many years, providing a place for meetings, worship, homecomings, and revivals.

Though for decades churches like the old Mountain Page Baptist Church had been offering worship services outside of what became the Saluda town limits, it was not until the town was established in 1881 that churches began to crop up within the town limits. Within the next 15 years, four churches were built, including the Methodist, Episcopal, Presbyterian, and Baptist churches. All four churches still provide worship services today and are vital to Saluda's religious community. Two small churches were built on the outskirts of town to accommodate the influx of the black population arriving to take advantage of the employment opportunities that came with the railroad and tourist boom of the late 1880s. However, with the cessation of the passenger train and the arrival of other modes of transportation, the black population diminished, and those churches no longer offer worship services.

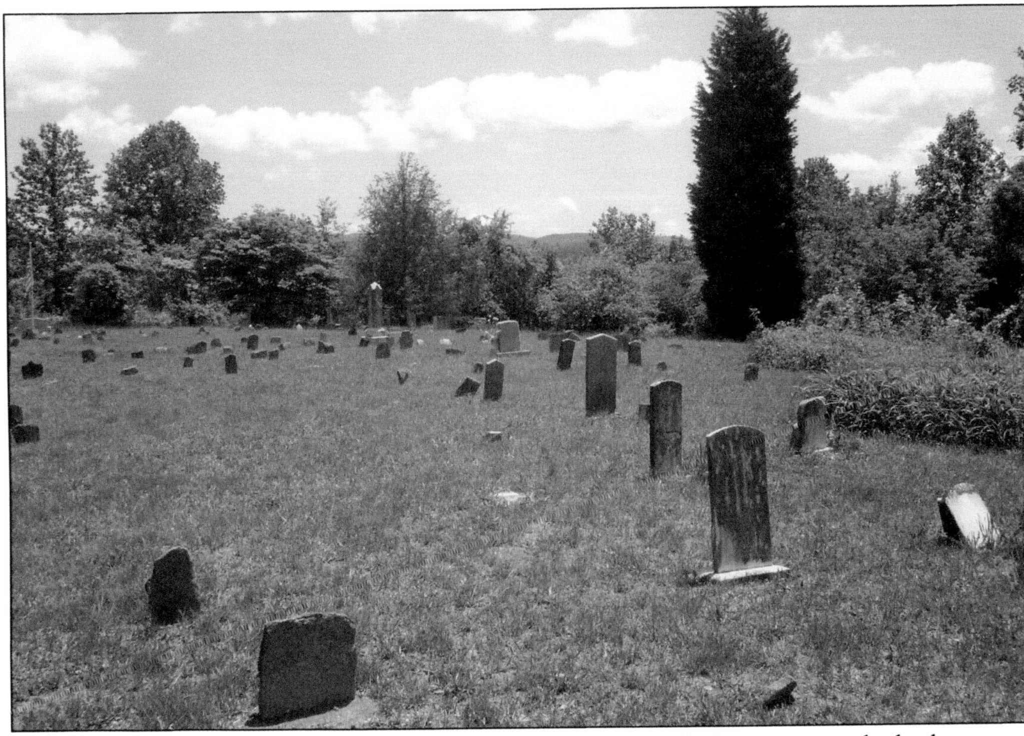

Legend has it that the Mountain Page Community was named after a man with the last name Page, who settled in the area when the land was still owned by the Cherokee. A log church was built in this community in the 1780s, sometimes referred to as the old Mountain Meeting House or the first Mountain Page Baptist Church. The log church burned in 1830 and a frame building was constructed in its place. Pictured above, the church cemetery dates to the 1780s and contains the graves of many of the ancestors of Saluda's families, primarily Paces, including Burrell Pope Pace, who died in 1816. Many of his descendants are buried alongside him, along with a few Thompsons and Hipps. The frame church eventually burned as well. Pictured below is a cinder-block building, located downhill but on the same property, constructed in the 1940s for funerals and occasional services. It contains the original handcrafted pews once used in the old Mountain Page Church. (Both, courtesy of Cindy Stephenson Tuttle.)

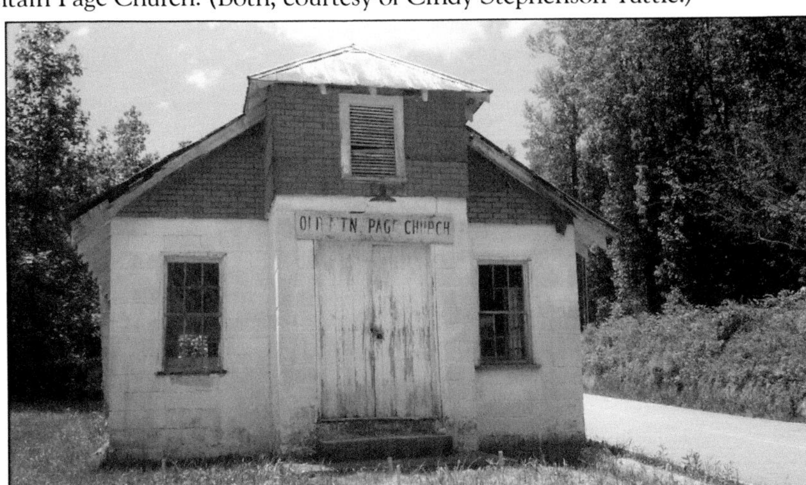

Due to a disagreement among congregants, several members left the first Mountain Page Baptist Church around 1830 and built another church less than a few miles from the first. The new Mountain Page Baptist Church was originally a wooden-frame structure; however, in 1936, the current church (shown at right) was built out of rock, which was quarried and laid by church members. The rock walls were built 18- to 24-inches thick. The bead-board ceilings in the Sunday school rooms came out of the old church. Its cemetery contains gravestones bearing common surnames of Saluda's people and a section for blacks. Records from the 1830s indicate blacks were welcomed as members. There are 10 Confederate soldiers buried in the cemetery. Up until recent years, baptisms were held in a creek at the headwaters of the Pacolet River, pictured below. (Right, courtesy of Cindy Stephenson Tuttle; below, William "Bill" Horace Russell.)

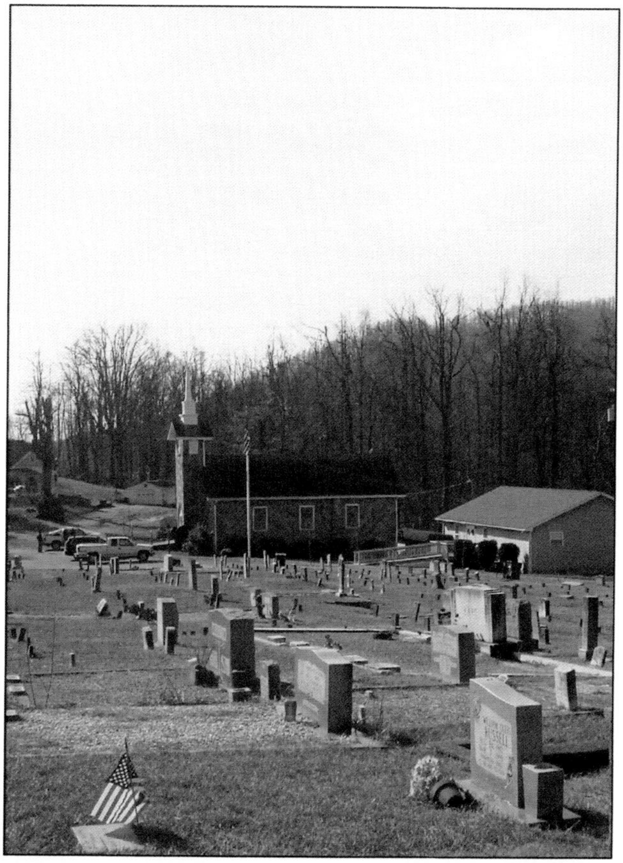

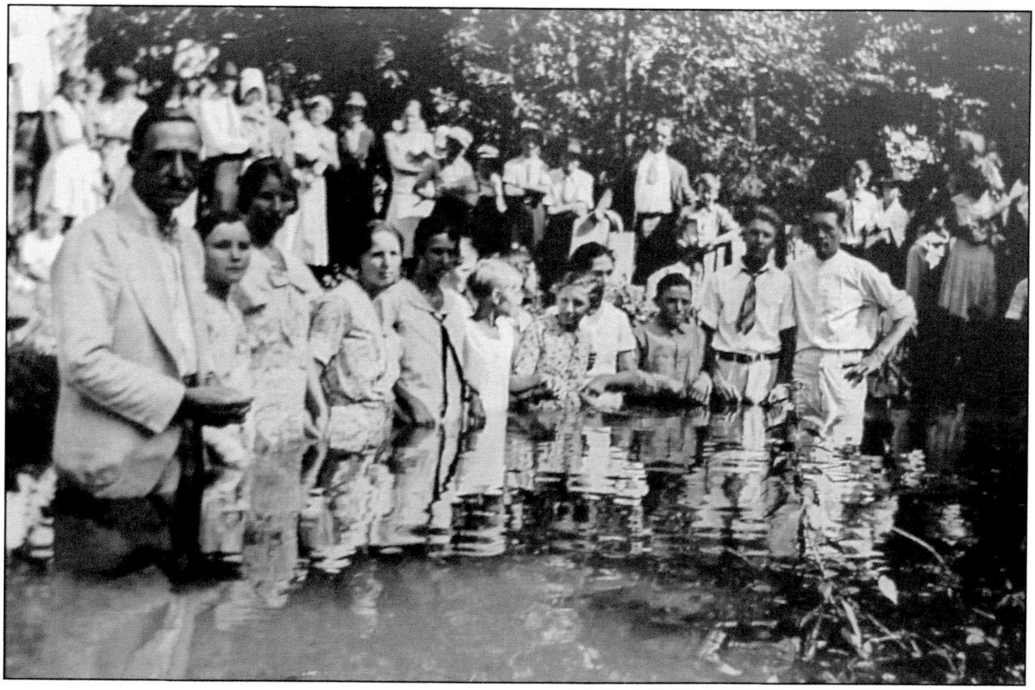

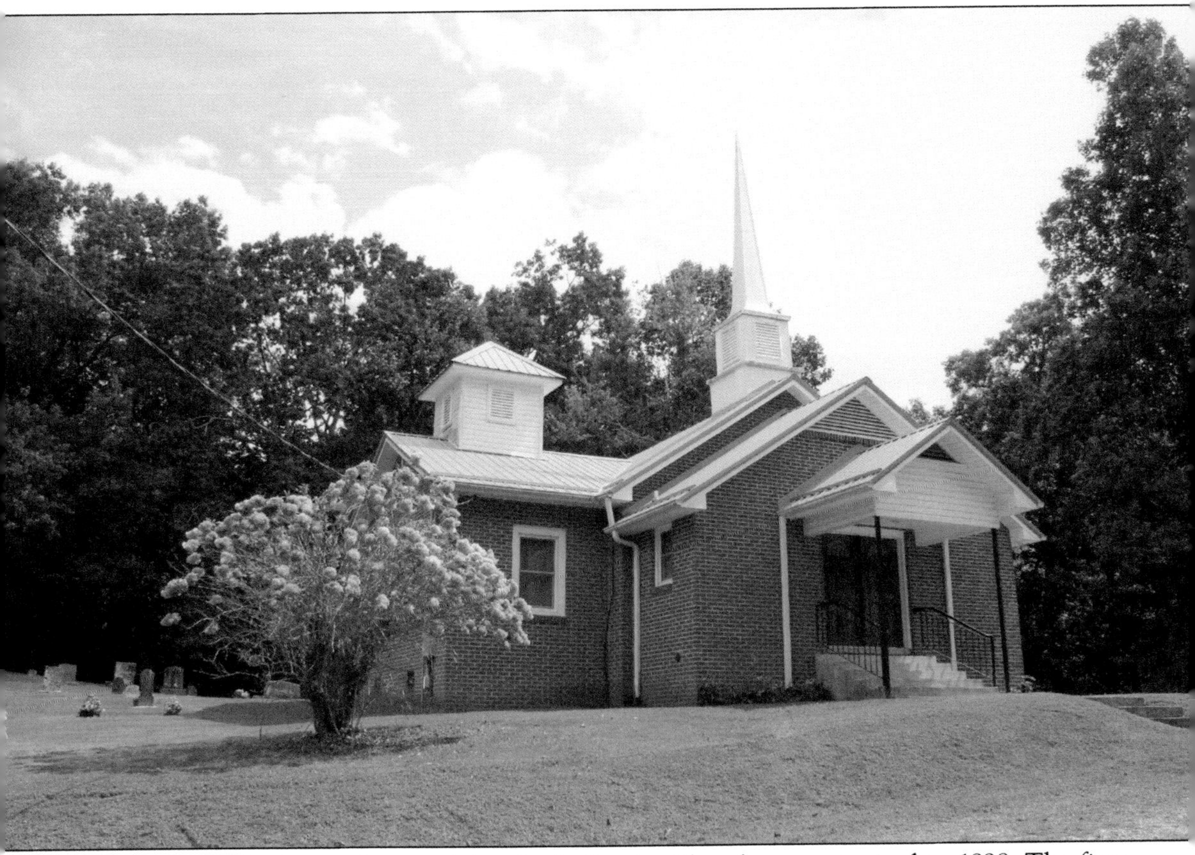

Located in Henderson County, Macedonia Baptist Church was organized in 1898. The first pastor was Rev. William Henry Jones. The church, pictured here in 2014, is the original place of worship, but it has been renovated and modernized. Charter member surnames were Fletcher, Williams, Revis, Arledge, Guice, Staton, Gordon, and Wagener. At least two Civil War soldiers are buried in the church cemetery, including Eli Arledge, born in 1826. On April 2, 1863, he married Mathursa Adeline Pace, and that same year he enlisted, joining Company A, 25th North Carolina Regiment. Under the command of Brig. Gen. Thomas Clingman, the 25th Infantry participated in some of the fiercest battles of the war, including the long Siege of Petersburg. Arledge was captured near Petersburg, Virginia, on April 2, 1865, which was his second wedding anniversary. He was held at Point Lookout, Maryland, until his release on June 22, 1865, after taking the oath of allegiance. Though he never joined the church, the rest of the family were charter members and a daughter, Lydia, taught Sunday school there for many years. (Courtesy of Cindy Stephenson Tuttle.)

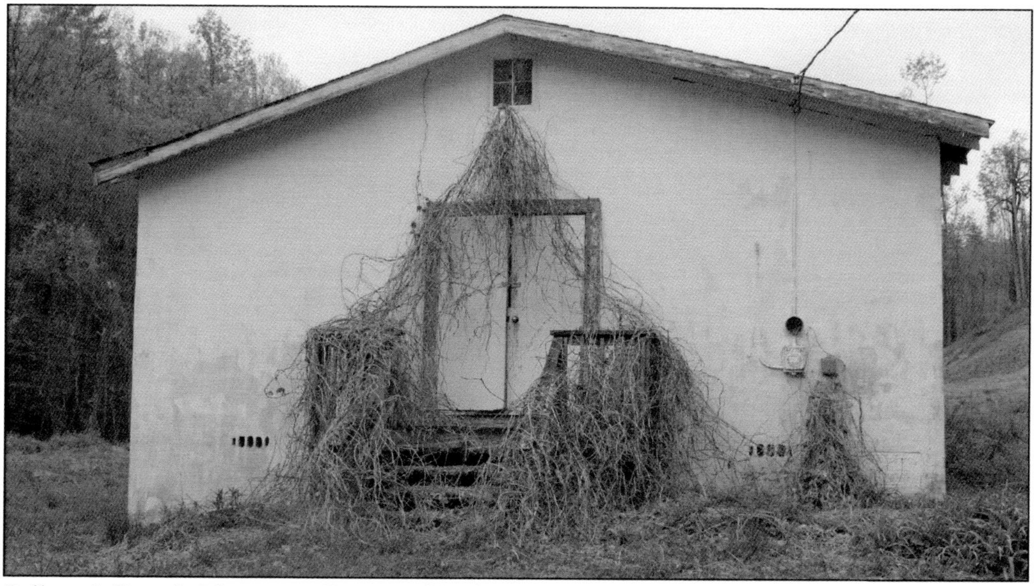

Sullivan's Temple Missionary Baptist Church was founded in 1947 by Phoebia Sullivan, a black woman who was said to have divine powers. She never preached, as it was not her calling, but her son James Sullivan became an assistant pastor. She claimed to receive her inspiration for healing from the book of Psalms. She died in 1956. Pictured here in 2011, her church has been left to decay. (Courtesy of Cindy Stephenson Tuttle.)

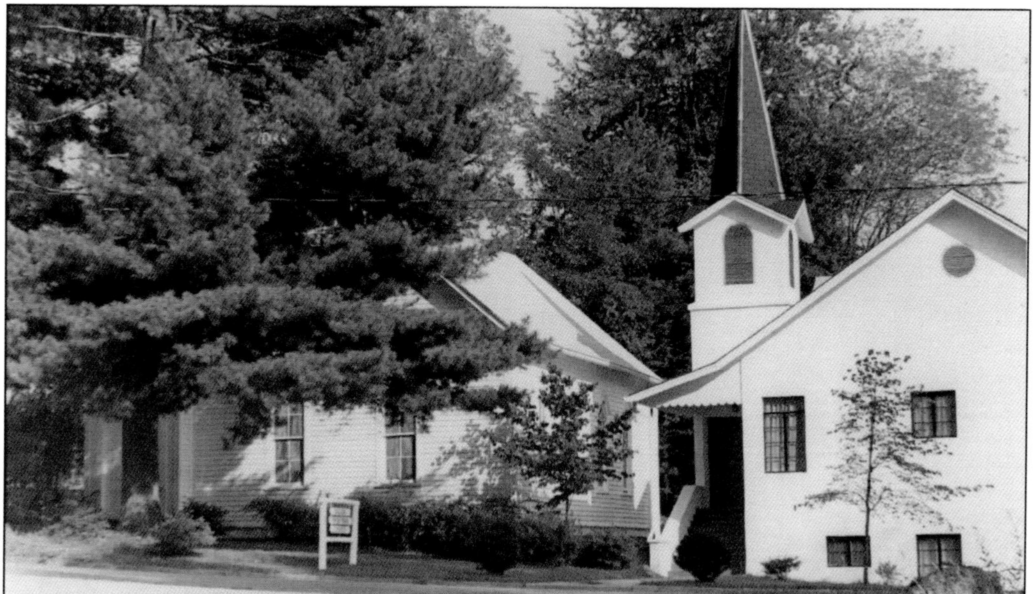

Considered a contributing structure for the Saluda Main Street Historic District's listing in the National Register of Historic Places, the Saluda Presbyterian Church was built between 1895 and 1896 as a multidenominational community church with funding from residents and summer people. It became a Presbyterian church in 1914. The pews were donated by Tryon Presbyterian Church, and the antique pulpit came from South Carolina when a church there closed. The picture above was taken in 1982 and shows the original church on the left and a newer addition to the right. (Courtesy of Martha Coates Ashley.)

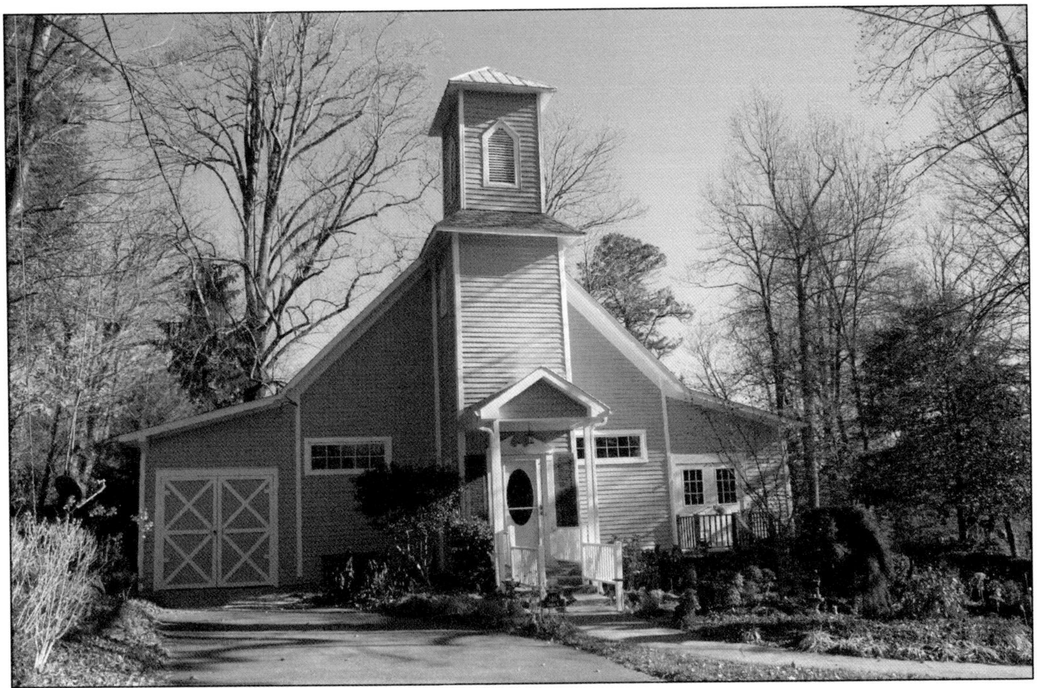

The First Baptist Church of Saluda was organized in 1888. Ransom Woodruff Pace, who had been pursuing the formation of a Baptist church in the town of Saluda, donated land and $100. In support, a revival was held by ministers James Blythe of Friendship Baptist Church and J.A. Staton of Refuge Baptist Church. Out of that revival came the original 28 members. The original church building was dedicated on October 31, 1894, with Pastor Blythe preaching the dedication service. In 1923, the church purchased the lot on which the present church now sits. A ground-breaking ceremony, pictured below, was held on October 9, 1955, for a multipurpose building, which was completed in 1956. A new sanctuary was completed in 1961, and it is still in use today. The original church, pictured above, is now the private residence of Corinne Gerwe. (Above, courtesy of Cindy Stephenson Tuttle; below, from the album of Lola Ward, courtesy of Judy Ward.)

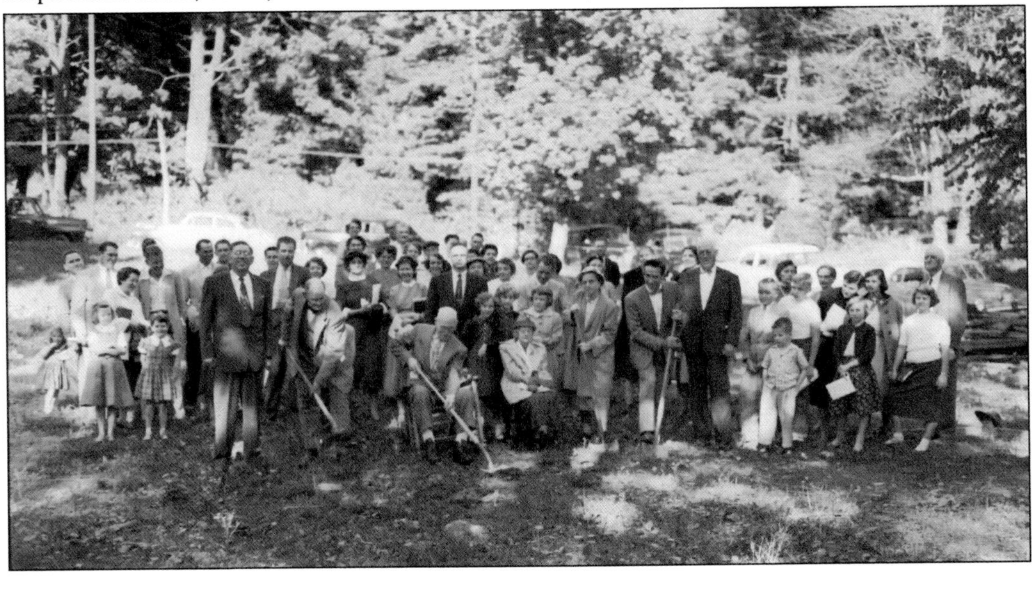

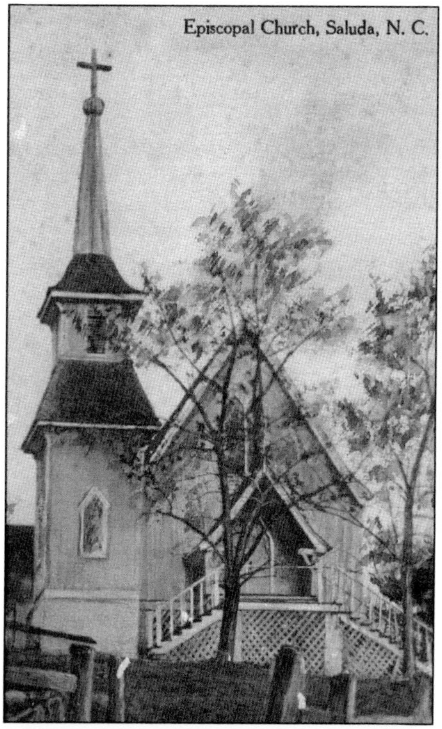

Placed in the National Register of Historic Places in 1982, the Episcopal Church of the Transfiguration is an excellent example of the Carpenter Gothic style. The church was finished in 1889 and formally consecrated in 1891. Rev. John DeWitt McCollough, an architect, carpenter, and builder, designed and planned the structure, raised money for its construction, and actually helped build a large portion of the church, with help from his sons, townspeople, and theological students from Sewanee Seminary. The small building features an exterior sheathed in board and batten siding, a handsome two-tiered bell tower, stained glass in pointed arch and lancet windows, and a richly wooded interior displaying original furnishings carved by Reverend McCullough. Today, membership of over 230 includes full-time and summer residents. A columbarium for deceased members was finished in 2014 along with restoration of the memorial garden. (Right, courtesy of Jim Boyle; below, courtesy of Episcopal Church of the Transfiguration.)

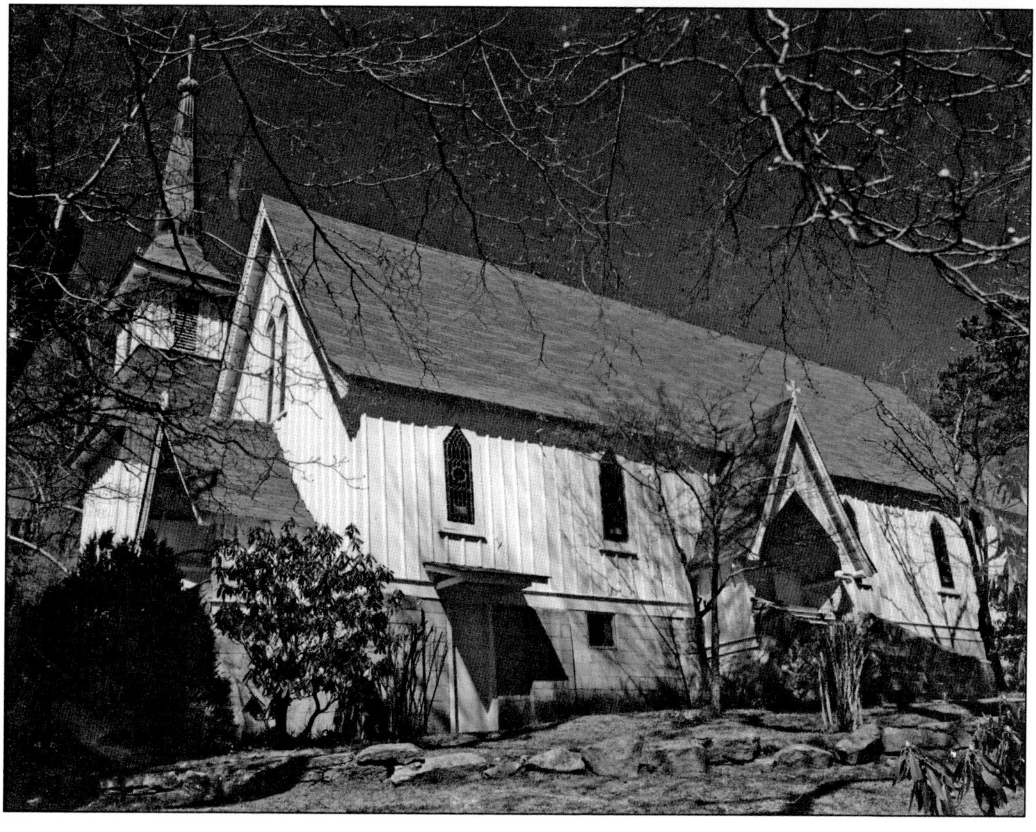

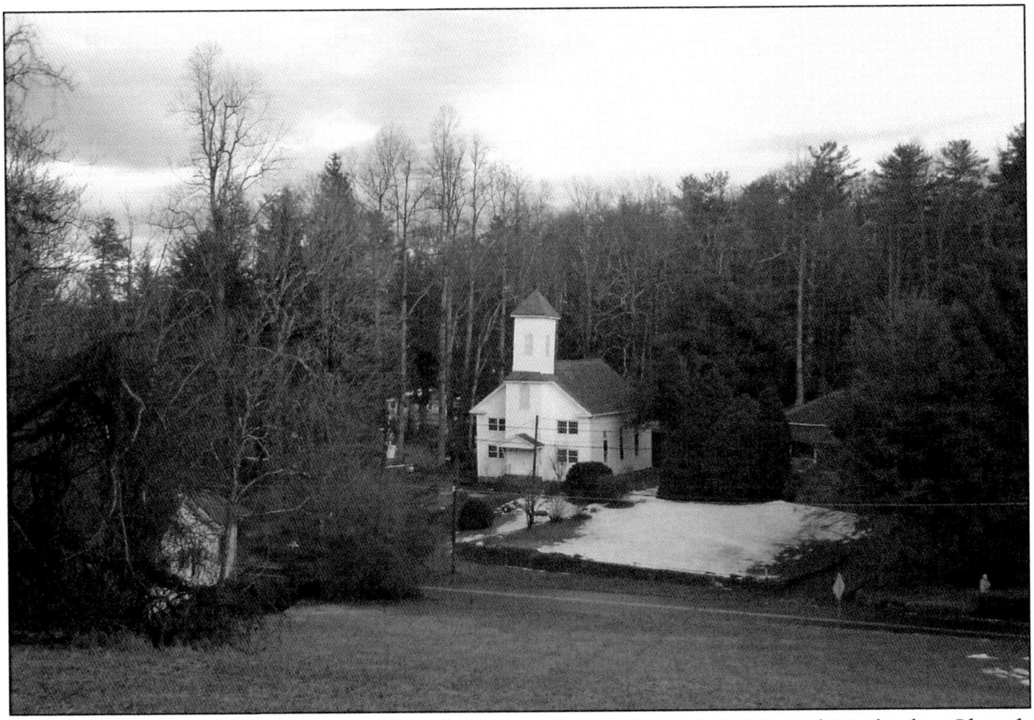

This modern view (above) from Smith Hill, is proof that the Saluda United Methodist Church has remained historically intact, despite it being the oldest of the four churches within the Saluda city limits. Organized by H.C. Tanner on land that he donated, the church opened in 1882 and was built across the street from his Mountain Home Hotel. It first operated on a "circuit" for Polk County, Saluda and Hendersonville. It is now in the Blue Ridge District and its minister serves both the Saluda and Columbus Methodist churches. The image below, taken on a snowy day, provides a closer look. (Above, courtesy of Cindy Stephenson Tuttle; below, courtesy of Saluda United Methodist Church.)

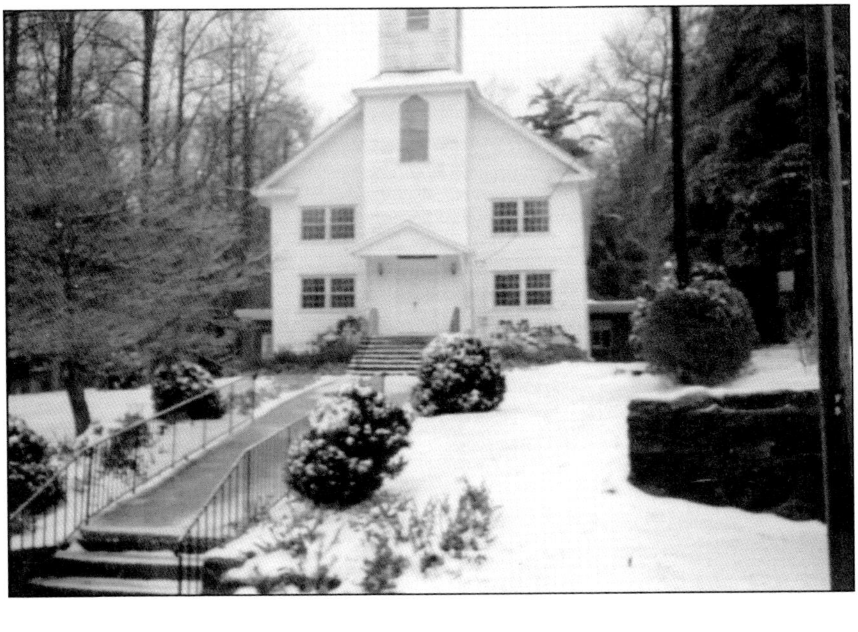

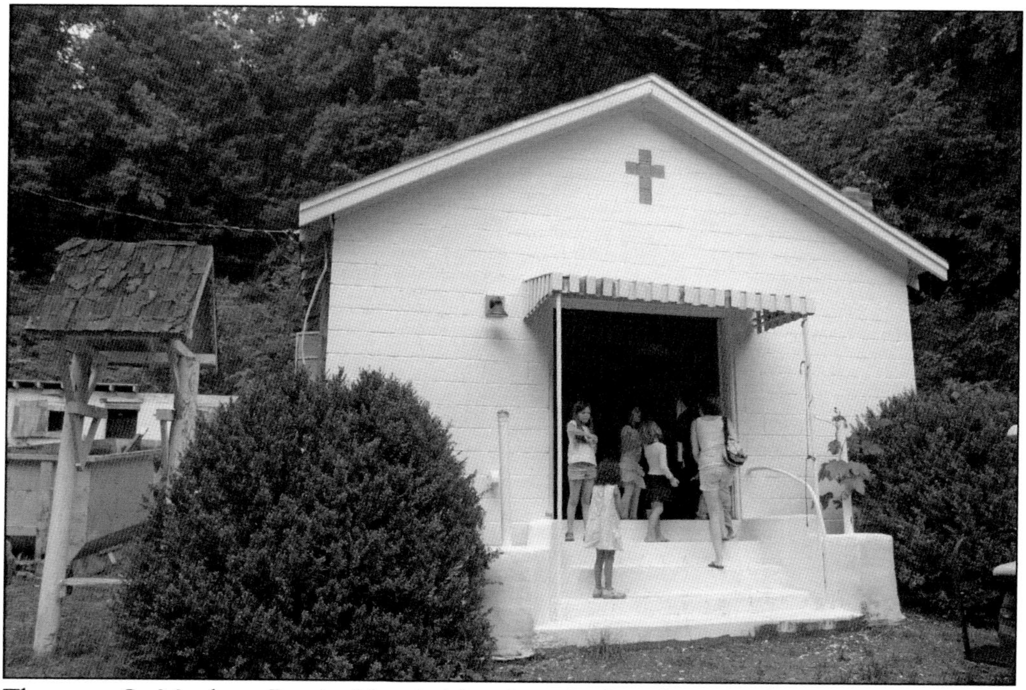

The newer St. Matthews Baptist Church (above) was built in the 1930s from cement blocks and is located across the railroad tracks from the original site. The church was home to a faithful African American congregation, many having relocated from South Carolina seeking work during the heyday of the railroad. Baptisms were often held nearby in a pond dug by hand, as shown in the photograph below of Rev. Lester Samuel Suber baptizing a member of his church. The church doors closed as the congregation dwindled, likely due to the lack of jobs when the passenger trains ceased to run. After sitting vacant for many years, Betsy Burdett purchased the church in 2014, along with its original cast-iron bell. She wishes to preserve its African American roots and use it to bring the community together for special celebrations. (Above, courtesy of Cindy Stephenson Tuttle; below, courtesy of Pearlie Suber Harris.)

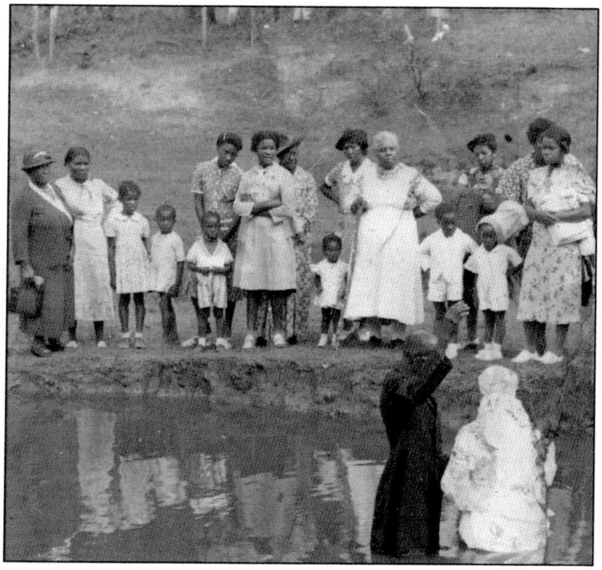

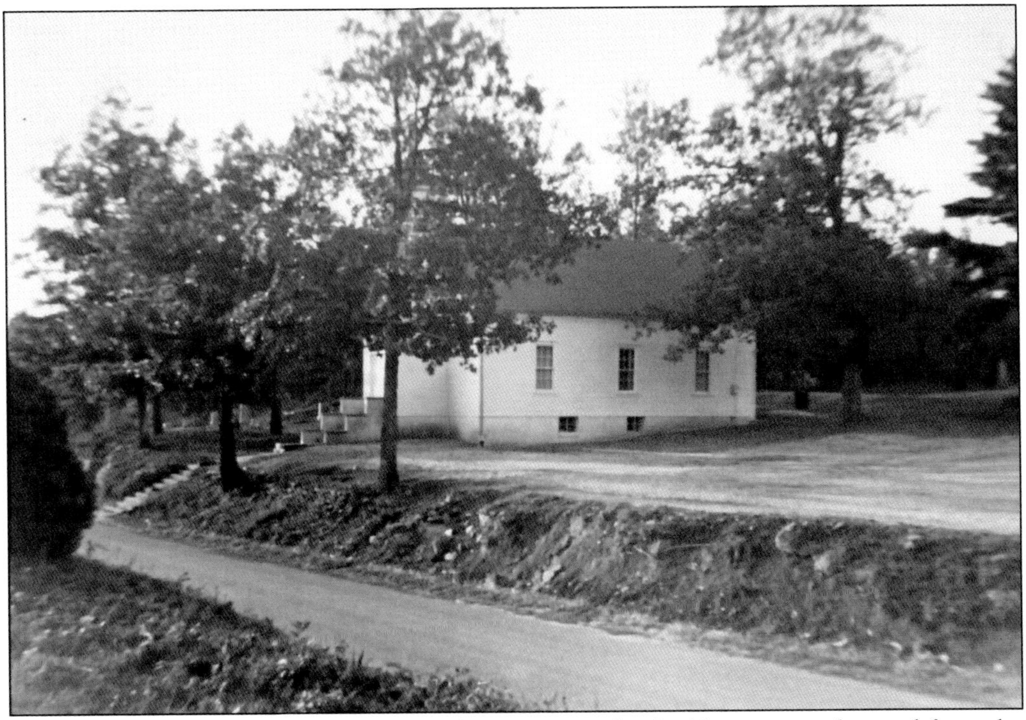

Friendship Baptist Church was organized in 1834 in a log building across the road from the current church (above) and is thought to be the second-oldest church in the Saluda township. The present-day church sits on the old Howard Gap Road, which now dead ends into Interstate 26. Originally, the church was called Forman's Chapel and was used by both the Methodist and Baptist denominations, with ministers alternating their services each week. The cemetery is older than the church with some dates from the 1700s hand-carved in stone. Local lore says that Indians and slaves may be buried there. The photograph above was taken in 1958. Rev. Henry "Hank" Vegter has been the pastor since 1964. The picture below is of a hymnal dated 1834, shared during a church tour held in 2011 in celebration of Saluda's 130th anniversary. (Above, courtesy of Mildred Thompson Skelton; below, courtesy of Cindy Stephenson Tuttle.)

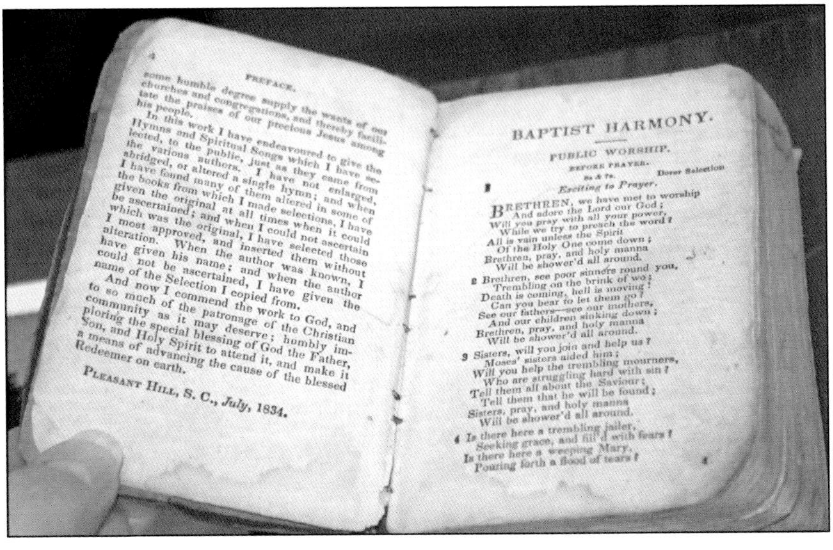

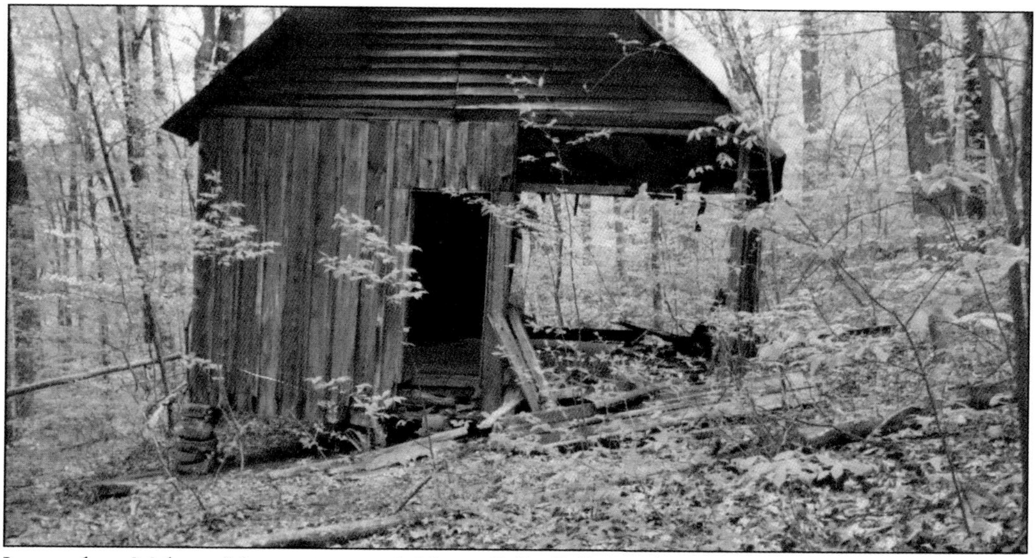

Located on Melrose Mountain near Melrose Falls, Fall Creek Baptist Church, organized in the mid-1920s, is now abandoned. Rev. James Broadus Middleton built the small church and was the preacher for 35 years. His payment for services was sometimes fruits or vegetables. There is a graveyard at the church with many unidentified stone markers, but there are markers for the Waters and Jones families, too. Reverend Middleton also ran revivals in western North Carolina and South Carolina. (Courtesy of the Polk County Historical Association.)

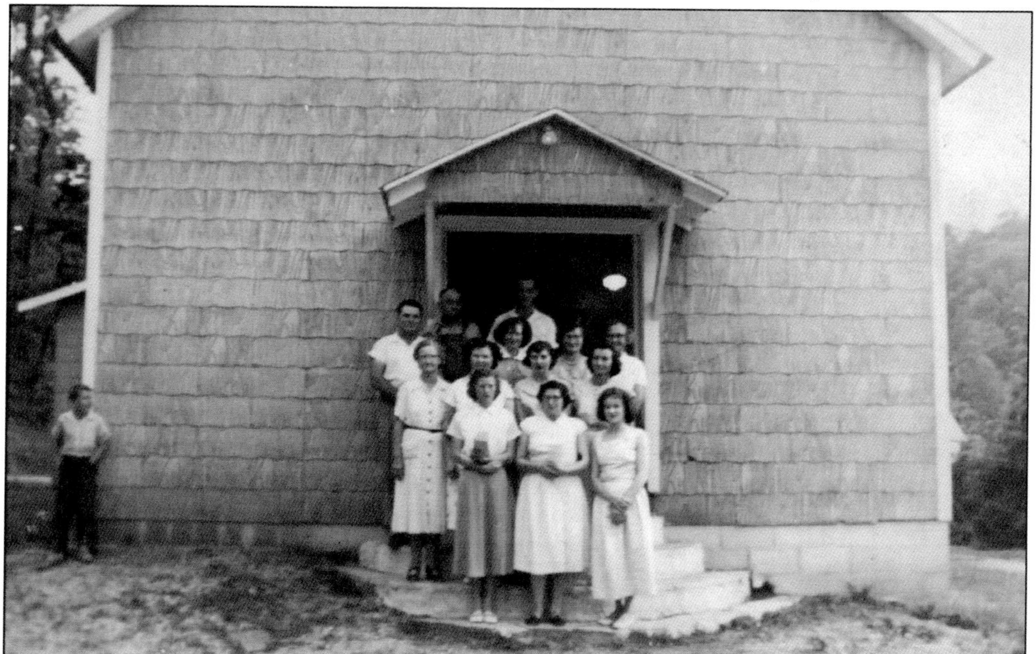

The Melrose population had grown since becoming an important commercial railroad junction. As a result, Fork Creek Baptist Church was organized in 1891 in a one-room schoolhouse located on a mountain one mile above the junction. The land was donated by Decatur Pace, and the new congregation elected Rev. J.R. Rhodes as their first pastor. The third and final brick church building was constructed around 1970. (Courtesy of James Metcalf.)

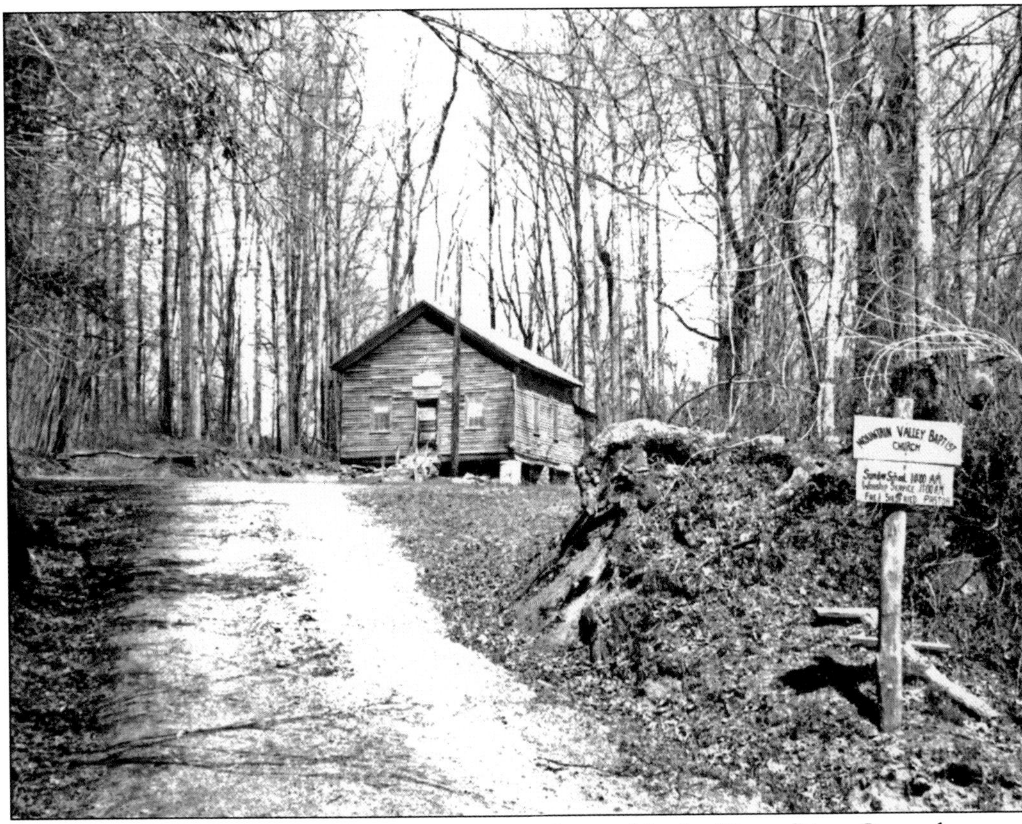

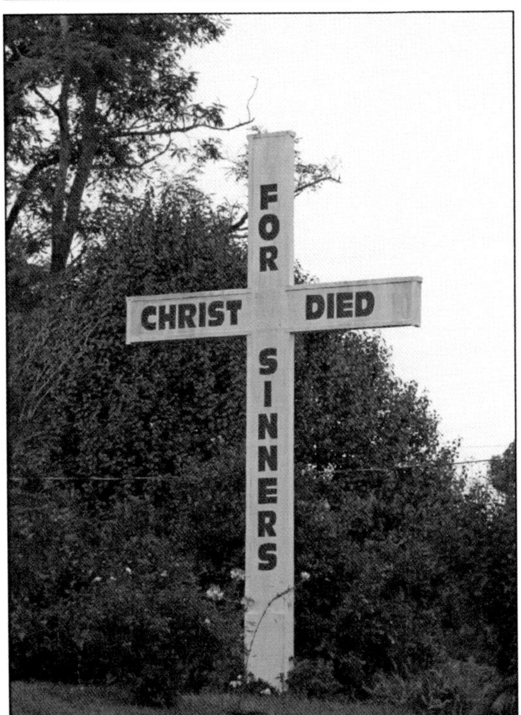

Located in the Green River Cove, the Mountain Valley Baptist Church was organized in 1887. Elder James Blythe was elected the first pastor, and 27 members formed the original church. Located up a narrow road, the steps to the church were made of stone and a latch string opened and closed the door for 100 years, until a knob replaced it in the 1980s. The pews were made of hand-hewn pine, put together with wooden pegs. (Courtesy of the Polk County Historical Society.)

Rev. Hank Vegter, pastor of Friendship Baptist Church for the past 50 years, has personally installed at least 100 crosses in North Carolina, South Carolina, Alabama, and Tennessee. The first cross was installed at Friendship Baptist Church over 20 years ago. According to Reverend Vegter, who still constructs the crosses today, he does so "as an effective means of revealing Christ and the reality of His salvation." This cross is located at a private residence off Ozone Drive. (Courtesy of Cindy Stephenson Tuttle.)

Seven

Saluda's Unique People

In 2010, the Historic Saluda Committee began to collect oral history interviews from longtime locals and summer folks. Each has been asked, "What makes Saluda so unique?" The most popular response? The people. Though the specific details have varied, all have expressed a genuine appreciation for friends and neighbors, citing various examples of neighborly good deeds. In this chapter, readers will notice a diverse mix of characters, but one will also see that many have captions reflecting the sincerity of these individuals to leave or to have left Saluda a little better than they found it.

For a town the size of Saluda, there are and have been many unique characters. Some have been mentioned repeatedly during oral history interviews. While writing this book, many new characters have been introduced as well. Due to the historical nature of Saluda, it is hard to walk the streets and not feel the presence of these characters, though many are long dead. These characters, ranging from the black woman who was a healer, herb doctor, mystic, and prophet, to the doctor who helped save the lives of countless infants with his medical knowledge, are the people that will forever define Saluda.

Another common theme echoed during the oral history interviews has to do with change. These neighborly people are the same ones that will warn a newcomer that they do not like change. Many have expressed frustration over the newcomers who come to Saluda and begin to try to change things. A frequent remark is, "If they liked it so much to move here, why do they want to change it?" or a favorite, often said by Charlene Pace, "The road that brought them in to town can take them out of town." The general feeling among Saluda folks is that a little change is okay but only a little, please.

A quote from Sourwood Sam, in the summer 1985 edition of the *Saluda Signal* sums it up: "There are some who were born or reared here and others who only appeared here, but we share common ground in our love for the town and the good life that has persevered here."

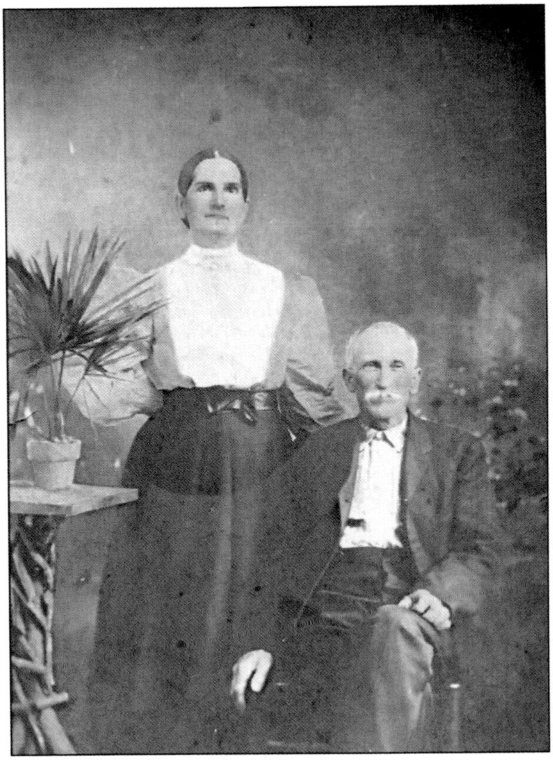

John "Wallace" Thompson is pictured here around the 1890s with his second wife, Louise Jackson Thompson. Wallace was born in 1851 to William "Will" Melvin Thompson and Arrena "Rener" Ballad Thompson. Wallace's first wife was Harriet S. Thompson. They were the parents of William Luther Thompson, who was known for his craftsmanship in home construction. All are buried at the Friendship Baptist Church cemetery. (Courtesy of Mildred Thompson Skelton.)

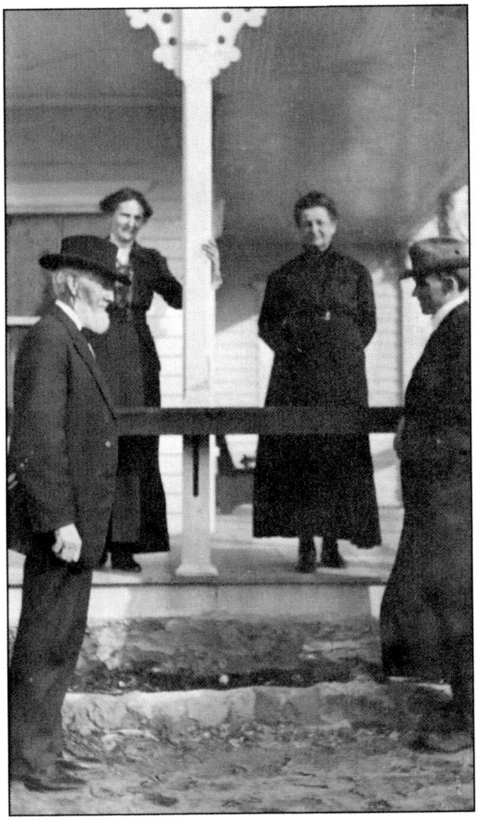

Pictured here are, from left to right, Ransom Woodruff Pace, unidentified, Emily Gilbert Pace (wife), and a Mr. Woodward (guest) standing on the front porch of the Pace House. According to family oral history, as the Pace House was being torn down in the 1960s to make way for the new nursing home, a two-story log cabin was found beneath all the additions. Trees on the property that had been brought over from England were torn down with the house. (Courtesy of Cindy Stephenson Tuttle.)

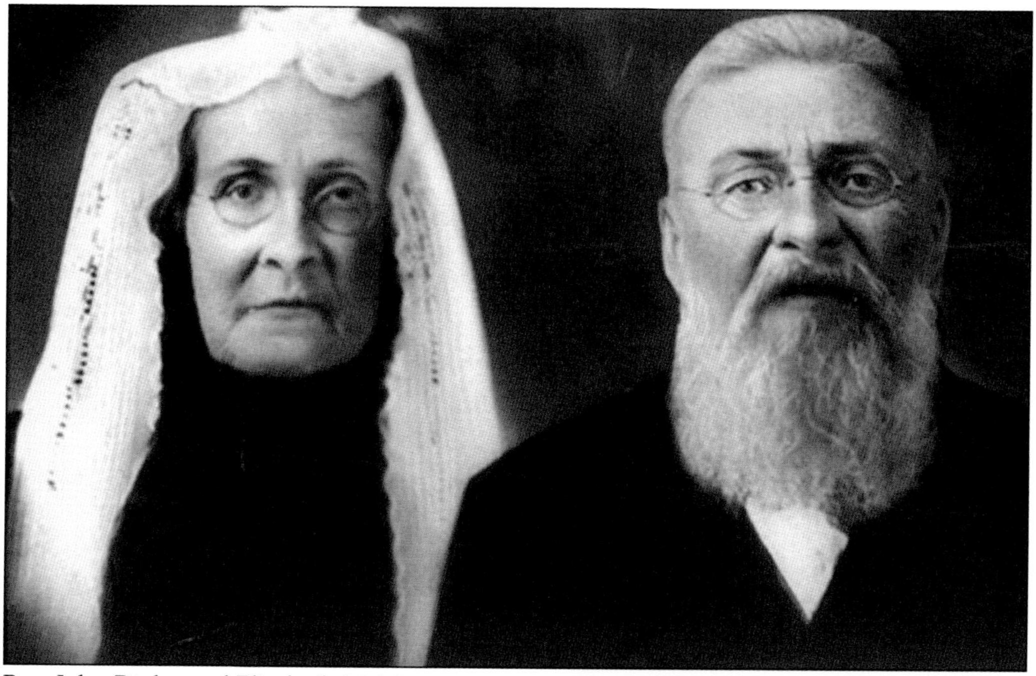

Rev. John Ripley and Elizabeth McMinn Heatherly, living atop Heatherly Heights, provided an observation tower for tourists and the first piped water into Saluda from a spring on their property. As a Confederate soldier, Reverend Ripley was captured and sent to New York. Released in 1865, he walked home to North Carolina. He became a circuit rider preacher and was known for sitting very straight in the saddle while riding a white horse. (Courtesy of Cindy Stephenson Tuttle.)

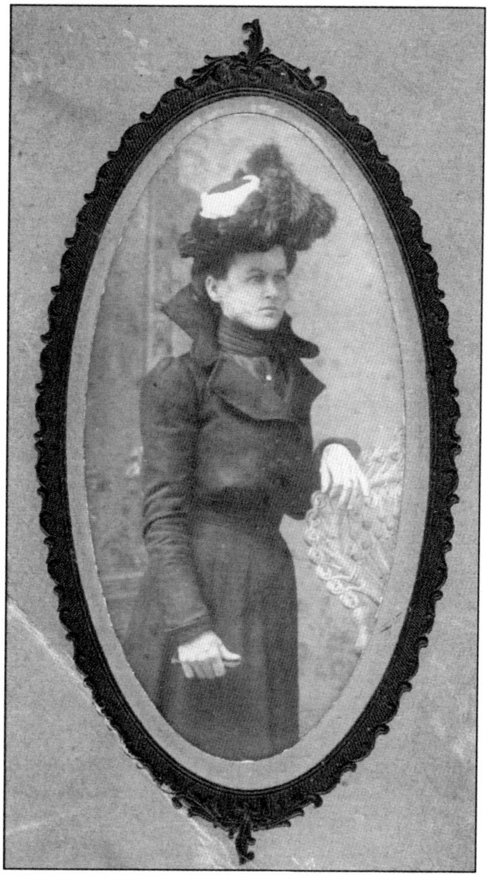

In this photograph, Nancy Margaret Gaines Hart, known as "Maggie," shows off her fine attire. Maggie, originally from South Carolina, was the second wife of James Leander Hart, affectionately known as "Daddy Hart." Married in 1911, the Harts had one child, Margaret Gaines Hart. (Courtesy of Jim Boyle.)

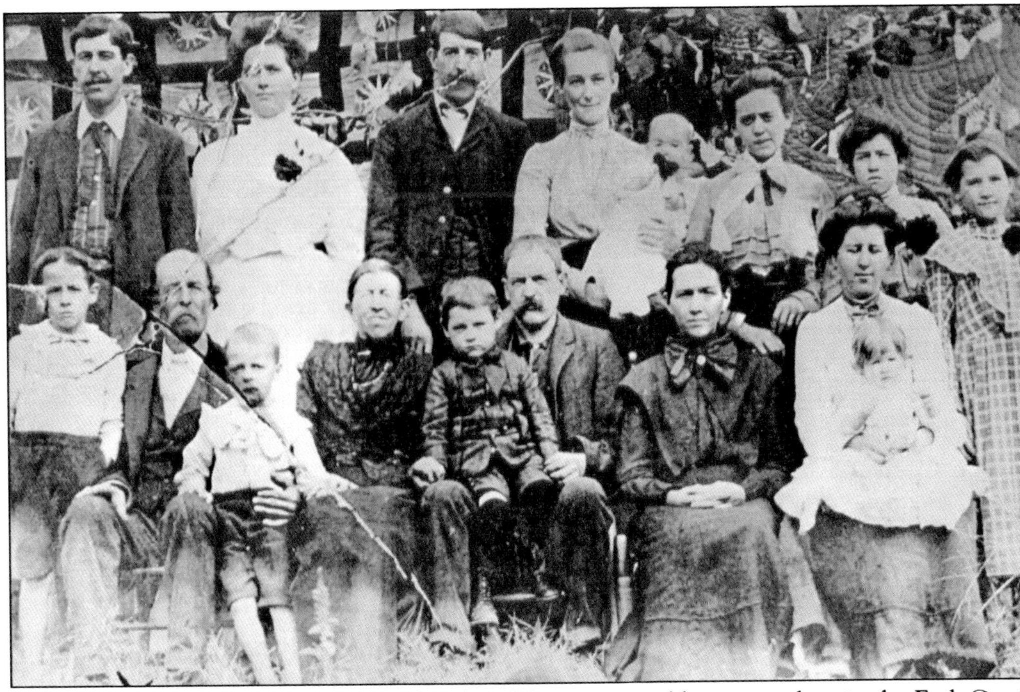

This early photograph of the Morgan family celebrating a wedding was taken in the Fork Creek community near Melrose Lake. Pictured here are, from left to right, (first row) Willie "Bill" Morgan, John Morgan holding Monroe Morgan, Salena Morgan, Ruben Morgan holding Lloyd Morgan, Julia Morgan, and Lenna Pace holding Dora; (second row) the wedding couple, Luther and Addie Morgan, Joe and Mary Morgan, holding Lilian, and Alethia, Odessa, and Myrtle Morgan. (Courtesy of Leon Morgan.)

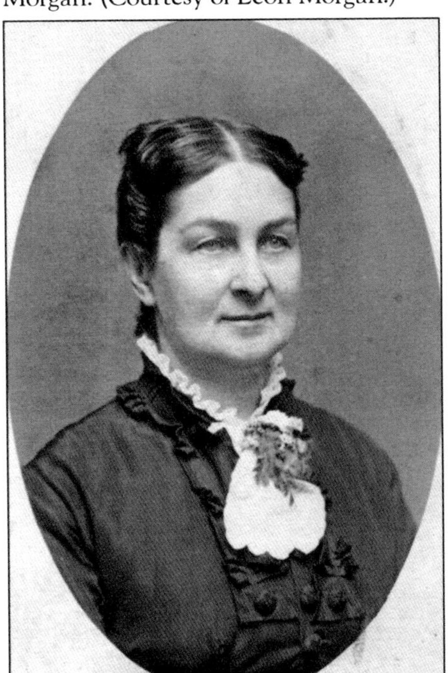

Unhampered by deafness at an early age and later crippled by arthritis, Emily C. Prudden founded 17 schools in western North Carolina and upstate South Carolina, including the Saluda Seminary in 1891. Prudden financed the school initially by selling used clothing and household items donated by supporters, and it was later funded by the American Missionary Society. Prudden also founded Oberlin Home and School, which later became Pfeiffer University. (Courtesy of Pfeiffer University.)

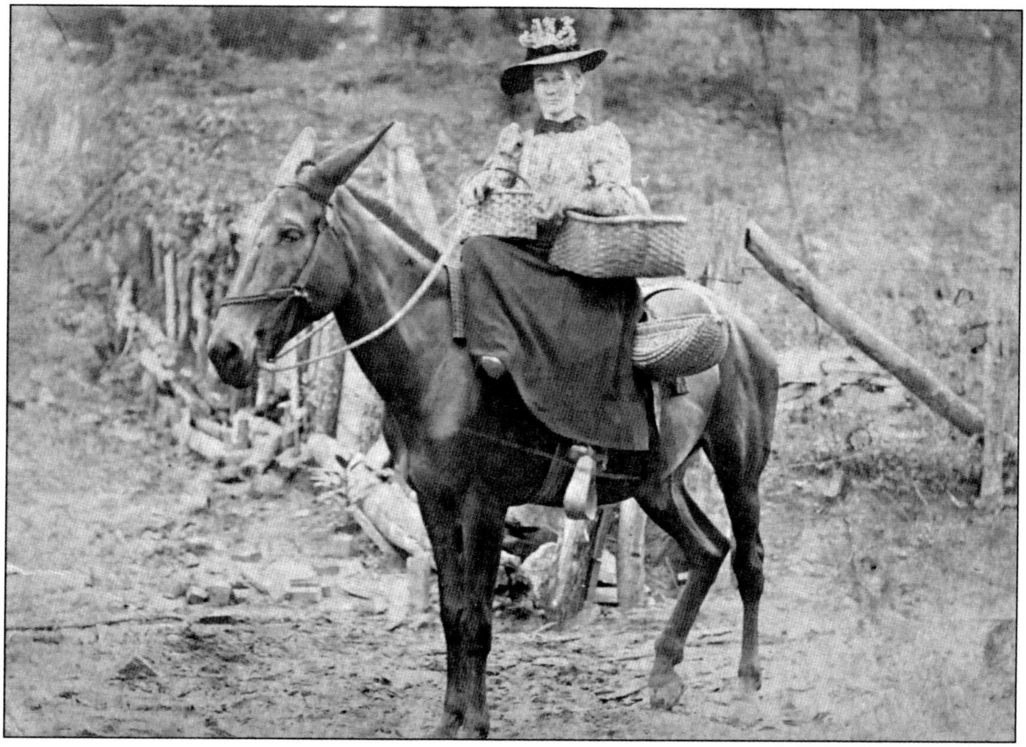

Common in the early days, horses and mules provided a principal means of transportation in and out of the deep coves around Saluda. Sally Henderson McMurray (above), from the Green River Cove, regularly rode by horseback up the long and arduous winding road to Saluda to sell her goods to merchants. (Courtesy of Mildred Thompson Skelton.)

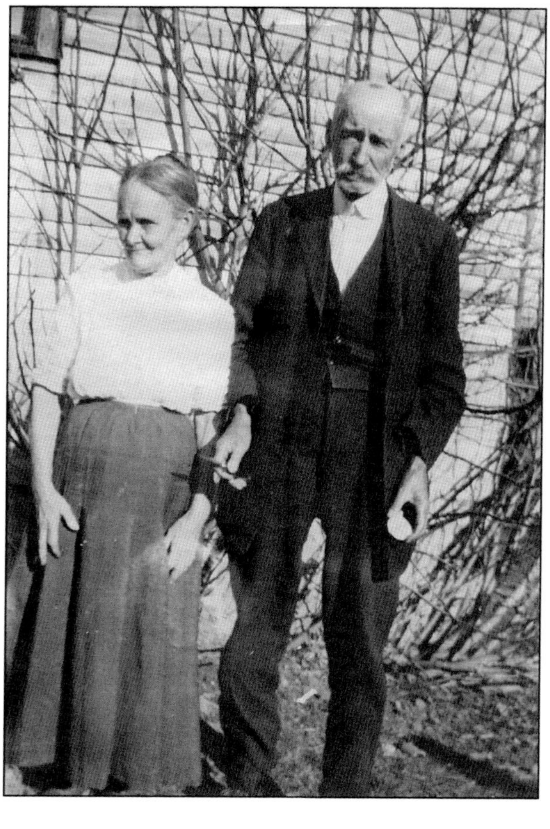

Pictured here, John Thomas Hipp was born in 1854, and his wife, Emily Dow Owens Hipp, was born in 1860. According to the 1920 census, they lived on Louisiana Avenue. The Hipps had 12 children and farmed for a living. (Courtesy of Caroline Hipp.)

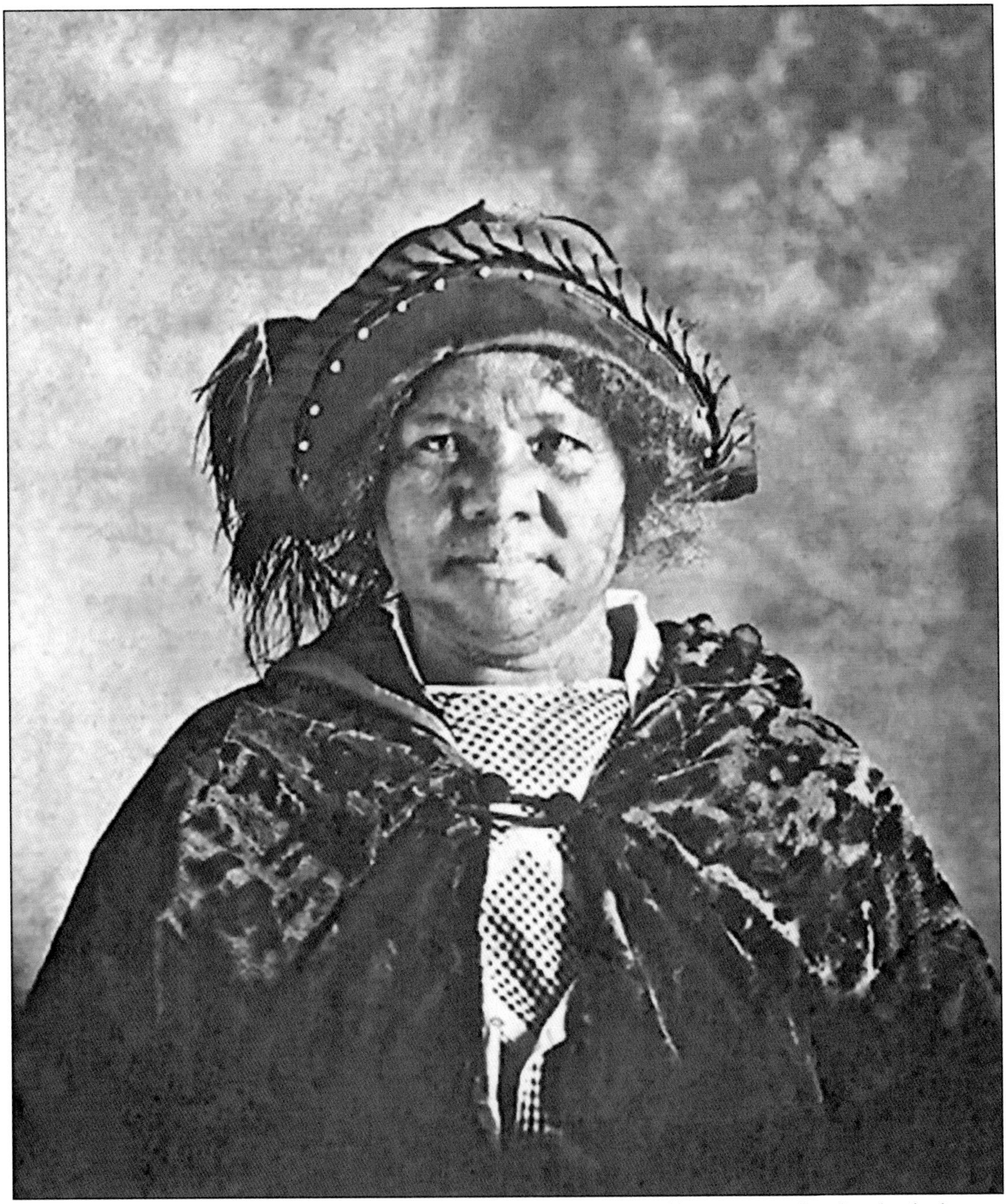

Born to former slaves in South Carolina, Madame Phoebia Sullivan was a healer, herb doctor, mystic, prophet, and leader in Saluda's black community. She arrived in Saluda in the late 1920s after the death of her husband, bringing with her 16 children, and it is said she adopted 20 more. According to her memoir, *From the Cradle to the Crutch*, she experienced her first vision in a dream on her ninth birthday, when she was given a Bible by a messenger and left with the power to heal by the laying on of hands. Those who believed often arrived at her door by the busload from all over the country. Founding Sullivan's Temple Missionary Baptist Church in 1947 was her greatest accomplishment. She often held grand celebrations on the church grounds, where a bounty of food was served, and all were welcome. According to the engraving on her tombstone in the black section of Mountain Page Cemetery and death records, she was born in 1855 and died in 1956; however, these dates conflict with her own memoirs. (Courtesy of Charlene Pace.)

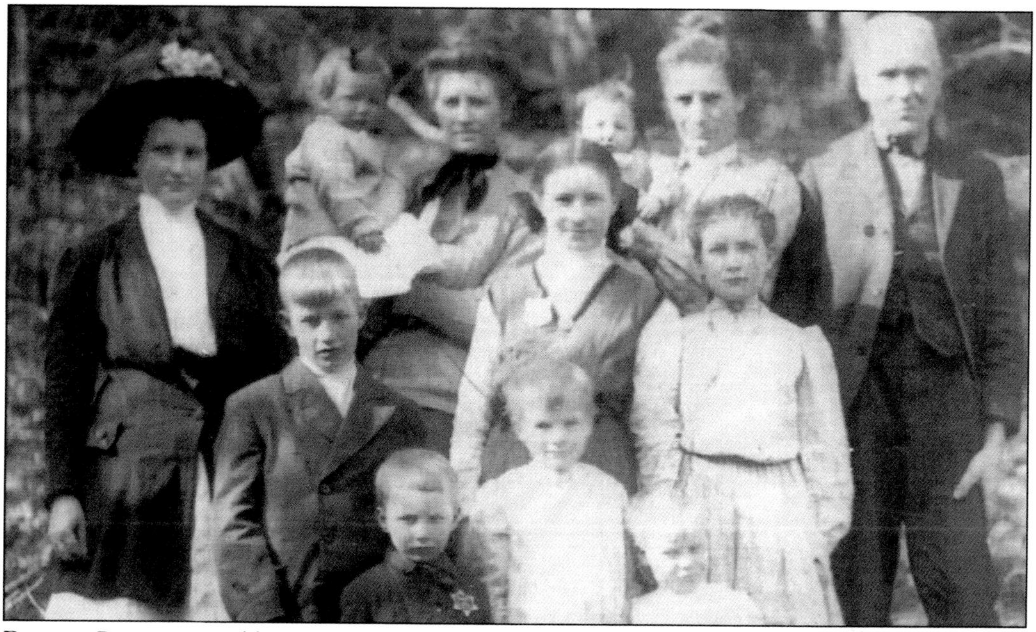

Decatur Pace, pictured here around 1912 with his second wife, Mary Burns, and their children, donated the land for the Fork Creek Baptist Church and became the first church deacon. In 1878, Pace, also a moonshiner, was involved in the shooting of Chief Deputy US Marshall Rufus Springs near Hogback Mountain. Another man was charged and later acquitted. (Courtesy of James Metcalf.)

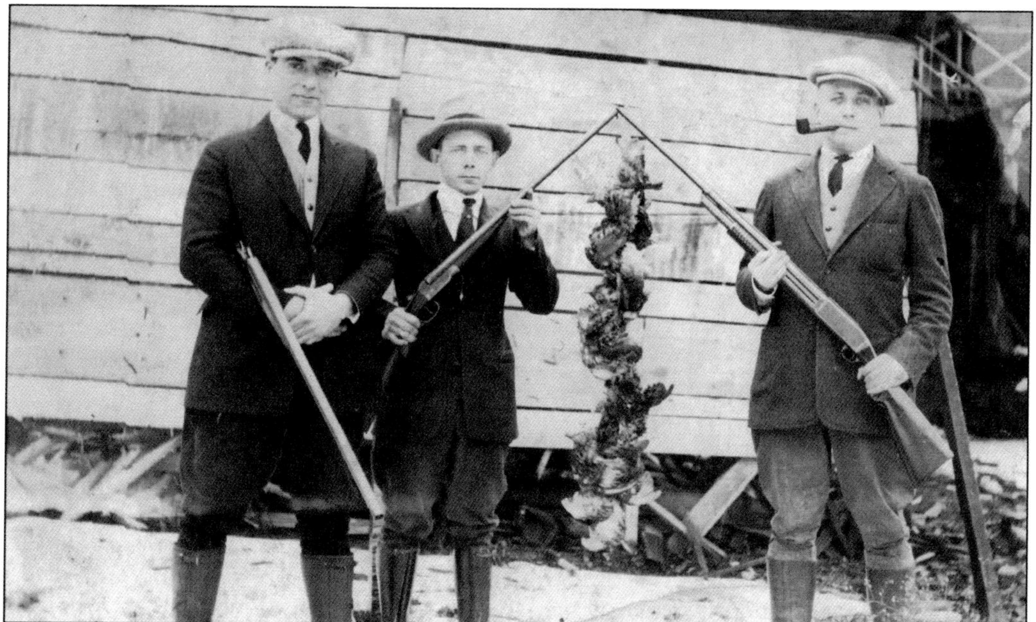

From left to right in the 1920s, an unidentified friend, John T. Coates Jr., and Radcliff Haffenden successfully undertook the popular pastime of hunting birds. Coates was very active in the civic life of Saluda, serving 12 years as mayor and operating several businesses. He helped organize the Saluda Lions Club and served as president. His family operated Crystal Springs. (Courtesy of Martha Coates Ashley.)

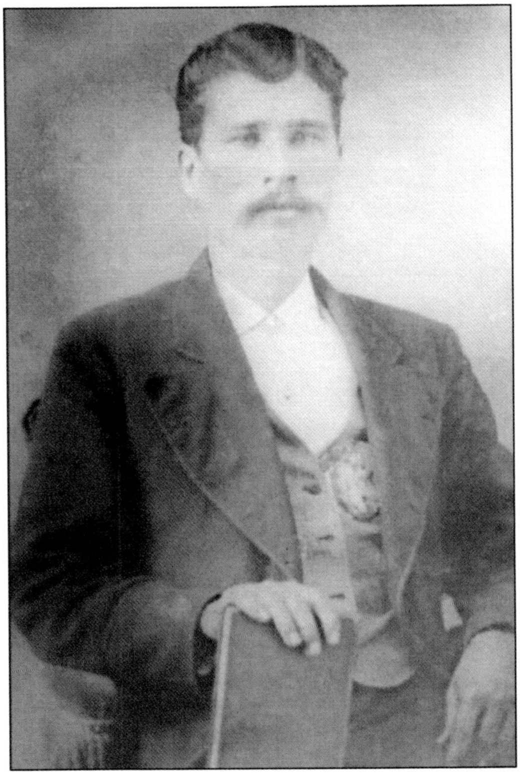

Born in 1854, George Washington Metcalf, hid family livestock in the woods during the Civil War to keep them safe from renegades and deserters who frequently robbed families of their precious commodities, and he later was employed as a prison guard over the convicts building the railroad. The 1880 Tryon Township census has him listed as living in the household of Edward Stansill, a railroad engineer, along with 31 African American convicts. (Courtesy of James Metcalf.)

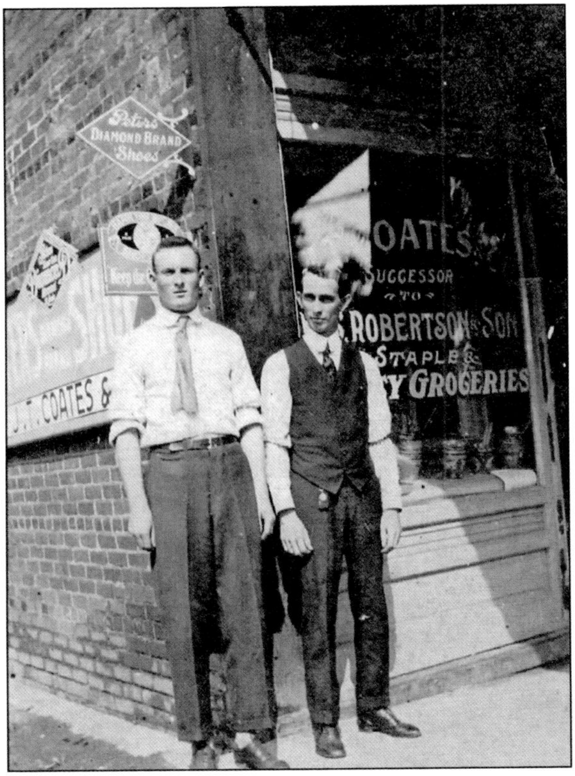

Clarence Pace (left) and W.C. Robertson (right) stand on the corner of Church and Main Streets, in front of what is now the city hall building. Pace was a switch-tender for the railroad at the primary safety track for many years, and Robertson was the longest-serving sheriff of Polk County, having served seven terms. He declined to run for reelection in 1908. (Courtesy of Charlene Pace.)

William Luther Thompson (right) and Otho Brownlow "O.B." Garren (below) are credited with building many of the fine Vernacular-style homes in Saluda. Luther was married to Sara "Alice" Cantrell Thompson and is well known for building Ryder Hall, the girls' dormitory for the Saluda Seminary, and a substantial addition to the Saluda Inn. In addition to other homes in town, he built several houses on Louisiana Avenue for family members. Not only a builder, O.B. Garren was a professional photographer and was one of the town's first mayors. Garren was married to Margaret "Maggie" Pace, daughter of Ransom Woodruff and Emily Gilbert Pace, who operated the Pace House. According to Polk County grantor books, O.B. and Maggie Garren conveyed 54 parcels of land, upon which many homes were built, from 1895 to 1930. (Right, courtesy of R. Clark Thompson; right, courtesy of Cindy Stephenson Tuttle.)

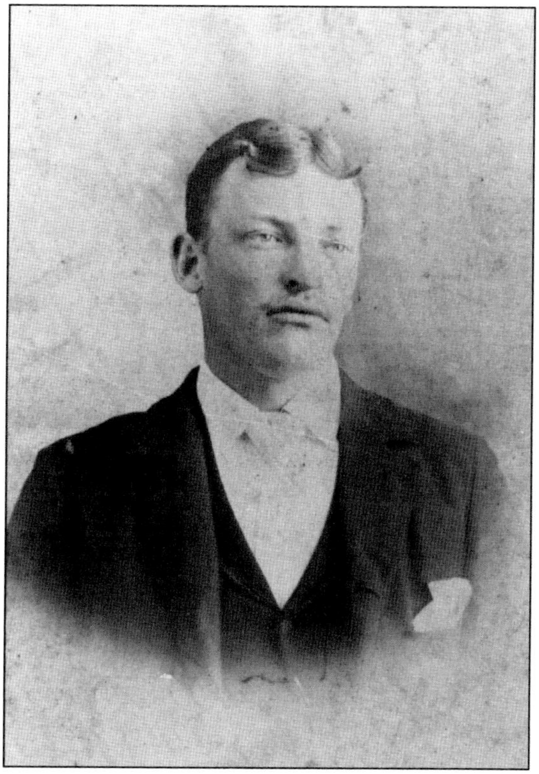

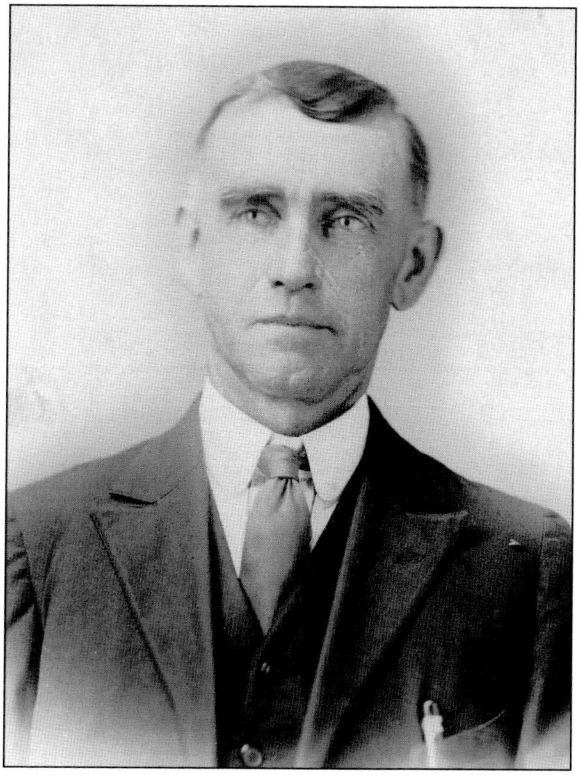

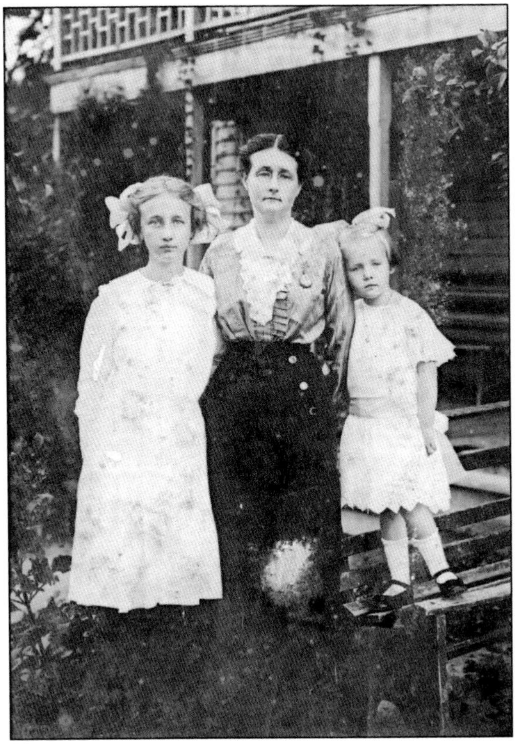

Pictured here is the family of O.B. Garren; from left to right are Lucile, Maggie, and Kathleen. Lucile was the town clerk for Saluda and married Fred Robertson. Maggie was widowed in 1940 and later married Rev. Daniel Earnhardt, minister of the Methodist church. Kathleen was an elementary schoolteacher and taught private piano lessons. She was married to J. Raymond Stephenson Sr. (Courtesy of Cindy Stephenson Tuttle.)

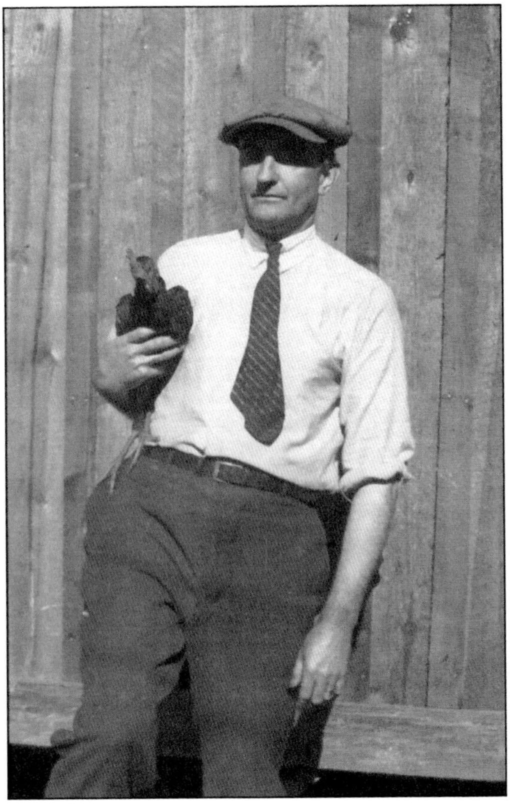

Jethro Garren was in the photography business with his brother O.B. Garren and is also credited with documenting early Saluda. They operated a photography gallery downtown. Their parents were Andrew and Elizabeth Morris Garren. Jethro never married and resided at the Pines, a boardinghouse owned by his sister Mattie Garren Hopkins. The Garren and Morris families can be found as early as the 1700s in western North Carolina. (Courtesy of Charlene Pace.)

James Leander Hart, affectionately known as Daddy Hart, was born in 1858. He worked for Andrew Tanner's crew that surveyed the land for the railroad and claimed to strike the first lick in building the town. Daddy Hart was a jack-of-all-trades, including acting as postmaster for 17 years. He operated a general merchandise store and was the town undertaker. Despite adversities, he was known for his soft heart. (Courtesy of Jim Boyle.)

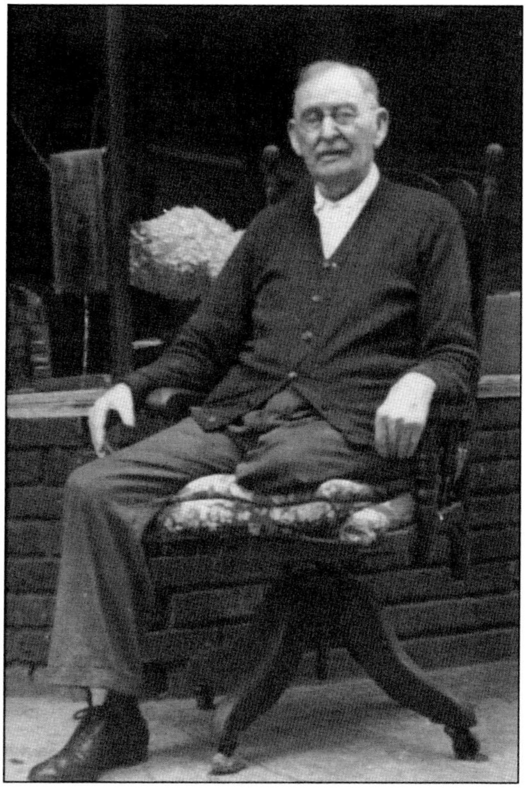

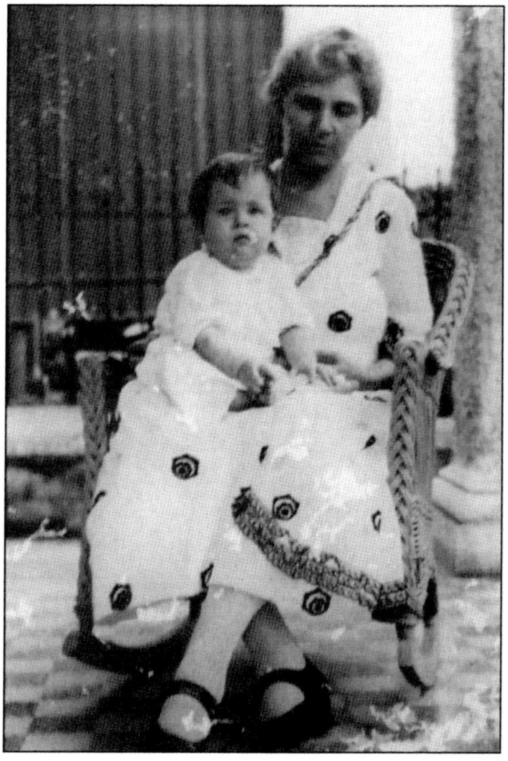

Pictured here is Henry Twiggs Jr. (left) and his mother, Bernice Twiggs, in the early 1900s. Henry Twiggs Sr. worked for the British Railways in Havana, Cuba, and the family came to Saluda every summer on a boat to Key West and changed to a train in Florida, which brought them to Saluda. The Twiggs purchased a home on Florida Street, and today the home is still owned by the Twiggs family. (Courtesy of Henry Twiggs Jr.)

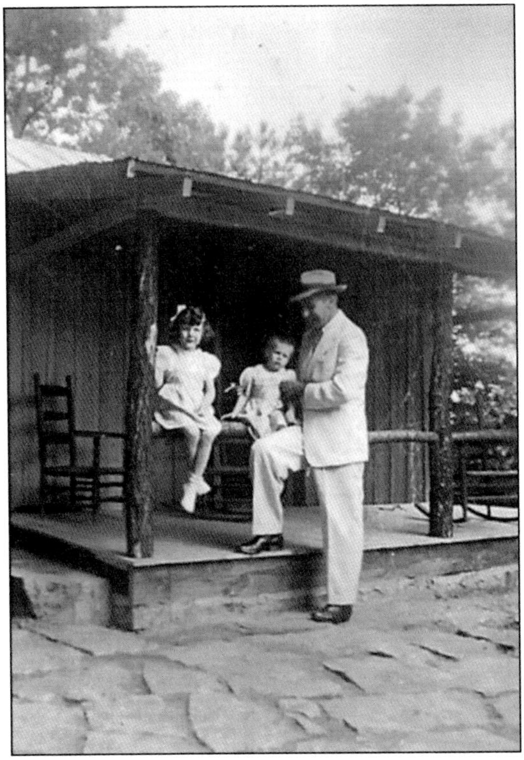

Edwin (Ed) Bennett Ogden Jr. is pictured here with two of his daughters, Nancy "Nicky" (left) and Mimi, at their cabin atop Piney Mountain. Ed and his wife, Nancy, were American citizens who had a family business in Havana, Cuba. In 1938, the Ogdens learned of Saluda through the Twiggs family, who also resided in Cuba. They were enamored of the area soon after their first visit. Nancy and Ed Ogden had two other daughters, Anita and Ellen (not shown). (Courtesy of Anita Ogden Moore.)

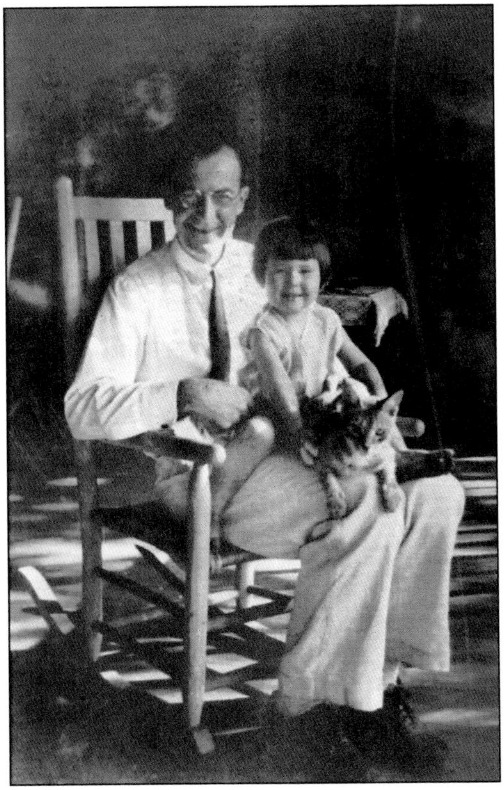

In this photograph, Martha Stoney Anderson rocks with her father, Rev. W.S. Stoney, who along with his wife, Martha Hunt Stoney, hired O.B. Garren to build a Prairie-style log cabin as a summer residence. Completed in 1928, they named it Happy Hut. Martha Anderson and her husband, Bill, eventually moved to Saluda permanently. Martha once said, "When I die I don't know where I will go since I am already in heaven!" (Courtesy of Martha Stoney Anderson.)

Ransom Taylor "Bud" Pace was known as the "Champion Father," for siring 29 children. Married three times, he buried two of his wives. He was born in 1858, and when he died in 1939 at the age of 81, he had 96 grandchildren and 50 great-grandchildren. Ransom is pictured here beside a large bell used to call his children home. An annual reunion is held annually for his descendents. (Courtesy of Charlene Pace.)

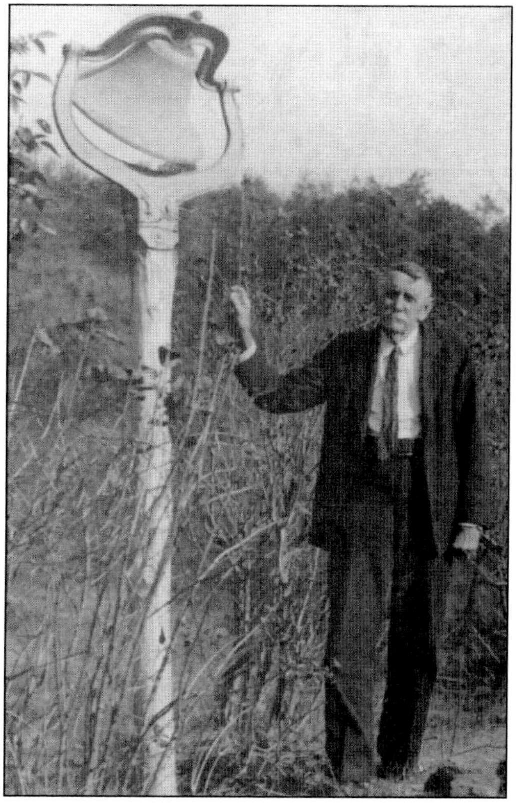

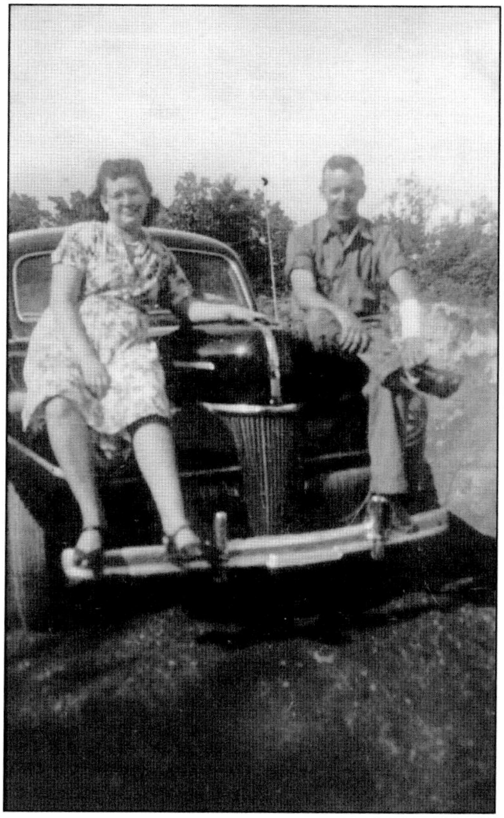

Charlene Wooten and James Baylus "J.B." Pace married in October 1947; his lineage traces back to the early 1800s when Burwell Pope Pace moved to the Saluda area. He traded this car in to build a house for his family of seven children. Of course, he was the 25th child of 29 children. Charlene is the keeper of the family history and is active in preserving Saluda history. (Courtesy of Charlene Pace.)

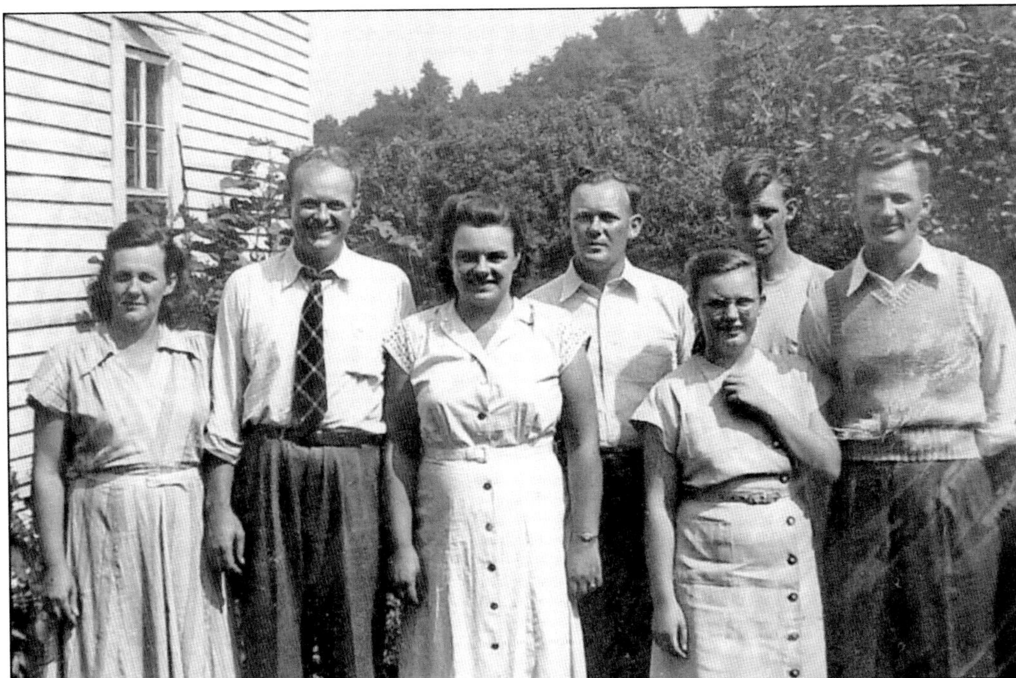

This late 1940s image of the children of Josiah and Roxie Johnson Holbert was identified as the last family photograph taken before leaving "the holler." Holbert Holler was filled in with dirt in order to accommodate the intersection of US 176 and Ozone Drive. From left to right are Lula Mae, Russell, Ruby Marie, Josiah Jr., Anne, Malcolm "Mike," and Willis "Bill," with the sweater vest. (Courtesy of Bill Holbert.)

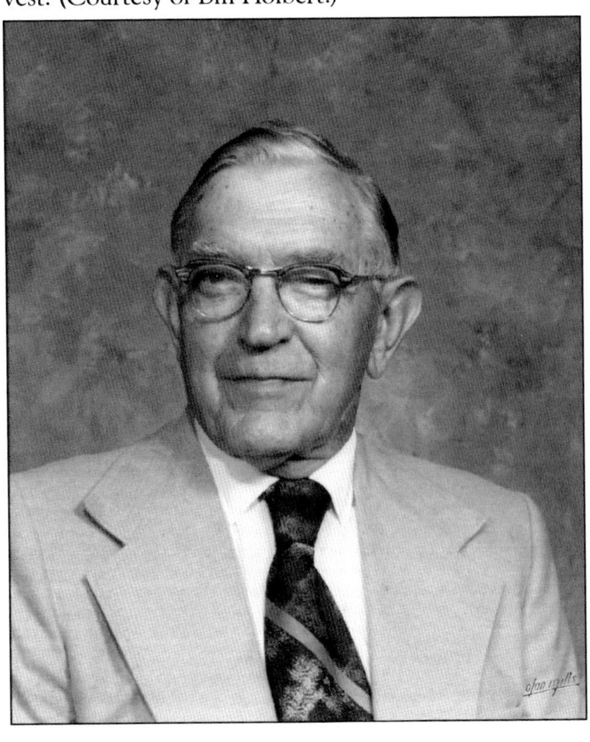

Richard Luther Thompson Sr., born in 1899, was the son of William Luther Thompson and a graduate of the Saluda Seminary. He chose to follow in his father's footsteps by becoming a builder and is responsible for several of the unique homes and structures in Saluda. (Courtesy of Betty Anna Thompson Brown.)

In 1913, Will Forrest, famous for his sense of humor, opened a barbershop and pool room downtown, which also offered showers, baths, dry cleaning, laundry service, and shoe shines. He was one of Saluda's most beloved citizens, evidenced by the number of folks who mention him during the Historic Saluda's oral history interviews. Forrest was also the source of endless fascination for many youngsters because of his wooden leg. (From the album of Lola Ward, courtesy of Judy Ward.)

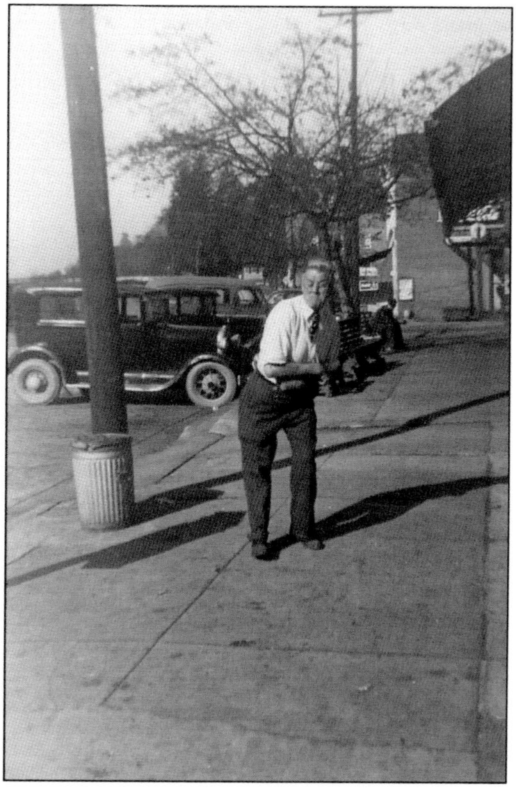

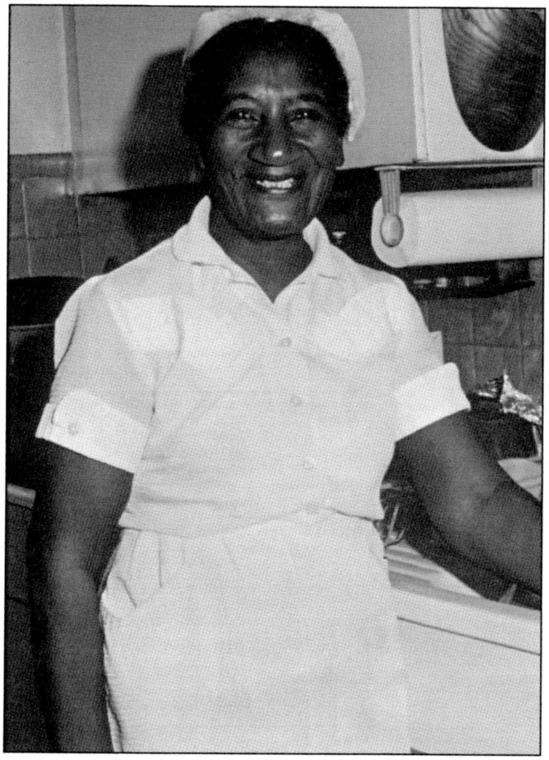

Rebecca Irving's father was the first black landowner and stone mason in Saluda. Her older sister Sophie was the first black child born in Saluda. Rebecca continued the family firsts as she was the first black Gentile to work at the Jewish-sponsored Sinai Hospital in Baltimore, Maryland, in the 1930s. Rebecca returned to reside in the Saluda Nursing Home until her death in 1982. (Courtesy of Charlene Pace.)

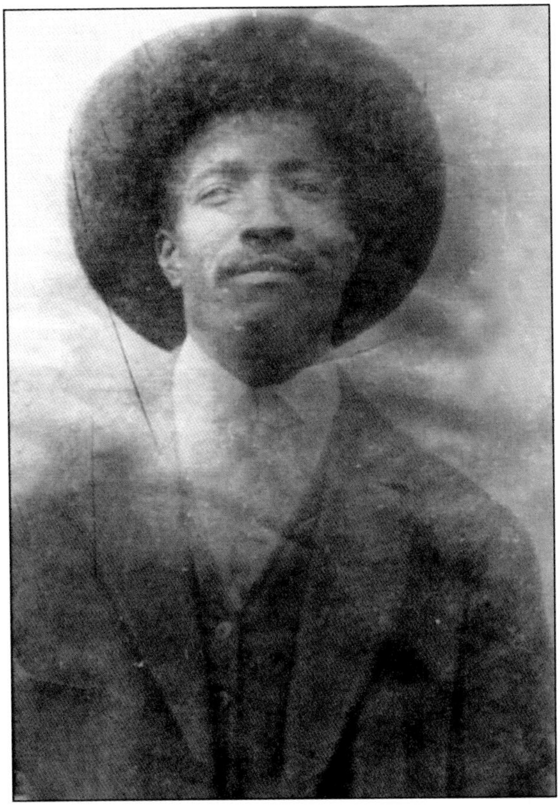

Pearlie Mae Suber Harris (below), daughter of a black Baptist minister, moved to Saluda in the 1930s as a very young child when her father, Rev. Lester Samuel Suber (left) was called to preach at St. Matthews Baptist Church. At a very young age, she worked for the wealthy white families who had second homes in Saluda. However, she was paid a fair wage and at times was the family breadwinner. Reverend Suber was always dressed in a white shirt, even when he was plowing the fields, and read stories out of the Bible as if it were a wonderful novel. Pearlie became an elementary schoolteacher in Greenville, South Carolina, and finished her master's degree at Furman University. Today, she comes back to Saluda to talk with the elementary school students about life in Saluda prior to the civil rights movement. (Both, courtesy of Pearlie Mae Suber Harris.)

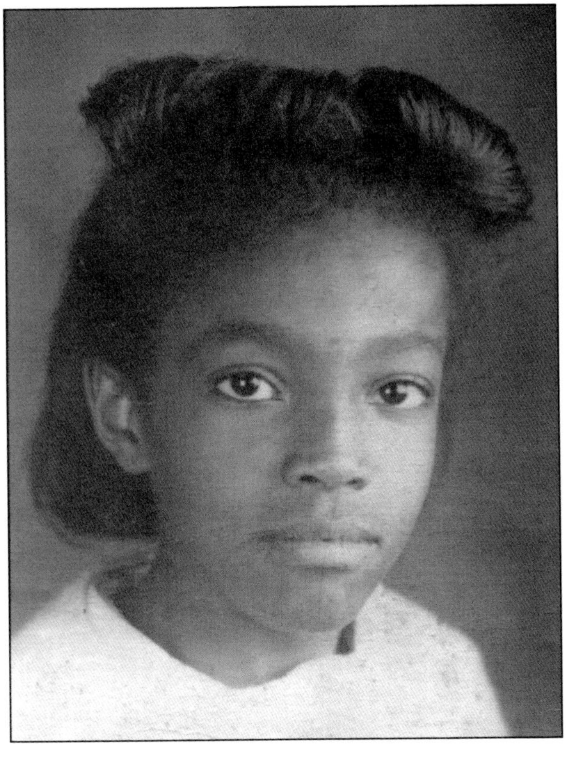

Dr. George Jones, local historian and genealogist, was 16 years old when this photograph was taken in 1936. Deciding he wanted to be a minister, he attended the Southern Baptist Theological Seminary in Louisville, Kentucky, and then volunteered for a chaplain's position in the US Army. He received a doctorate degree in history on the GI Bill and founded the Henderson County Genealogical and Historical Society in 1983. (Courtesy of Martha Jones Denka.)

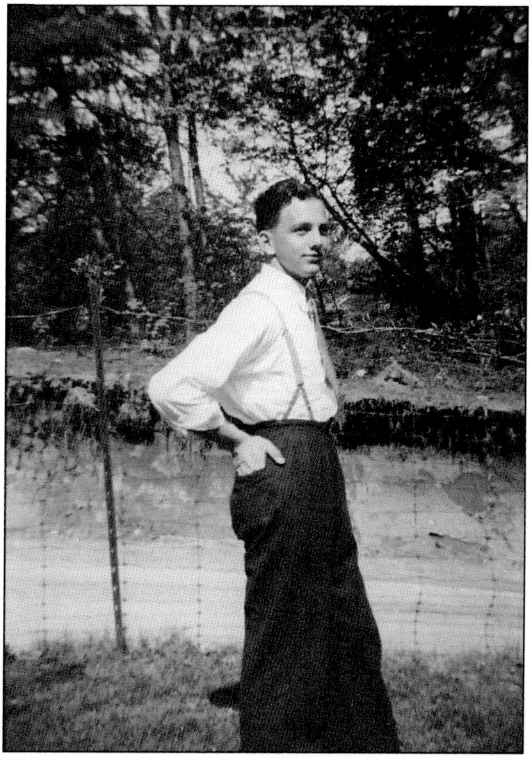

This photograph is of the 1939 graduating class of Saluda High School. Pictured here are, from left to right, (first row) Frances Pace, Mildred Thompson, Malachi Goforth, Beatrice Pace, and Lois Johnson; (second row) J.A. Nabors, Jeanette Pace, Catherine Pearson, Odessa Pearson, and Arthur Elewes; (third row) school principal Dr. John G. Michael. (Courtesy of Mildred Thompson Skelton.)

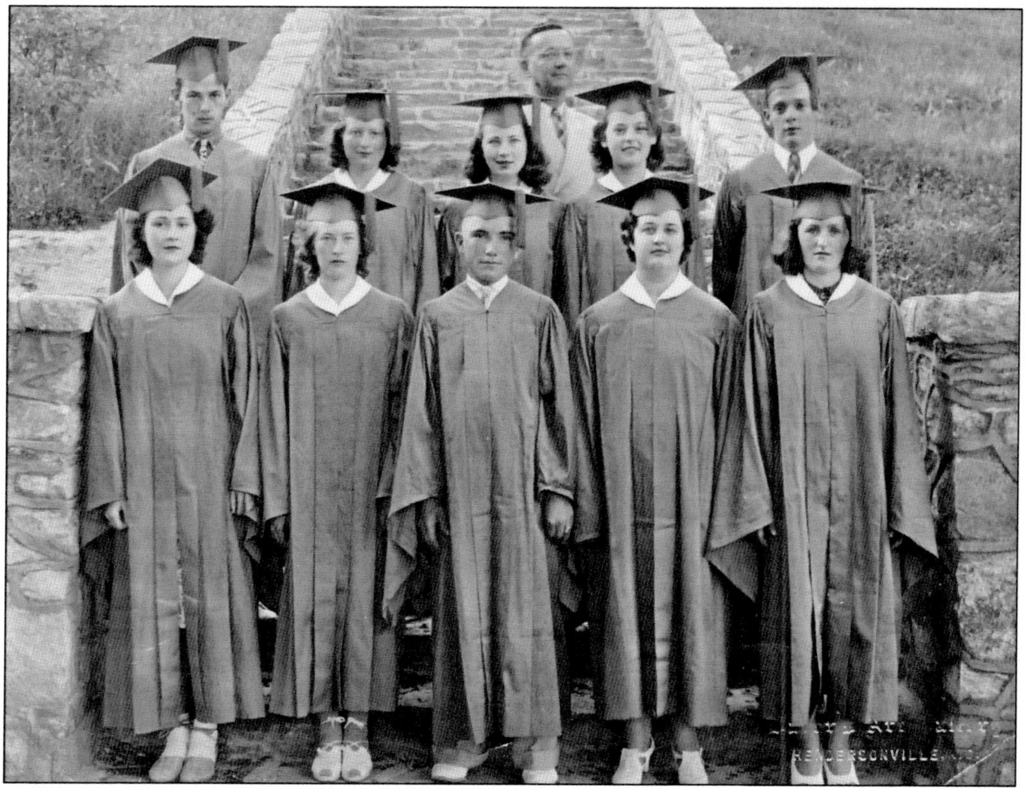

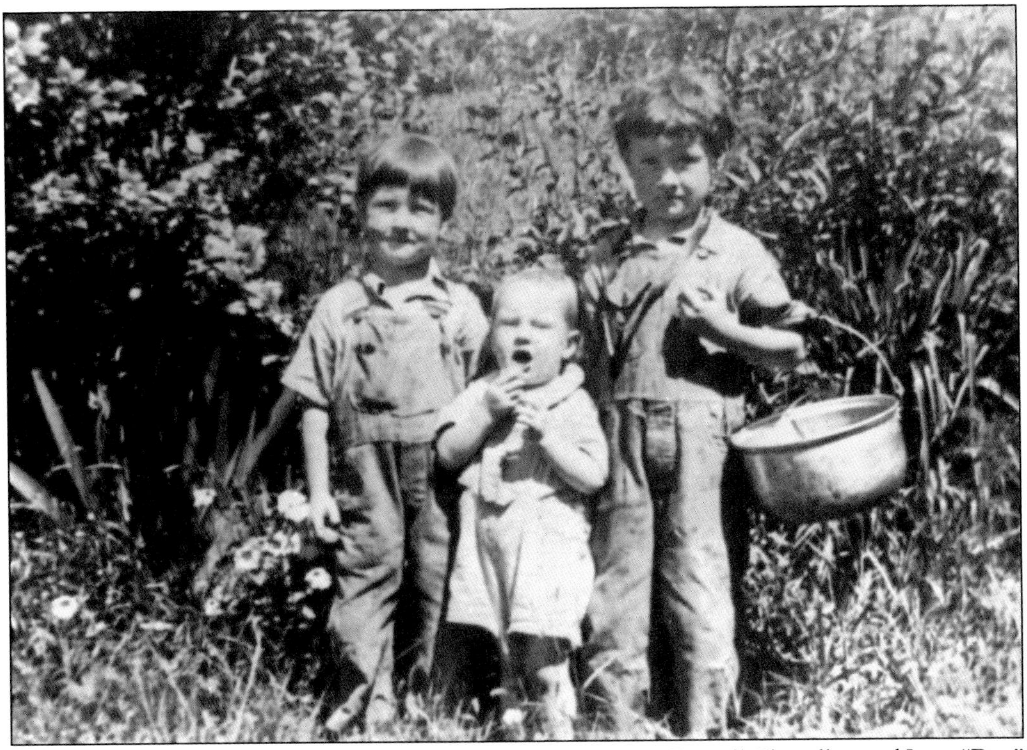

From left to right, William "Bill" Horace Russell, LaFaye "Faye" Russell Chandler, and Jerry "Doc" Morris Russell have shared their bittersweet oral histories of growing up in Saluda. Bill is the author of *In Times Gone By*, a chronicle of his life. Chandler obtained her nursing degree and became a caregiver. Doc obtained multiple college degrees, including a doctorate in education, taught school, and served as the principal of Saluda School. (Courtesy of Faye Chandler.)

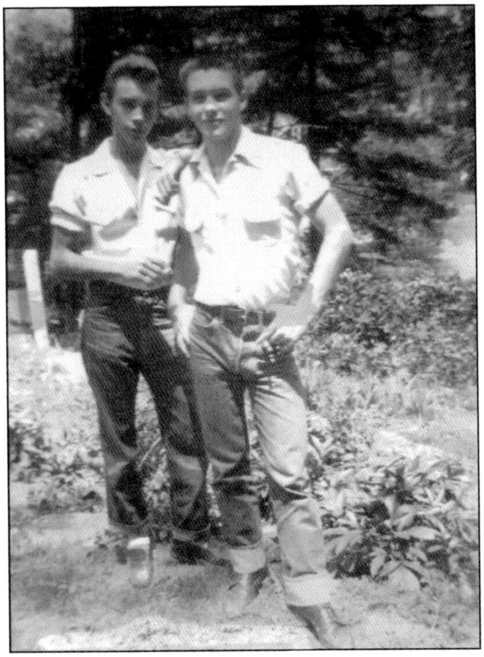

Pictured here in the 1950s are close friends John T. "Jack" Coates III (left) and William "Billy" Gaston Edgerton Jr. (right). Coates attended Wake Forest University and returned to Saluda to live, venturing in real estate and insurance. Edgerton attended college and served in the US Army. His parents, William Sr. and Vernon Thompson Edgerton, lived on Louisiana Avenue for over 50 years. Prior to Edgerton's death in 1999, he worked at Thompson's Store. (Courtesy of Thompson's Store.)

Walter McQueen Stephenson was born in Saluda in 1911 and died in Shreveport, Louisiana, in 1993. The son of Joseph Hoge Stephenson and Minnie May Guice Stephenson, his nickname was "Tarzan," and he went on to fame by becoming a professional baseball player. A the age of 24, he broke into the major leagues and was a catcher and pinch-hitter from 1935 to 1937 with the Chicago Cubs and Philadelphia Phillies. (Courtesy of Cindy Stephenson Tuttle.)

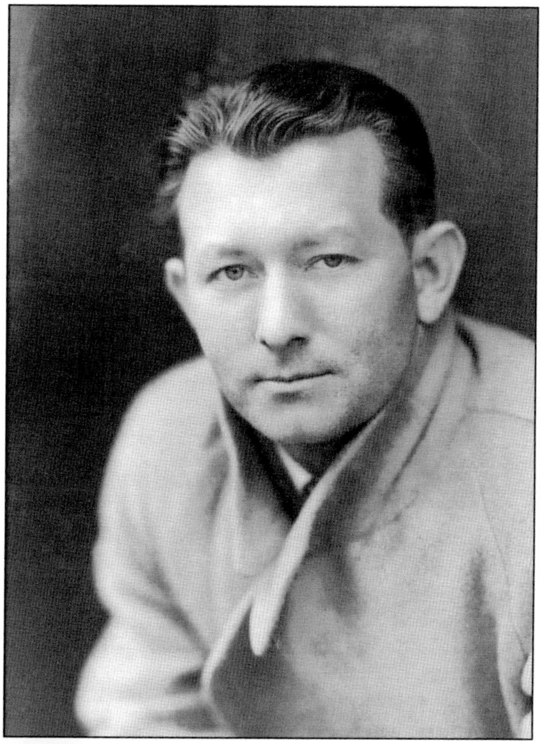

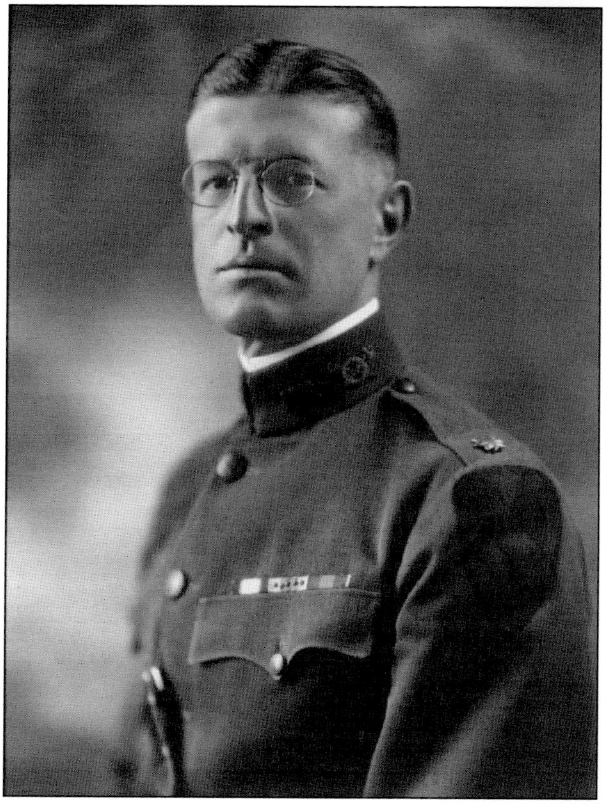

Brig. Gen. Vincent Meyer, pictured here as a major, was a close acquaintance of Maj. Gen. Edward Postell King Jr., who owned a house located near Shand Hill. Mary King, his sister, inherited the house in 1958, and the Meyer family came with her in the summers to help her keep up the house. General King was the commanding general on Bataan during World War II and surrendered his troops, which led to the Bataan Death March. (Courtesy of Kim Meyer Ford.)

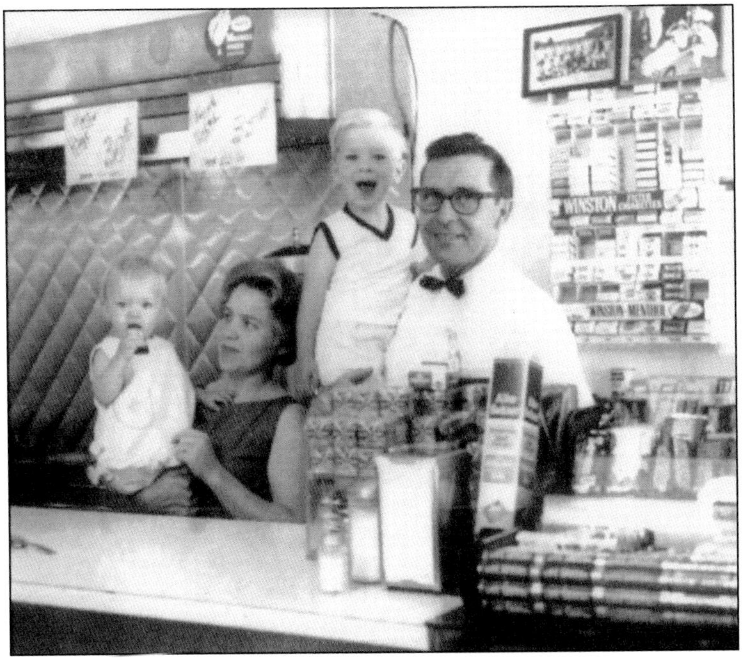

Jack and Ursi Veil Ward are pictured here with their two children, Sara and Roger, at Ward's Grill, located within Thompson's Store. Ursi came from Germany in 1957 and married Jack in the 1960s. Every morning at 6:00 a.m., Ursi would help open the grill before she went to work as a nurse in Tryon. Jack Ward was raised along with his younger brother, Charlie Ward, working in the store. In 1994, Jack passed away at the age of 67. (Courtesy of Thompson's Store and Ward's Grill.)

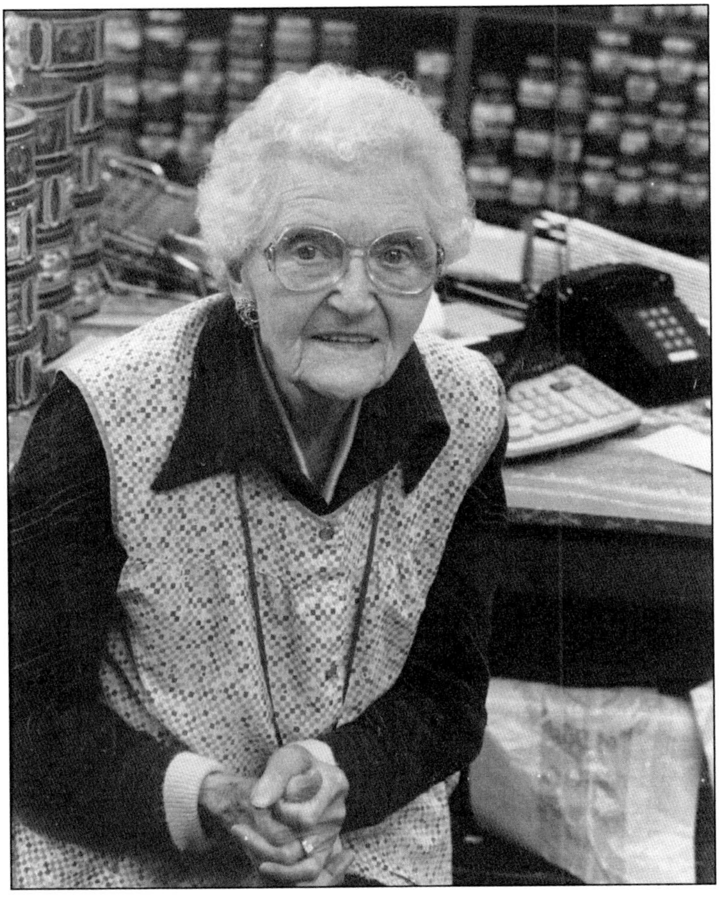

Lola Thompson Ward is pictured here at the family business, Thompson's Store. The store was the town's information hotspot for generations, and folks called to find out everything from the weight of new babies to the funeral arrangements of old-timers. Lola was the very heart of it all, stationed on her stool up front by the cash register, well into her 90s. She died at the age of 103. (Courtesy of J. Landwher.)

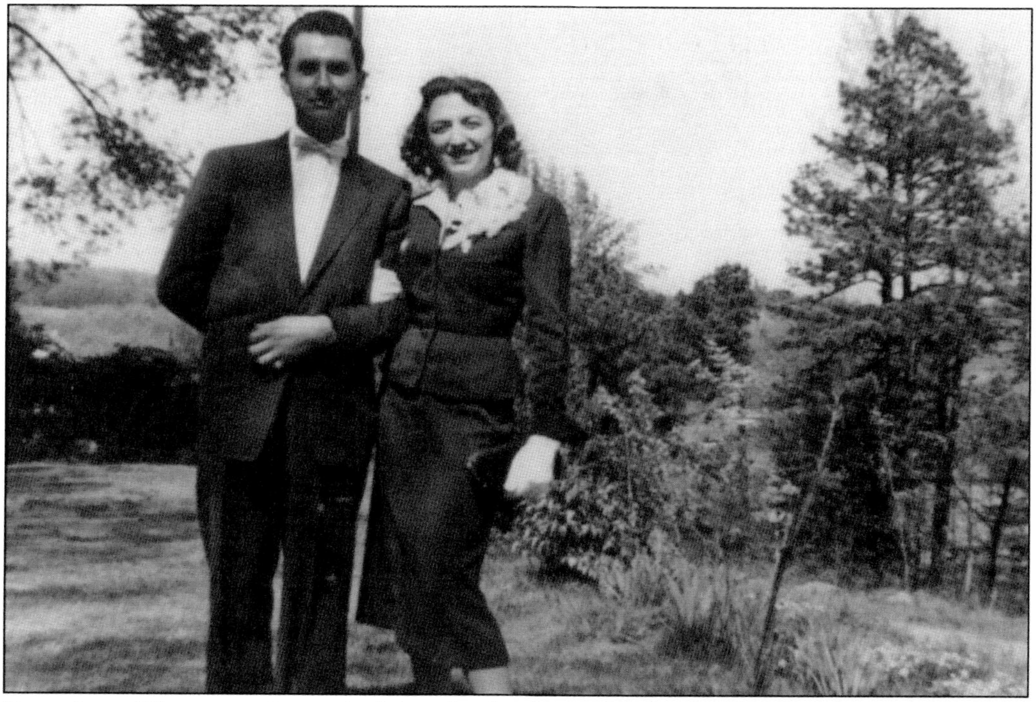

Betty Anna Thompson Brown (right) is the daughter of Richard and Atlas Johnson Thompson Jr. and granddaughter of local builder Luther Thompson and Alice Cantrell Thompson. She graduated from Saluda High School, Brevard College, Appalachian State, and Western Carolina, with degrees in radio, television, and criminal justice. She met her husband, Joe Brown (left), at a local basketball game. She was an English teacher for 45 years, and her husband retired from Bigelow-Sanford after 51 years. (Courtesy of Betty Anna Thompson Brown.)

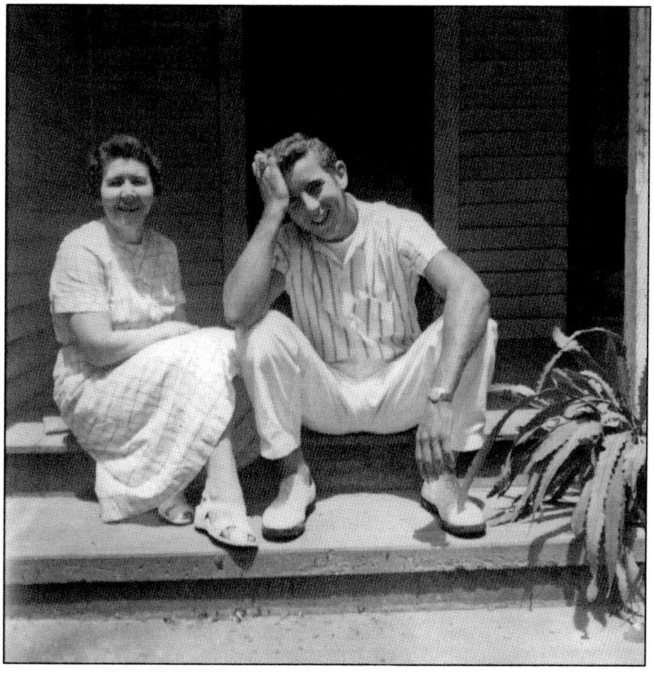

Taken during the summer of 1958, R. Clark Thompson (right) sits on the front porch of his Pine Street home with his mother, Mary Lillian Pack Thompson. Clark was 18 and had just returned from a year in Florida, seeking his fortune as a construction laborer. Clark's father, Roy Alonzo Thompson, was also in the construction business, as was his grandfather Luther Thompson, known for his fine carpentry work in Saluda. (Courtesy of R. Clark Thompson Jr.)

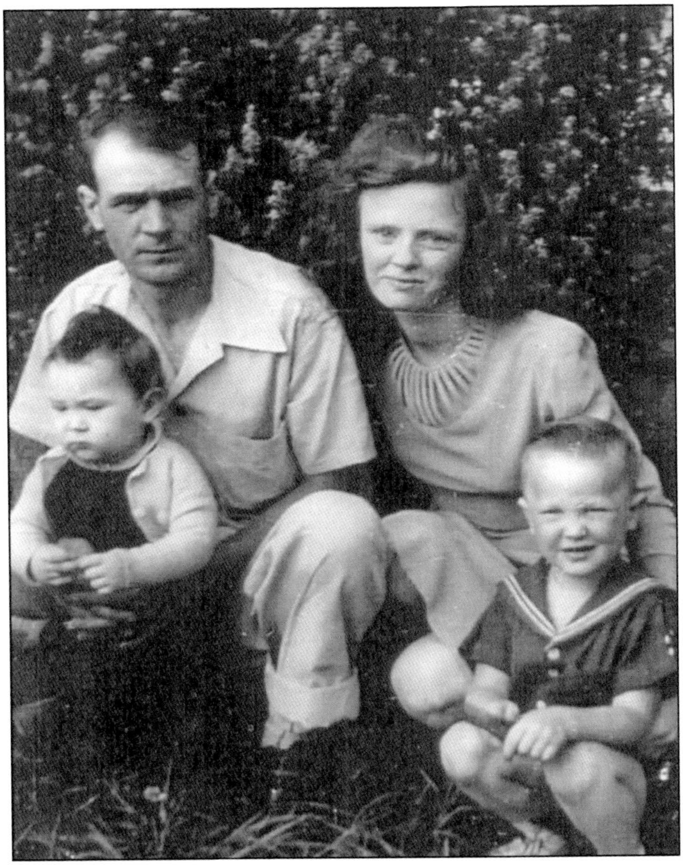

Pictured here in 1949 are, from left to right, Ronnie Morgan, Leland Morgan, Lucy Russell Morgan, and Leon Morgan. The Greenville watershed now covers the land where their home once stood. Lucy worked at the hosiery mill in Saluda, and Leland was a master carpenter and cabinet maker. (Courtesy of Leon Morgan.)

Posing from left to right are Bud Morgan, Jess Morgan, Leland Morgan, Ralph Morgan, and Lawrence Summey. This photograph was taken at the William Reuben and Rosa Metcalf Morgan home. (Courtesy of Leon Morgan.)

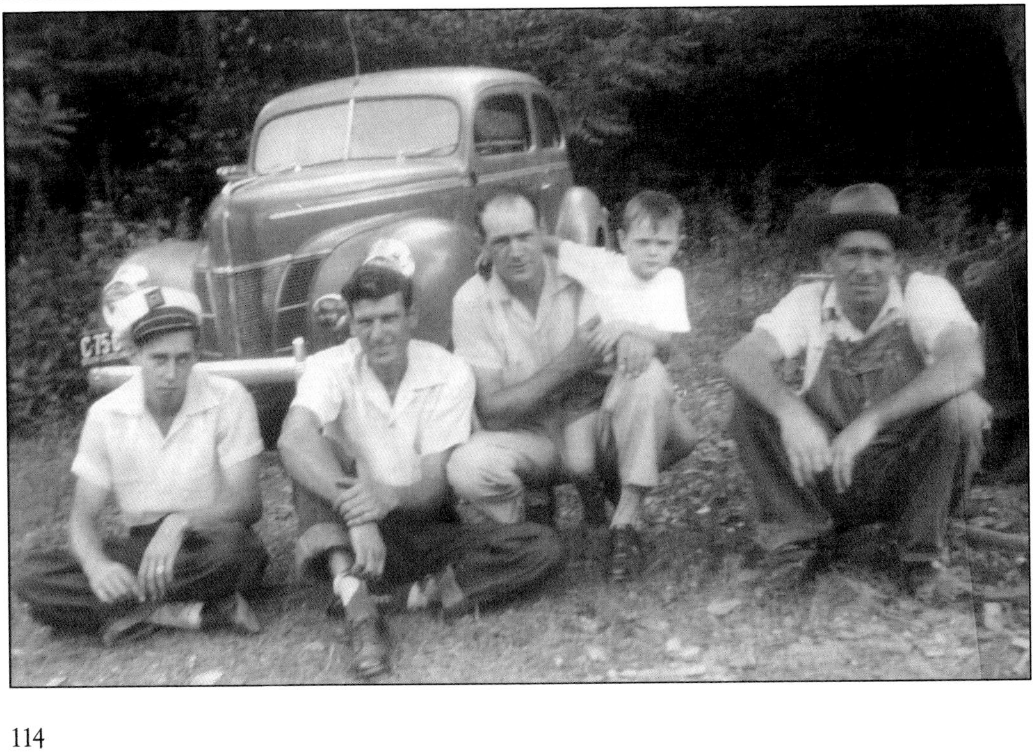

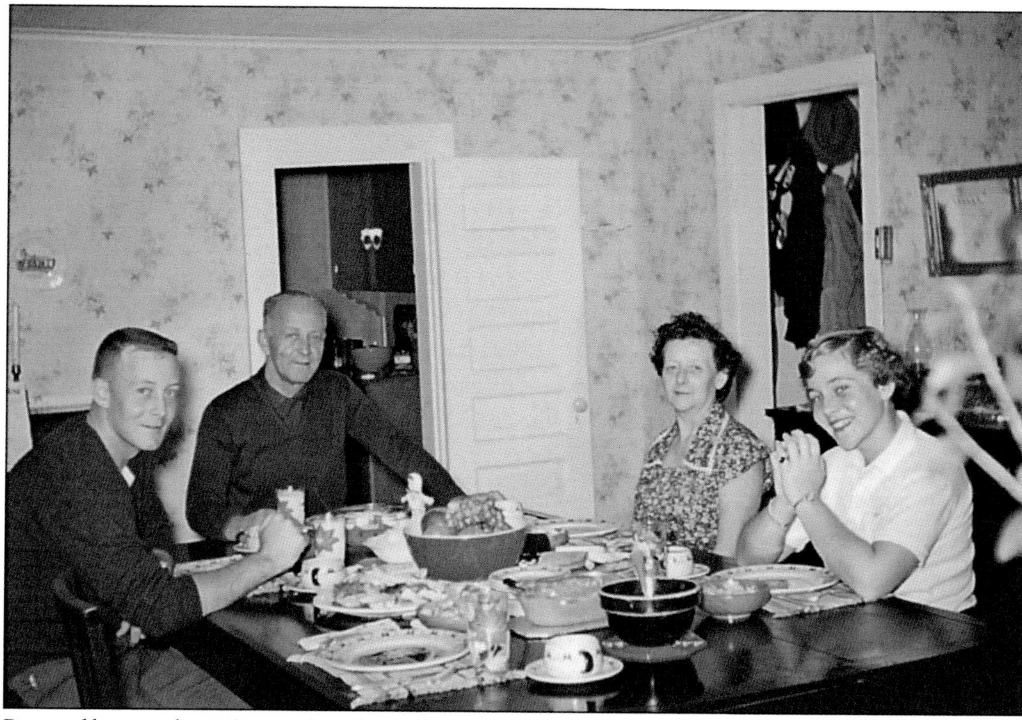

Pictured here in the 1950s are, from left to right, Joseph "Joe" Raymond Stephenson Jr., Joseph Raymond "Raymond" Stephenson Sr., Kathleen Garren Stephenson, and Lucille "Lu" Ann Stephenson. Raymond was chair of the Polk County Board of Education, chair of the Saluda Lions Club, and served in the North Carolina Senate in the late 1950s. Both Joe and Lu left Saluda after college. Lu studied and served her country abroad. (Courtesy of Cindy Stephenson Tuttle.)

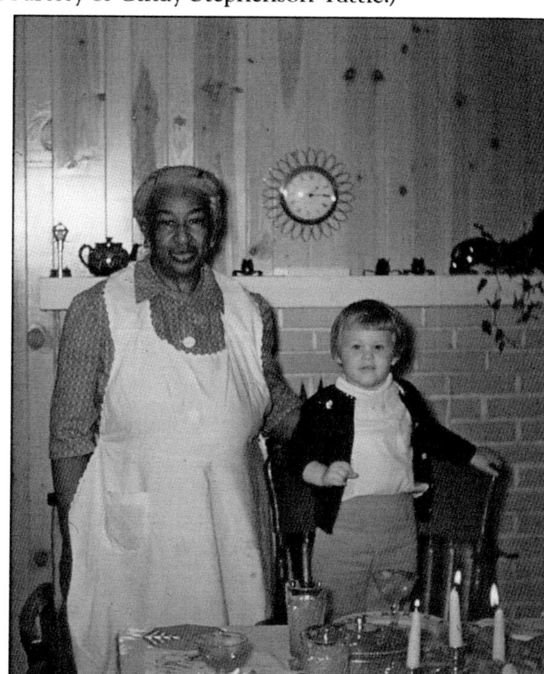

Ada Means (left) and Cindy Stephenson (right) pose at the Stephenson farm on Thanksgiving Day in the early 1960s. Means was a cook and nanny for the family for many years. Means, born in South Carolina in 1883 to freed slaves, was married to Isaac Means, a local barber. A member of St. Matthews Church, she died in 1967 and is buried at Mountain Page Church. (Courtesy of Cindy Stephenson Tuttle.)

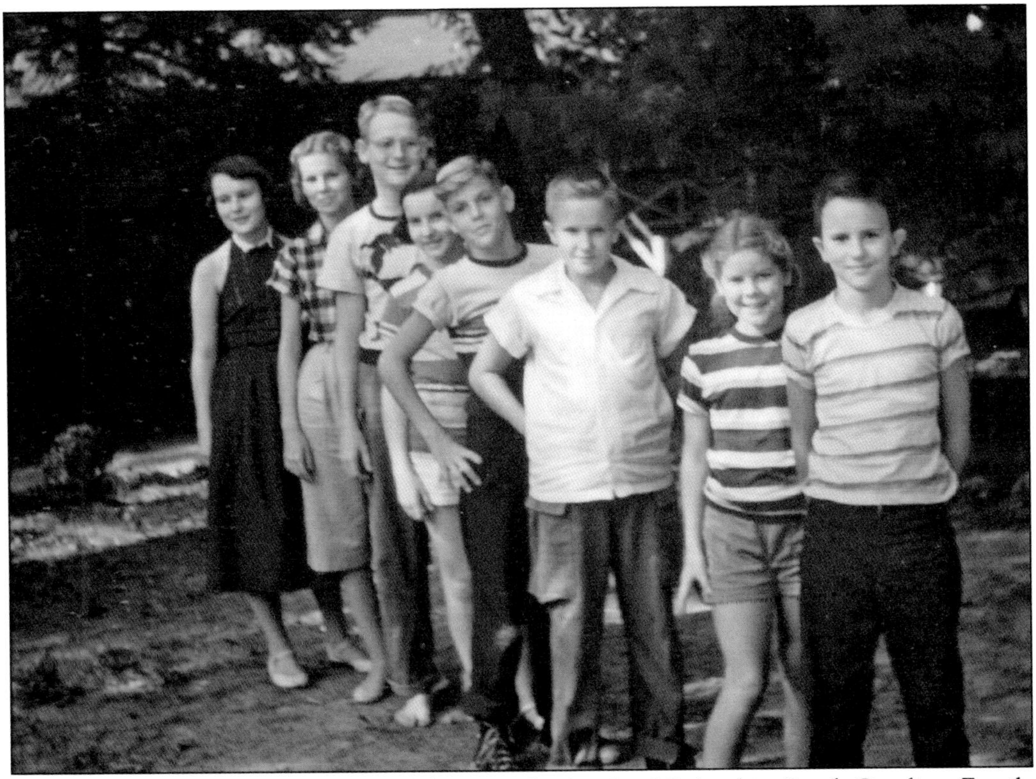

SIBMMASE was the Saluda retreat of the McNulty family of Columbia, South Carolina. Family patriarch Gene McNulty claimed the name was an Indian word for "man marry, much trouble," but it was formed with the first letters of his grandchildren's names when the property was bought. The home burned in 1966 but was rebuilt by Alex and Eliza Dickson to reflect the character of the original structure. (Courtesy of Gene and Lesesne Dickson.)

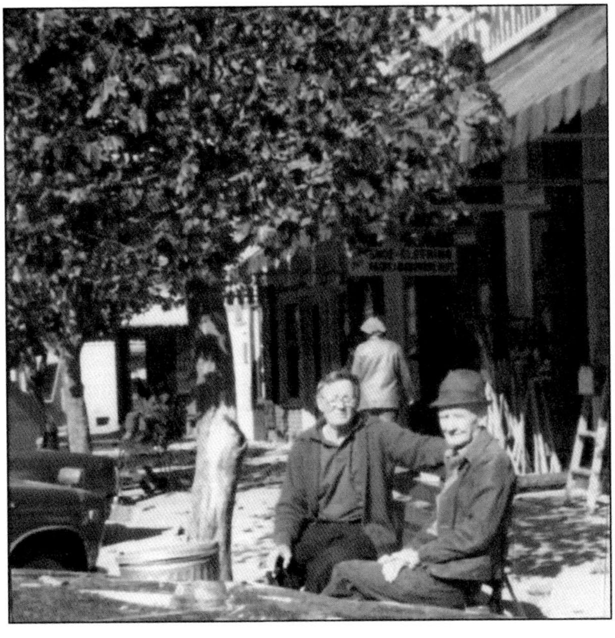

Ralph Hipp (left) is sitting with Arthur "Ott" Hawthorne Hipp (right) on Main Street in front of Thompson's Store. Ralph joined the Army and married Laurence Claire Etienvre in Paris, France, after World War II. According to Ralph's family, they lived in Beaufort, South Carolina, but Ralph's heart was always in the mountains. He looked forward to Coon Dog Day every year to reunite with his family and friends from childhood. (Courtesy of Caroline Hipp.)

In the mid-1960s, actor Pat Hingle (left) visited his friend Roy Ward (right), who was ill. As a boy, Hingle lived with his grandparents E.M. and Maggie Patterson. In the 1930s, he loved to stand by the railroad tracks in town and wave to his grandfather, a railroad employee, as he drove a steam engine. Hingle is best known for his role as Commissioner Gordon in the first four Batman films. (From the album of Lola Ward, courtesy of Judy Ward.)

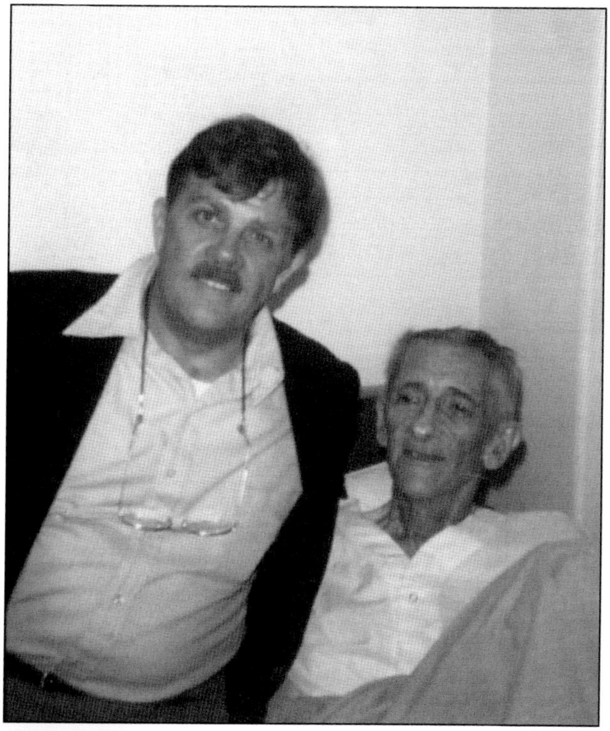

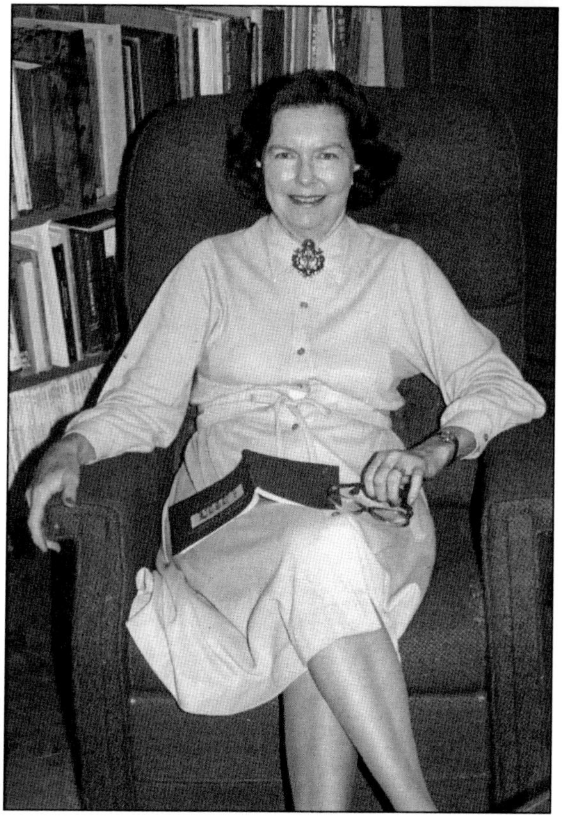

Anne Riggs Osborne was born into a military family and continued the tradition of moving often by marrying an Air Force doctor. Finally settling in Augusta, Georgia, she wrote for the *Augusta Chronicle* and *Augusta Magazine*. Spending summers in Saluda, she had her own writing cottage where she wrote novels and histories, including *Storm in the Backwoods*, *The Episcopal Church of the Transfiguration*, and *The South Carolina Story*. Osborne coauthored *Saluda NC 100 Years 1881–1981* with Charlene Pace. (Courtesy of Peg Osborne Henneke.)

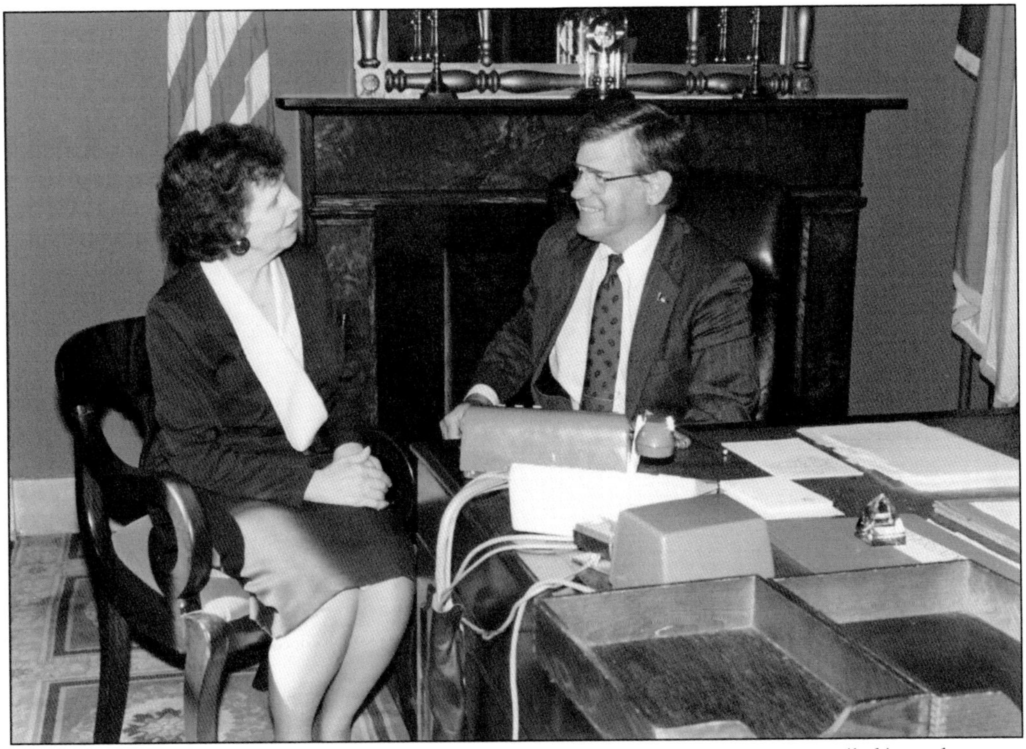

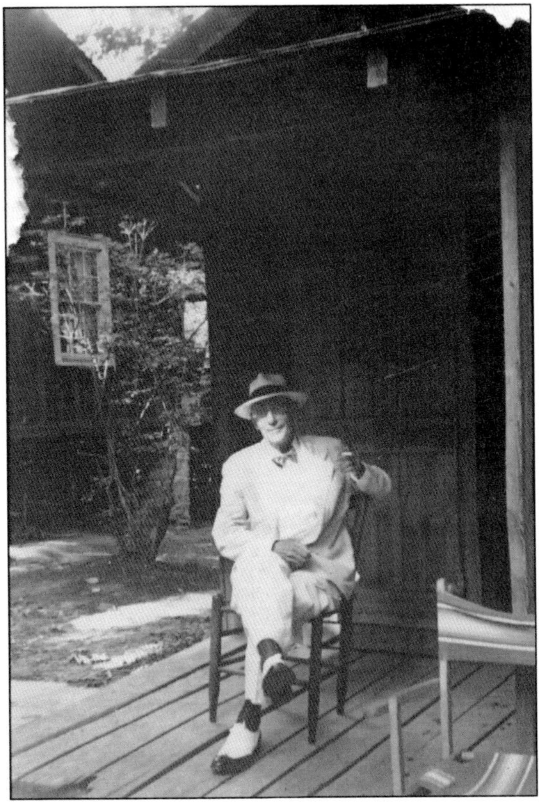

Ruby Thompson Hooper (left) made history in 1984 as the first woman to run on a major party ticket for governor of North Carolina, an office she sought again in 1992. After her 1984 primary opponent James Martin (right) was elected, he appointed her deputy secretary of the North Carolina Department of Human Resources. In this 1991 image, Governor Martin accepts her resignation as she seeks the nomination of Republican gubernatorial candidate. (Courtesy of the State Archives of North Carolina.)

Charles O. Hearon Sr. was the editor of the *Spartanburg Herald* and had a summer home on Scout Camp Road. His newspaper articles helped promote interest and participation in the Spartanburg Baby Hospital and Infants' and Children's Sanitarium, aiding mothers and babies suffering from the summer heat of the lowlands. He gave the Palmetto Council Scout Camp additional acreage along Casey's Branch for expanding the camp to the present-day Camp Bob Hardin. (Courtesy of Chuck Hearon.)

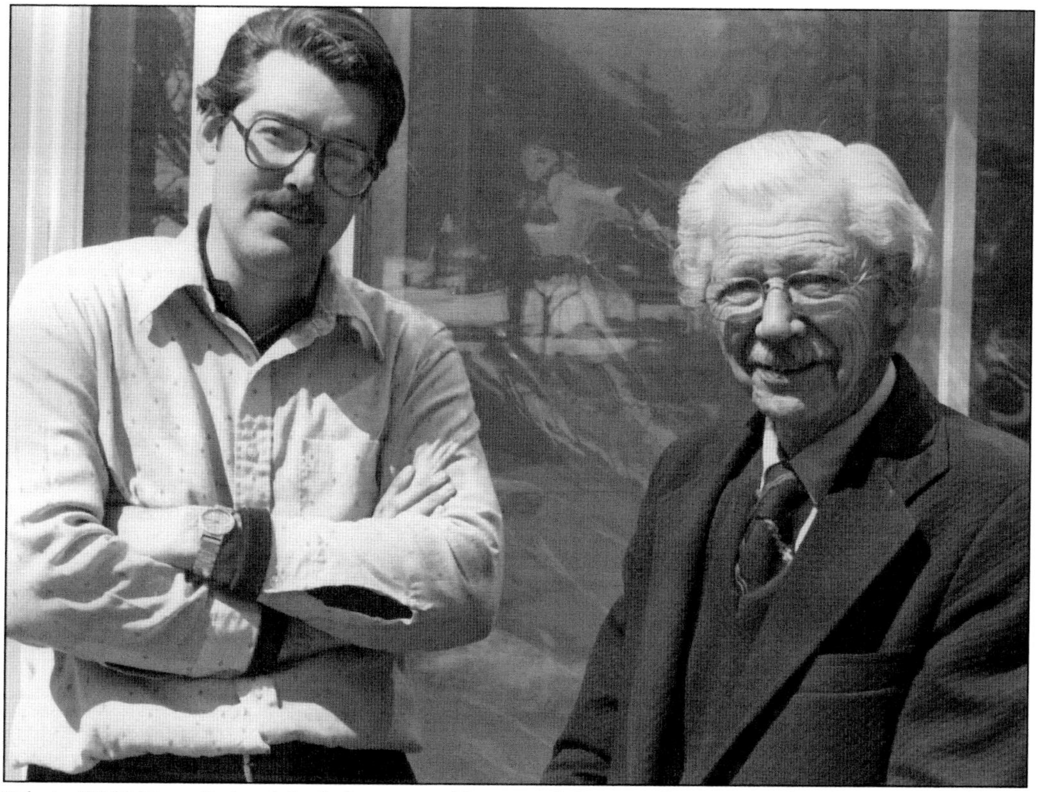

Edwin "Ed" Cater Leland (right), pictured here with his son E. Cater Leland Jr. (left), not only owned and operated the Saluda Mountain Telephone Company from 1936 to 1990, but was active in civic affairs. He became the first president of the Saluda Lions Club, was a member of the Saluda Board of Commissioners, and served as mayor of Saluda. His son followed in his father's footsteps, serving as mayor. (Courtesy of E. Cater Leland Jr.)

Perry Como, pictured here with local resident Janis Sutherland, loved Saluda and spent many summers at the vacation home he bought in 1980. He was welcomed without being overwhelmed by the low-key community. One story about the very private Como was that he called a friend in Saluda to sing "Happy Birthday," and the response was, "Perry, I didn't know that you could sing!" The Orchard Inn still has a plaque over his favorite table. (Courtesy of Susie Welsh.)

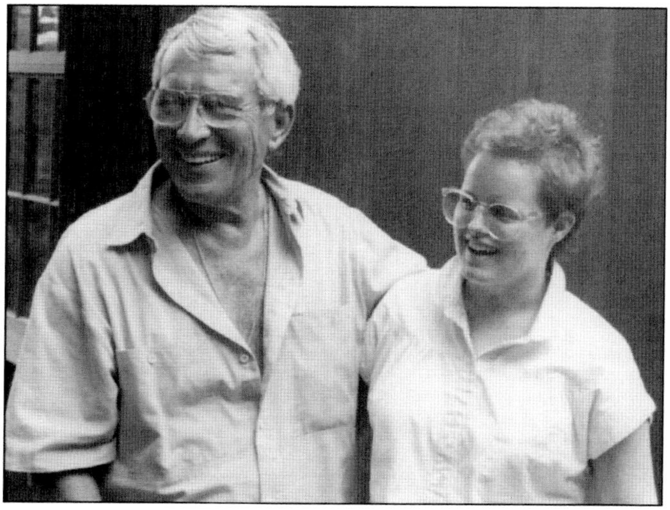

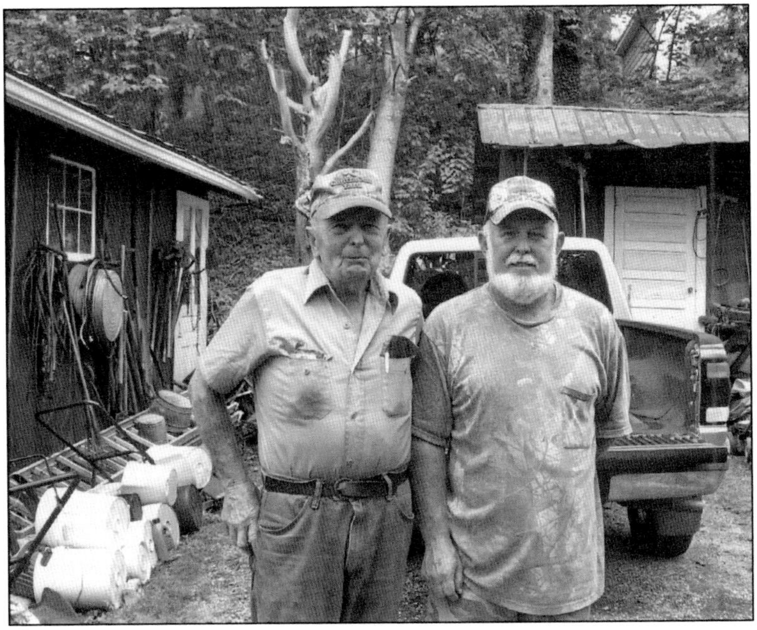

Horace Pace (left) and his son Gary (right) stand next to Horace's workshop at his home. Horace, one of 29 children born to Ransom Taylor Pace, was an avid hunter and loved spending time hiking and fishing along the Green River. Known for telling stories about his adventures, he claimed to be one of the few who knew where the devil's footprint is etched in rock along the riverbanks. (Courtesy of J. Landwher.)

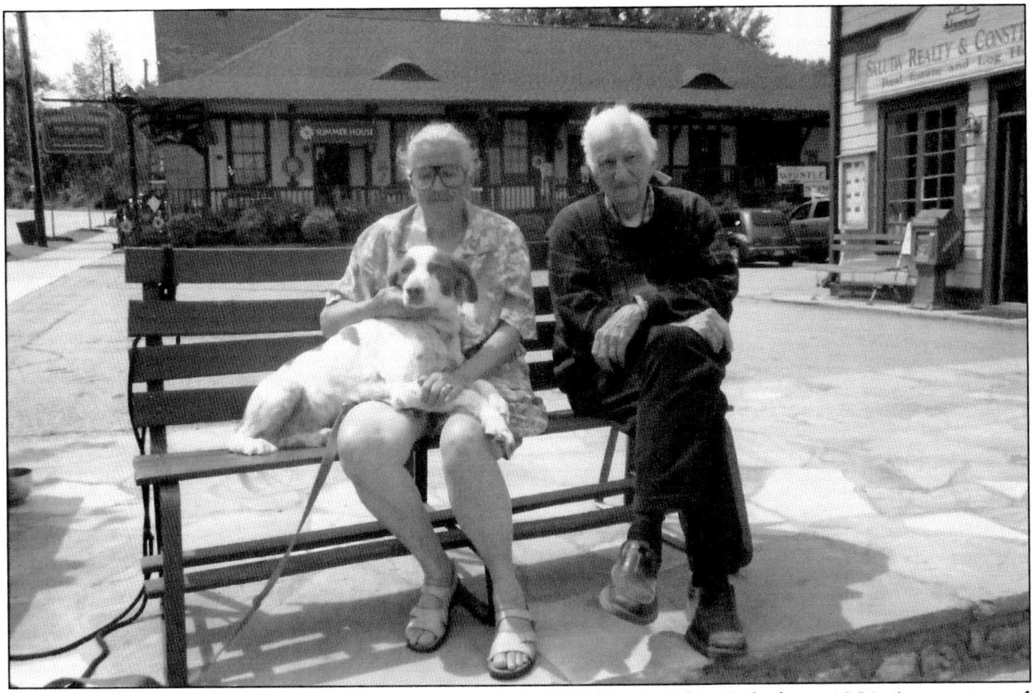

Pictured here with their dog Huddy, Dottie and Roy Eargle moved to Saluda in 1981. Active in real estate development, they saw various projects through sometimes difficult circumstances. They purchased and moved the train depot downtown and bought and restored the historic Woods House and opened it as an inn. In 1986, Dotty obtained state funds so that the tin facing and trim of Saluda City Hall could be restored. (Courtesy of Carolyn Ashburn.)

Living to his 103rd year, Foster Archer was a true renaissance man. As an architect, he built unique, handcrafted houses in Saluda and was known for constructing stairs with treads wider than normal, which made the stairs seem less steep. His reasoning, "I have big feet and I was tired of them not fitting on a step." He had a lifelong interest in health and body building and was the author of *Wild Fields* and *Down with Up and Up with Down*. (Courtesy of Libby Archer.)

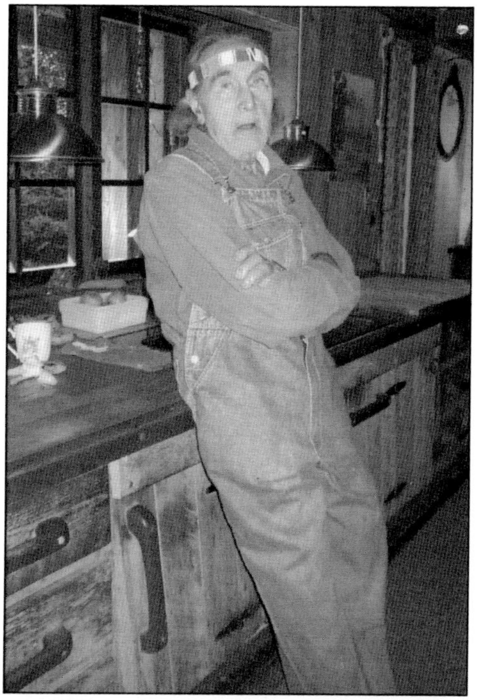

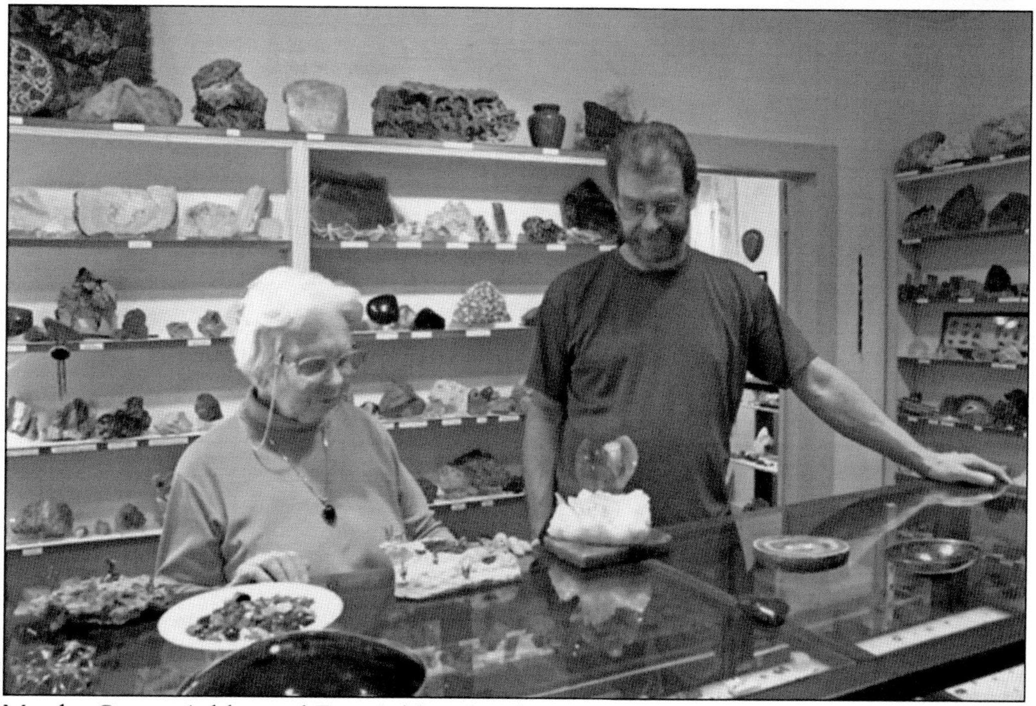

Martha Coates Ashley and Eric Ashley, daughter in-law and grandson of W.C. Ashley, are pictured in the reassembled Polk County Rock and Mineral Museum located inside the Ashley home. The museum closed in 1973, and its contents were packed into boxes, which stayed under the Ashleys' home for nearly 30 years. Though not open to the public, Eric and his father, Allen Ashley, reassembled the museum in the early 2000s. (Courtesy of Chuck Hearon.)

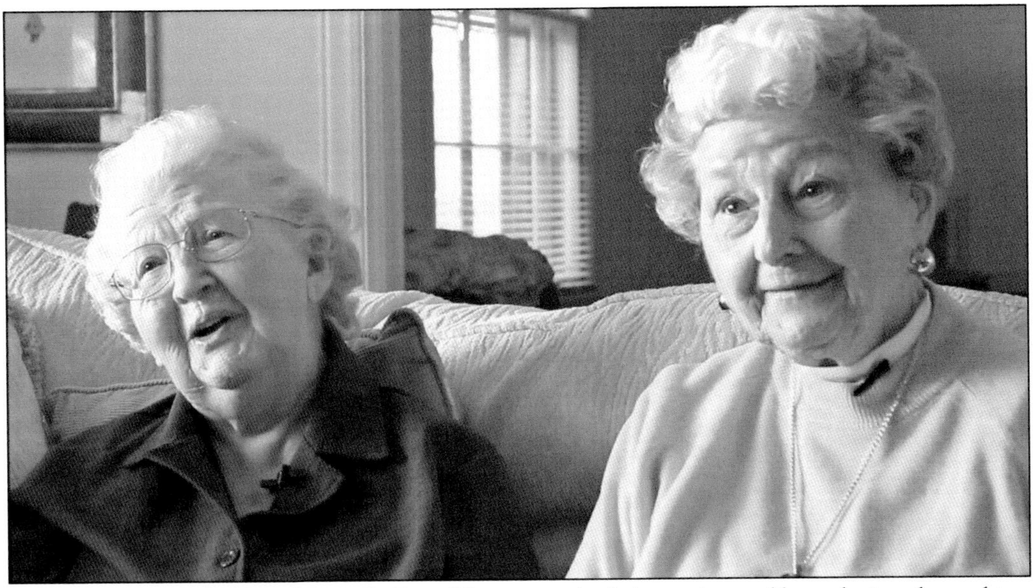

Ruth Pace Lawter (left) and Betty Jo Pace Thompson (right) are pictured here during the making of the 2011 oral history film documentary *Home, Hearth and History: Stories of Old Saluda*, as they talked about growing up in Saluda. Daughters of Herbert and Maude Pace, the family operated a large dairy farm, and as children they helped to deliver the milk all over town, twice daily, using a pony and buggy. (Courtesy of Kim Clark.)

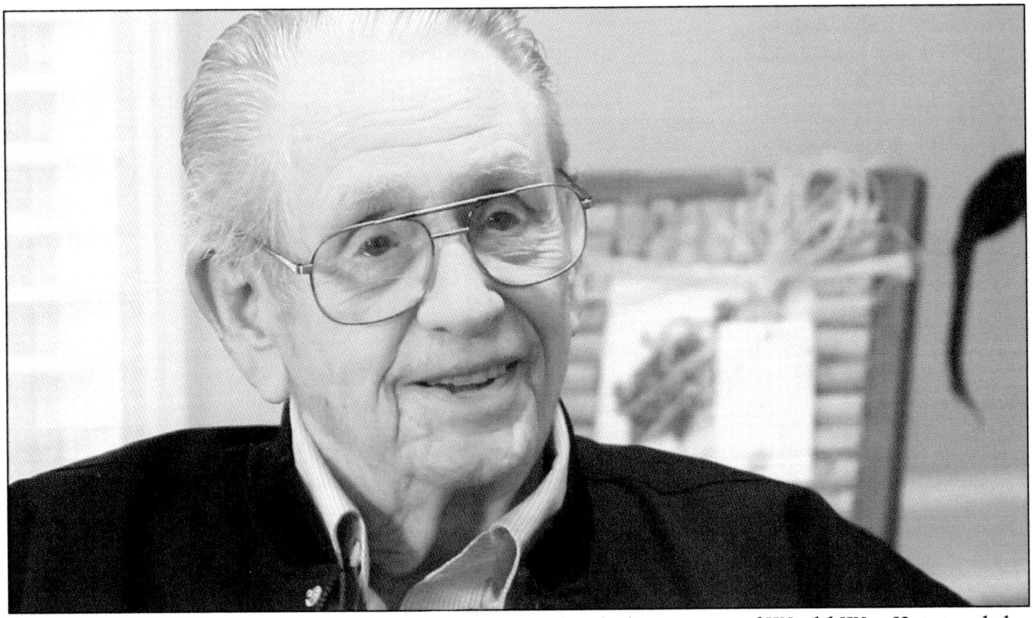

John Rhodes, often referred to as the most decorated Saluda veteran of World War II, joined the US Army and fought from Normandy through France with Patton's Second Division. Injured multiple times during the war, he received two Purple Hearts and the Bronze Star. Rhodes retired from the City of Saluda as maintenance supervisor in 1992. Married to Ruth Middleton Rhodes, John was a man of great patience and kindness. (Courtesy of Kim Clark.)

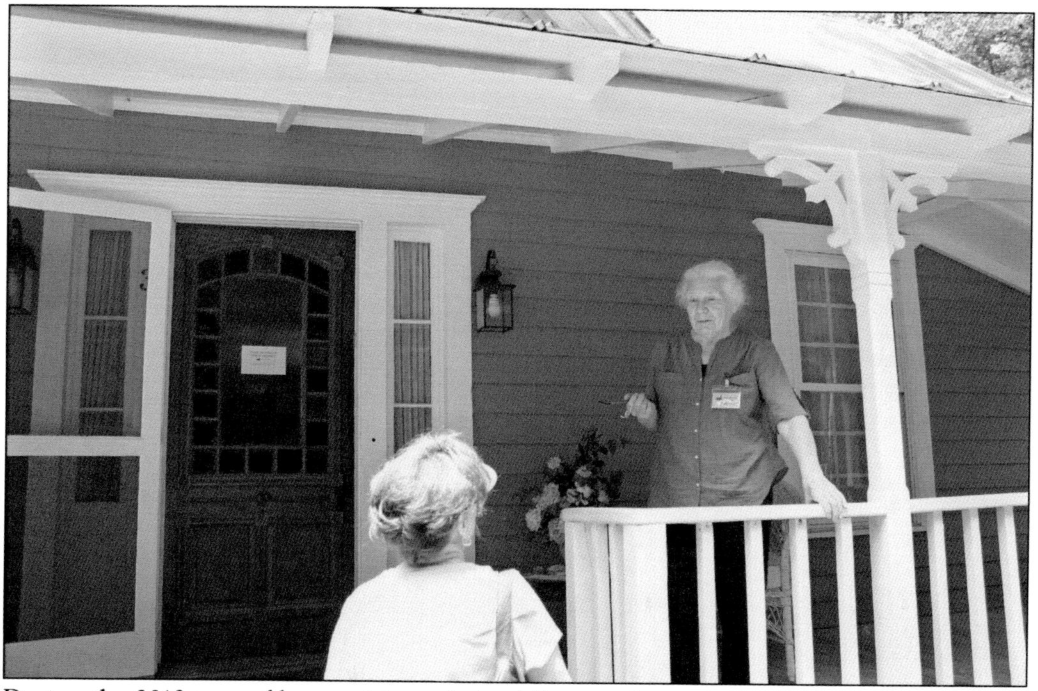

During the 2013 tour of homes, Nancy Leland Barnett discusses the history of the home of Augusta Louise Leland, her grandmother, located on Henderson Street. Barnett's love of nature led her to study biology in college, and after raising her eight children, she earned a degree in horticulture. She is president of the Saluda Community Land Trust, working diligently to improve the community by providing trails, removing kudzu, and educating the public about conservation efforts. (Courtesy of Cindy Stephenson Tuttle.)

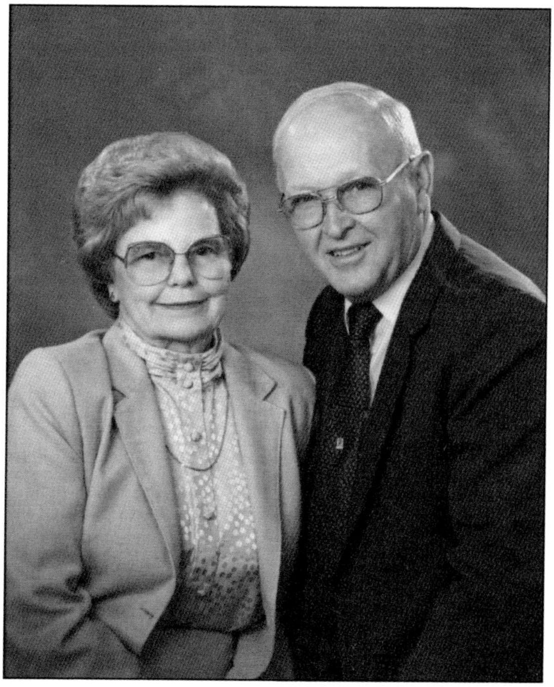

Clyde and Hattie Conner, who resided for many years on Gaffney Street, took this photograph in celebration of their 50th wedding anniversary. Clyde was an unofficial greeter for the town of Saluda. When he met people in the post office or on Main Street, he always had a joke and smile for them. A veteran of World War II, he served in the US Army in the European theater (Courtesy of Bevie Conner Walker.)

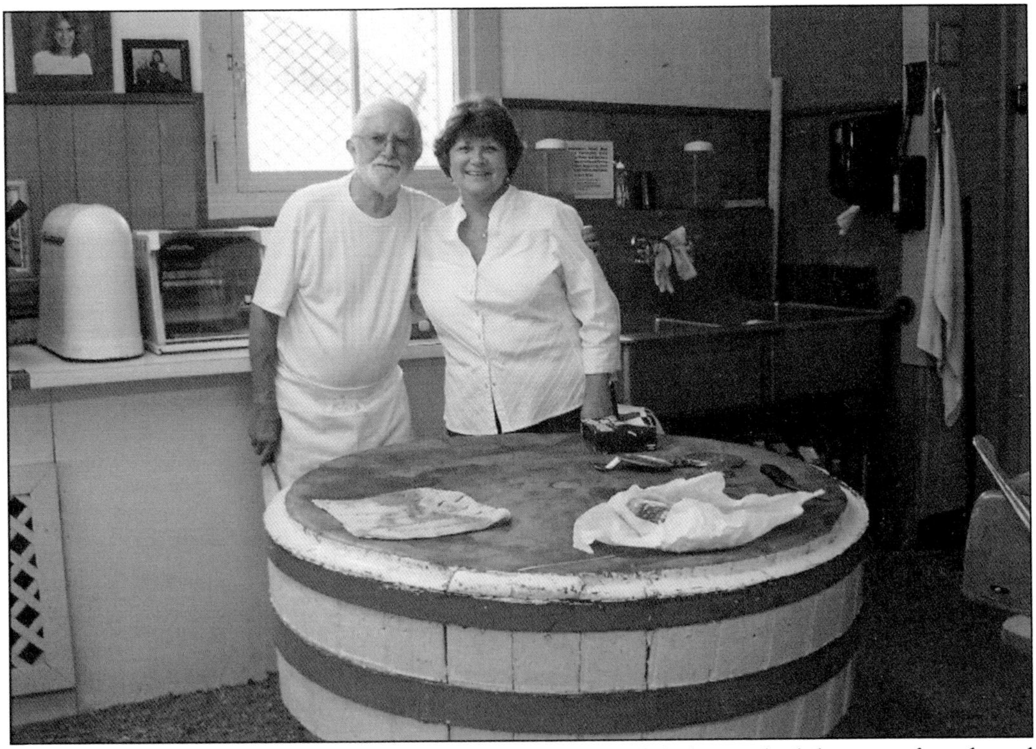

Charlie Ward (above left) was best known for whistling while he worked, hugging friends and strangers alike, and calling everyone "buddy," while working at his family's business, Thompson's Store and Ward's Grill. Charlie, with his wife, Judy, retired and sold the family business in 2007 to spend time with his family. In 2008, Charlie passed away. The business was only out of the family's hands for a few years, when Charlie's cousin Clark Thompson (below right), pictured here in Ward's Grill, and Judy partnered to acquire the business when it came up for sale again. It officially reopened in 2011. The store and grill have seen numerous renovations and expansions over the last few years, including a complete refurbishment of the second floor. Because of Clark and Judy, Thompson's Store and Ward's Grill remain a fixture of historic downtown Saluda. (Above, courtesy of Judy Ward; below, courtesy of Cindy Stephenson Tuttle.)

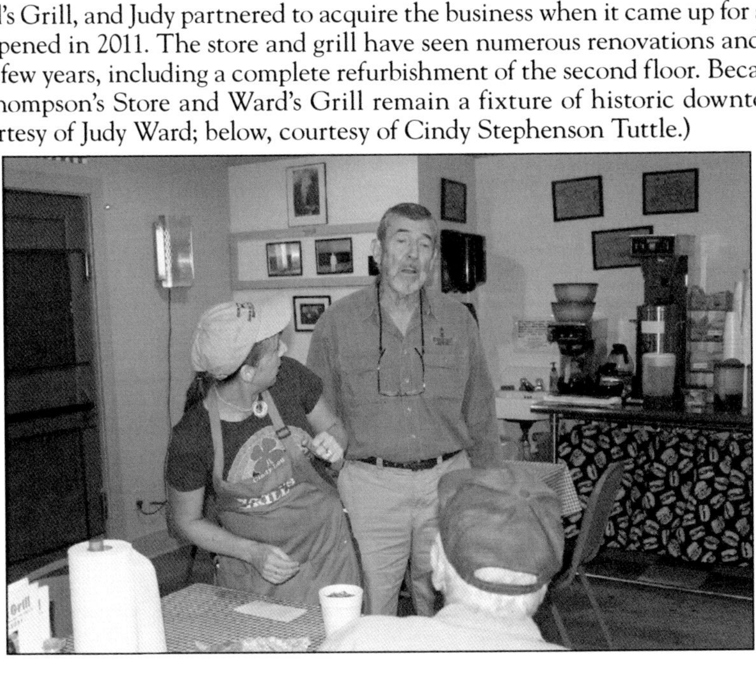

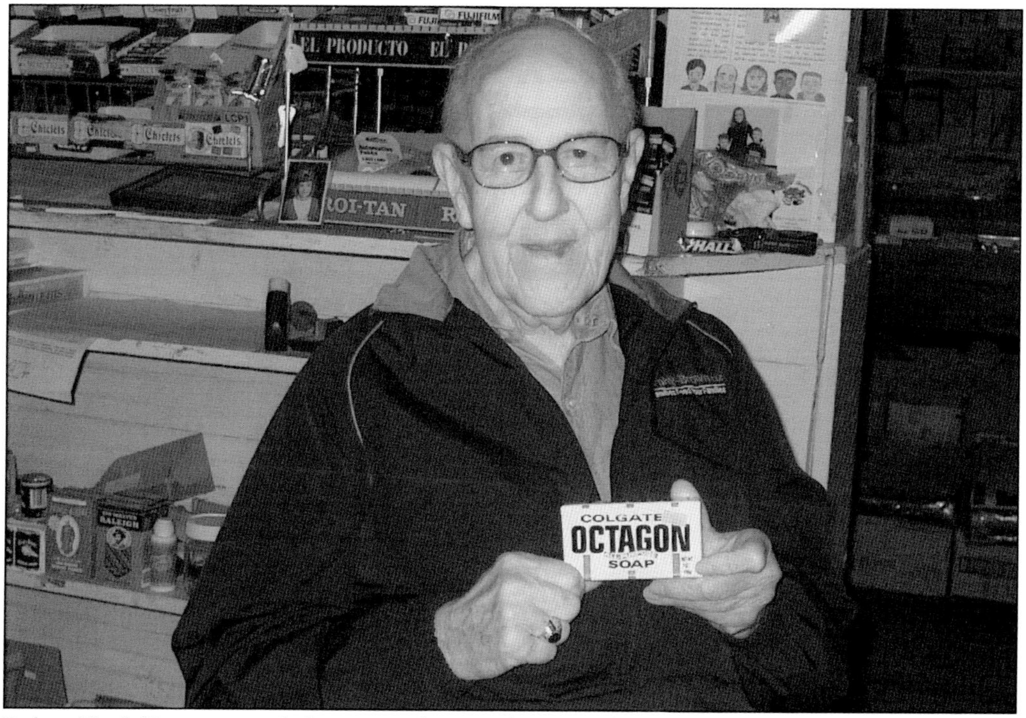

Robert Hugh Pace, pictured above, was the son of M.A. and Mintie Guice Pace. He was married to Betty Lou Maynard Pace, and his sisters were Lessie Pace Thompson, Eunice Pace, and Euva Pace Franklin, and his brother was Nolan Pace. Though the business was a family affair, at his death in 2010, Robert had outlived his family of origin, leaving him the owner and sole proprietor of M.A. Pace General Store, a landmark Saluda institution that his father had founded in 1899. Known for his friendly smile and cheerful personality, he had a deep and extensive knowledge of Saluda's history that he loved to share with his customers. The Morgan family, pictured below, stands in front of the M.A. Pace Store holding a picture of its namesake. The Morgans, distant cousins of the Paces, purchased the business in 2011 and have carried on the tradition of the Pace family by continuing to share the history of Saluda with their customers. From left to right are Tangie Ciarvolo, Judy Morgan, Cynthia Pace, Leon Morgan, Tammy Frisbee; Tonya, Wally, and Lathan Pace. (Above, courtesy of Cathy Jackson; below, courtesy of Cindy Stephenson Tuttle.)

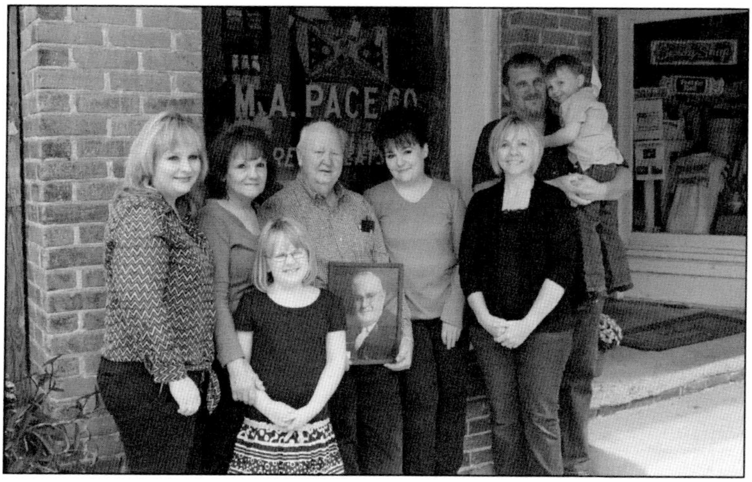

Bibliography

Anderson, Ruth. *Saluda Signal*, June-July 1996, Vol. XI No. 12.

Bennett, D. William, ed. *Polk County, North Carolina History*. Tryon, NC: Polk County Historical Association, Inc., 1983.

Clodfelter, Frank. "Saluda, Where You Either Run the Train or the Train Runs You!," *Trains, the Magazine of Railroading*, November 1984.

Craig, Susan Leland. *Saluda Magazine*. 1936–1938, Vol. 1–3.

Dupuy, Edward L. and Emma Weaver. *Artisans of the Appalachians*. Asheville, NC: Miller Printing Company, 1967.

FitzSimmons, Frank. *From the Banks of the Oklawaha, Vol. III*. Hendersonville, NC: Golden Glow Publishing Company, 1979–1998.

Giles, Jennie. "Saluda Grade Seen Its Share of Runaway Trains," *Spartanburg Herald-Journal*, May 28, 1993.

———. "Settling County History," *Hendersonville Times News*, April 16, 2006.

Hale, Arthur. *Howard Gap Road, 1725 to 1925: Between Spartanburg, S.C. and Asheville, N.C.: Predecessor to US-176 and I-26*. Tryon, NC: Polk County Historical Association, 2001.

Kirkpatrick, W.S. "Mystery New Deal Rug Now Worth $7,500," *The Atlanta Journal* and *Constitution Magazine*, August 30, 1964.

Leland, E. Cater. *The Descendents of John Heatherly (1769–1854)*. Flat Rock, NC: self-published, 2010.

Osborne, Anne, and Charlene Pace. *Saluda, N.C.: One Hundred Years, 1881–1981. Vols. I & II*. Saluda, NC: Holly Hill Publishers, 1981.

Pace, Herbert E. *50 Years Ago Around Saluda*. Saluda, NC: self-published, 1957, 1977, 1998.

Parris, John. "Saluda to Observe its 100th Birthday, Roaming the Mountains," *Asheville Citizen-Times*, February 1, 1981.

Patton, Sadie Smathers. *Sketches of Polk County History*. Spartanburg, SC: The Reprint Company Publishers, 1999.

Scherping, Carlann, Through Our Eyes, Images of Saluda's Historic Homes Part II and The Railroad, 2001–2002; Through Our Eyes, The Faces of Saluda, 2002–2003; Through Our Eyes, The Images of the Churches of Saluda, 2005–2006, (fourth grade assignment at Saluda Elementary School.)

Warner, Eugene. "Mother-Son Team Makes Pretty Rugs," *Asheville Citizen-Times*, January 22, 1967.

About the Historic Saluda Committee

HISTORIC Saluda Est. 1881

This project was a joint effort led by Cindy Stephenson Tuttle and Mary Ann Hester, members of the Historic Saluda Committee. Cindy is a part-time resident with deep roots in Saluda. Her father, Joseph "Joe" Raymond Stephenson Jr., was raised in Saluda, while Cindy grew up spending summers and holidays at her grandparents' farm on the Howard Gap Road. She developed a deep appreciation for Saluda's history by listening to her grandmother Kathleen Garren Stephenson Jelley recite family lore, including stories about her great-grandfather O.B. Garren, whose photographs are featured in this book. Burrell Pope Pace, a founding father of Saluda and Peter Guice, for whom the Green River Bridge is named, are both her fourth-great-grandfathers. She is the executive director of Stokes Partnership for Children and lives full time in King, North Carolina, but hopes to retire in Saluda with her husband, Brad. She chairs the oral history project and is the founder and cochair of the Historic Saluda Committee.

Mary Ann Hester is a freelance writer and public relations consultant. She has a master's degree in journalism from the University of Minnesota and has worked across the country as a researcher with the Mayo Clinic, as corporate marketing director for C&S Bank in Atlanta, and as a mystery traveler for internet travel company 10Best. A native of Greenville, South Carolina, she moved to Saluda three years ago without having spent a night in the town or knowing anyone who lived there. She feels Saluda embraces and charms with its fascinating history and individuals.

The Historic Saluda Committee was formed by a group of concerned citizens who wished to preserve the historical integrity of the town. In June 2010, the Saluda city commissioners voted to make the committee an advisory committee to the city, and seven committee members were appointed. The Historic Saluda Committee held its first official meeting on July 9, 2010, the day before Coon Dog Day. Appointed committee members during the creation of this book were Greaton Sellers (chair), Cindy Stephenson Tuttle (cochair), Mary Ann Hester, Charlene Pace, Caroline Farris, Carolyn Ashburn, and Ammie Weymer. Lynn Cass served as the Saluda city commissioner representative.

For more information about the oral history project or any other projects of the Historic Saluda Committee visit www.historicsaluda.org.